MEDIÆVAL CONTRIBUTIONS
TO MODERN CIVILISATION

MEDIÆVAL CONTRIBUTIONS TO MODERN CIVILISATION

A SERIES OF LECTURES DELIVERED AT
KING'S COLLEGE UNIVERSITY OF LONDON

EDITED BY

F. J. C. HEARNSHAW M.A. LL.D.

PROFESSOR OF MEDIÆVAL HISTORY IN THE UNIVERSITY OF LONDON

WITH A PREFACE BY

ERNEST BARKER M.A.

PRINCIPAL OF KING'S COLLEGE

KENNIKAT PRESS, INC./PORT WASHINGTON, N. Y.

MEDIEVAL CONTRIBUTIONS TO CIVILIZATION

Originally published in 1921
Reissued in 1966 by Kennikat Press

Library of Congress Catalog Card No: 66-25917

Analysed in the ESSAY & GENERAL LITERATURE INDEX

PREFACE

GIERKE, in an arresting sentence which, once read, is caught and embedded in the memory, speaks of the great Leibniz as one " who in so many directions went deeper than his contemporaries, and who, perhaps for that reason, so often turned his eyes backward toward mediæval ways of thought." If this be a true saying, and if to go backward to the Middle Ages is to go deeper into the *vraie vérité des choses*, it is a wise man's duty to turn mediævalist. And at any rate some of those who have hazarded the adventure have brought back lessons of some price and of much influence. Gierke himself has found in mediæval theory and practice a lesson concerning groups—their spontaneous origin and growth; their underived and inherent scope of action —which, filtered through the genius and the style of Maitland, has influenced on the one hand ecclesiastics such as Dr Figgis, helping them to a vindication of the rights of ecclesiastical societies, and on the other hand publicists such as Mr Sidney Webb and Mr Cole, who have found comfort and countenance in Gierke's teaching for their advocacy of the rights and powers of trade unions. Above all, prior to Gierke, of a more native strain, with a wood-note of his own, there is William Morris. He went back to the Middle Ages for the true notion of art, which for him was of the nature of folk craftsmanship—" made for the people and by the people, as a happiness to the maker and the user." And he found in the Middle

Ages not only the true notion of art, but also the true notion of the social life of man—the notion of fellowship, which he expanded in *The Dream of John Ball*; the fellowship which is heaven, and the lack thereof hell, "and the deeds that ye do upon the earth, it is for fellowship's sake that ye do them . . . and each one of you part of it."

The mediæval contributions to modern civilisation, which are the theme of this book, are twofold. There is the contribution of the idealised Middle Ages, magnified, mirrored, and roseate in the reflective thought of modern man concerning the Middle Ages. This is their contribution as it appeared to Morris, or as it appears to Mr Belloc, or Mr Chesterton, or the votaries of guild socialism. It is a contribution made not by the actual Middle Ages, but by a projection of the Middle Ages on an ideal screen by an idealising mind. It *is* a contribution, but it is an indirect contribution; it moves the mind and stirs the spirit of men, but the motion and the stirring are those not of the Middle Ages themselves, but rather of a certain antiquarian idealism—an inverted Utopianism, as it were, leading men to find the Utopia, or Nowhere, of the future in what one may call a Never Was of the past. But besides this indirect and ideal contribution—none the less real because it is indirect and ideal—there is the direct and actual contribution of the Middle Ages as they actually were. It is this contribution which is the peculiar theme of this book.

That contribution is very real, and very profound. The Middle Ages are the pit from which we were digged, and the rock from which we were hewn. They are the beginnings and the origin of the things that exist to-day; and "if one should look at things as they grow from the

6

beginning," said Aristotle, "it would be the best method of study." The Parliament of England, as Professor Pollard has lately taught us, can only be understood in the light of its whole evolution. The law of England is embedded in the Middle Ages. Our architecture is still mediæval: if we build Houses of Parliament or churches to-day, we build something which perhaps our mediæval forefathers would not have built, but something, too, which we should not have built as we have built it if they had not built before us. Economically we have travelled far from the Middle Ages: the open-field village with its common pasture and common life, the guilded town with its mysteries and its apprentices— these things are gone, and between them and us stretches the deep abyss cut by the Industrial Revolution of the eighteenth century—perhaps the greatest revolution in the daily life of man of which history bears record. It may be that here we have travelled too far from the Middle Ages: it may be that, sooner or later, we shall turn back to some of their ways. Even if we do, the structure we build, whatever the similarities or the imitation, will be fundamentally new; and in the field of economics it will remain true that we must think of the relation between ourselves and the Middle Ages in terms not of analogy or affiliation, but of difference and contrast.

I am proud to add any words of mine by way of preface to the lectures printed in this volume. The lectures were delivered in the autumn term of 1920, as part of the general scheme of public lectures at King's College, which has been in operation (and, I am happy to think, in fruitful operation) for some years past. They were planned by Professor Hearnshaw: seven of them were delivered by

PREFACE

members of the staff of King's College; three were
delivered, in a generous collaboration, by members of
the staff of University College and of Bedford College.
They bear testimony to the vitality of historical study
in London; and their appearance is opportune at a time
when the University of London is founding an Institute
of Historical Research—the first of its kind to be founded
in this country—for the advanced study of history. The
study of history has a natural home in London, rich as it
is both in its own history and in its accumulated store of
the records of the general national life. London is modern
—sometimes, one feels, terribly modern; but London is
also mediæval. So long as Westminster Abbey stands,
so long are the Middle Ages incarnate in stone among us,
and the age of faith, and of the beauty that was based on
faith, is not yet entirely dead. With its own past, and with
its rich records, London is a natural home of mediæval
studies. But mediæval studies can flourish on any soil.
They can flourish, as they do abundantly, in Manchester:
they can also flourish across the seas, in Boston and in
New Haven, at the Universities of Harvard and of Yale.
This book is a testimony to their vigour; and I trust that
it will be welcomed by mediævalists everywhere for the
sake of the subject which they all love.

ERNEST BARKER

KING'S COLLEGE
UNIVERSITY OF LONDON
March, 1921

CONTENTS

CONTENTS

MEDIÆVAL CONTRIBUTIONS TO MODERN CIVILISATION

INTRODUCTORY

THE MIDDLE AGES AND THEIR CHARACTERISTIC FEATURES

I

ARE the Middle Ages worth studying? The full answer to that question would involve answers to the larger questions, Is any history worth studying? Is anything worth studying? Is life worth living? This is not the place, however, to enter into a discussion of these vast themes. Something must be taken for granted. It must be assumed that existence has a meaning and a value; that education has a function and an end; that history of some sort or other has its part to play in the educational scheme. The question is thus narrowed down to the practical issue, whether or not the Middle Ages can claim attention as compared with other periods, ancient or modern. What is the test of worth in history? How can we determine our choice of time or topic?

Lord Morley provides us with a useful criterion. "I do not," he says, "in the least want to know what happened in the past, except as it enables me to see my way more clearly through that which is happening to-day." That is a severe yet perfectly clear and rational test—the test of present utility. It is severe; for in its demand that history should pour direct illumination through the opaqueness of politics, it refuses to recognise as adequate several pleas for the study of history which have been urged or admitted by modern educationists. Even Professor Ray Lankester, no friend of history, concedes from the depths of his armchair that it is a legitimate form of amusement; Messieurs Langlois and Seignobos, while denying its political value, maintain its indirect worth as an instrument of intellectual culture; Principal Caird places its chief service in the sphere of ethics ; Emerson treasures it metaphysically as an interpreter of microcosmic man. On all the grounds urged or admitted by these eminent men it would be possible to make out a good case for the study of the Middle Ages : their records are intensely interesting and diverting ; they are rich in thought-compelling problems ; they are mirrors of conspicuous and unrelieved virtues and vices ; they are radiant with macrocosmic illumination. But there is no need to take advantage of these pleas. Lord Morley's test may with confidence be applied in all its severity. The study of the Middle Ages can be defended on the strictly utilitarian ground that it is indispensable to the up-to-date man of affairs who wishes to see his way clearly " through that which is happening to-day."

It is not, of course, contended that a knowledge of the Middle Ages is nearly so important to the modern politician as is a knowledge of more recent times. The problems of the present have for the most part taken shape in the crowded and critical century that has succeeded the overthrow of Napoleon and the Vienna resettlement of Europe: a close acquaintance with the history of the period since 1815 is undoubtedly the most urgent need of the statesman who desires intelligently to serve his own generation and to further the interests of posterity. But the study of the history of the nineteenth century reveals the fact that no full comprehension of the questions which agitated that era is possible unless they be traced back to their sources in far earlier times. It was, indeed, in the Middle Ages that most of them had their rise. It was then that the modern national states were formed ; it was then that the rivalries of French and Germans, Russians and Poles, Magyars and Southern Slavs began ; it was then that religion became militant here on earth, and that the secular conflict between the Crescent and the Cross was inaugurated ; it was then, in a word, that Western civilisation as we know it came into existence. To those, therefore, who would penetrate beneath the surface of things some study of the Middle Ages is essential.

Yet we must keep our sense of proportion. If we deprecate undue disparagement of the Middle Ages, we must not make exaggerated claims on their behalf. We have to steer the sane and reasonable *via media* between the excessive contempt poured upon them by the radical modernist, and the uncritical adulation with which they are idealised and idolised by the modern reactionary. Milton dismissed their conflicts with the sneer that they were "battles of kites and crows"; an eighteenth-century rationalist boasted that he knew nothing of those ages which knew nothing ; even the Dean of St Paul's in his brilliant Romanes lecture on "The Idea of Progress" speaks of them as "the longest and dreariest set-back that humanity has ever experienced within the historical period . . . a veritable glacial age of the spirit." These utterances represent the extreme of depreciation. By those who adopt this attitude the Middle Ages are commonly spoken of as the Dark

Ages. On the other hand, and especially within the last few years, writers have arisen to whom the Middle Ages appear as the only ages of light. Such modern reactionaries carry appreciation to the extreme of romance ; they injure the cause of history by their excessive claims and their irrational prejudices. Three examples must suffice : they are culled from the recent writings of Messrs G. K. Chesterton, H. Belloc, and A. J. Penty. Mr Chesterton in 1917 wrote what he called *A Short History of England*. Reviewing it in *The Observer*, with less than his usual felicity, Mr Bernard Shaw commended it as " something like a history of England." It deserved the qualified praise which Mr Bernard Shaw gave to it; but it deserved it on quite other grounds than those which he assigned. It was, indeed, nothing like a history of England ; but it was very much like Mr Chesterton's other writings. To say that is praise enough. For few literary men of the present day are more marvellously skilled in standing (literarily) upon their head, and describing in inverted language the topsy-turvy scenes which they behold from this depression. Mr Chesterton perceives in " popular tradition " the norm of historic truth, and he proclaims that " it is especially in the matter of the Middle Ages that the popular histories trample upon the popular tradition." He then proceeds to revive the " popular tradition " of a mediæval " merrie England " free from Puritans, utilitarians, vegetarians, and teetotallers. What Mr Chesterton in his *Short History* does for England, that Mr Belloc does for Christendom as a whole in his *Europe and the Faith*. He treats the Reformation as a disaster, and speaks of everything that followed it as " modern and therefore part of a decline." He idealises the Middle Ages as the period of unmitigated orthodoxy and unpolluted beer. He burns with enthusiasm

14

for the Roman tradition, both imperial and ecclesiastical, as it maintained its dominance throughout the thousand years which divided Justinian from Charles V. Mr A. J. Penty in his *Guildsman's Interpretation of History* does not share Mr Belloc's passion for Rome. On the contrary, Roman law (of any detailed knowledge of which he is obviously entirely innocent) is his *bête noire*; to its reception in England he attributes the greater portion of the evils of modern capitalistic society. But he too, on economic rather than religious grounds, exalts the Middle Ages. He sees in them the golden period of healthy agriculture, artistic industry, and equitable commerce, embodied in a society grouped naturally according to its productive activities.

The truth about the Middle Ages lies somewhere midway between the gloomy depreciation of the modern rationalists and the fantastic over-glorification of the young idealists. The Middle Ages were not dark, but were illuminated by a light which enabled those who walked by it to attain heights of holiness rarely reached by men either before or since. They were not a mere episode in the history of the race, a breach in the continuity of classical civilisation; they had strongly marked characteristics of their own, and they added elements of incalculable worth to the spiritual heritage of mankind. They were not even a 'set-back' or retrogression, if rightly viewed. For the Græco-Roman culture which for a time they submerged was far from perfect in its quality, and those who shared its advantages were few. When after a thousand years of partial obscuration it re-emerged in the modern day, it came with a moral content which it had never before possessed, and it came—by means of printed page and popular university—to an immeasurably larger public than it had reached in the old world.[1]

But if it be true that the Middle Ages were not dark, or fruitless, or unprogressive, it is also true, on the other hand, that they were far removed from the ideal. They were no golden epoch to which we should seek to return. They were centuries of extreme hardship, of chronic war, of devastating pestilence, of recurrent famine, of prevailing ignorance, of degrading superstition, of paralysing terror, of furious passion and consuming lust. Only through the fires of fierce adversity and the waters of penitential discipline did they purge themselves of their more enormous faults, and prepare the world for the higher and more widespread civilisation of the modern day.

It is the purpose of these lectures, first, to give some account of the life and work of the Middle Ages ; secondly, to estimate their permanent contribution to the culture and humanity of the present day; thirdly, to ask how far it is possible or desirable in these late complex times to revert to the simpler ideas and the more primitive institutions of our mediæval progenitors. Can we, or should we,

[1] The defect of all the civilisations which up to the present the earth has known is that they have been the possession of the few. This is not the fault of the few, for the masses of mankind have never yet shown themselves capable of civilisation. The masses of mankind have always been, and still remain, barbarians. They see enough of culture to perceive that it immensely enhances the value of life, making it indeed worth living; they emulously and eagerly seek to capture it ; they fail to do so, and then in envious fury they destroy it. Every great civilisation so far has been overwhelmed by barbarians, whether invaders from without or insurgents from within. But each time a new civilisation rises from the wreck of the old it is shared by a larger community. The progress of humanity, if cyclic, is continuous : it is of the nature of a rising tide, each wave reaching a point higher than the last. History justifies a sober optimism. A historian who loses his faith in progress ceases to be a historian and becomes a philosopher or a—— But, no, I must not even appear to speak disrespectfully of high ecclesiastical dignitaries.

attempt in any measure to revive the patristic theology;
rehabilitate the scholastic philosophy; restore Byzantine
or Gothic art; return to mediæval literary models; re-
establish the communal ideals of monastic education;
recover the rigid organisation of feudal society; rebuild
the shattered fragments of the guild system of industry; go
behind the modern State with its monopoly of sovereignty,
and try to revive the corporations which in the Middle
Ages shared with the political authority the loyalty of the
Christian man?

To this course the present lecture is merely preliminary
and prophetic. It aims at performing the function of the
chorus in the Greek drama, viz., that of introducing the
protagonists and indicating the scope of the play. In
particular it proposes, first, to define the Middle Ages;
secondly, to specify the chief periods into which they
naturally fall; and, thirdly, to mark some of their characteristic features.

II

The term 'Middle Ages' implies a threefold
division of universal history into the sections (1) ancient,
(2) mediæval, (3) modern. This division was first adopted
in the eighteenth century, and it has persisted to the
present time. Of late, however, it has been subjected
to some severe criticism. Professor Freeman, for example,
objected to it because it obscured what to him was the
fundamental fact of history, viz., its unbroken continuity:
although he was a professor of modern history, he refused
to be bound by restrictions in date; he treated as modern
everything that had happened since the call of Abraham;
his chief interest centred round the eleventh-century
Norman conquest of England; the only things that he

17

regarded as really ancient and obsolete were such things as the rule of the Turk in Europe and the conservatism of Bishop Stubbs. Again, and still more recently, Mr H. G. Wells in his *Outline of History* has discarded the threefold division because of its lack of proportion. Mr Wells begins his study of mankind 600,000 years before the Christian era; hence, to accept the traditional classification would be to construct a time-chart divided into three sections in the ratio of 4 inches (modern), 10 inches (mediæval), and 167 *yards* (ancient). Which is absurd! And yet in practice Mr Wells does not diverge from the normal so much as might have been expected. The story of the unrealisable æons of antiquity to the time of the Roman Empire occupies almost exactly one-third of his work; the second third carries us to the Reformation; the remaining aliquot part is devoted to the last four centuries. The disproportion in duration of time is nicely counterbalanced by the increase in the fulness of the records and the growth in interest and importance. The old division vindicates itself against the charge of irrationality. As against Professor Freeman's charge of schism it can also make a good defence. For continuity is by no means the most conspicuous feature of history. The connexion of one civilisation with another is often obscure; it is a matter of faith rather than of sight; belief in it is a deduction from the axioms of science, and not an induction from observed phenomena. The phenomena which strike the eye from time to time are apparent breaches of continuity, and of these breaches two are particularly prominent. The first is that which presents itself in the fifth century of the Christian era, when the Roman Empire in the West is submerged by barbarian invaders: the Europe of A.D. 550 is immeasurably different from the Europe of A.D. 450. The

18

second is that which presents itself in the fifteenth century of the Christian era, when the great geographical discoveries of Vasco da Gama and Columbus open up new worlds to the wondering eyes of the West : the Europe of A.D. 1550 is a continent changed almost beyond recognition from the Europe of A.D. 1450. It would be a perverted view of history which, in its effort to discover the continuity which no doubt existed during these periods of rapid transition, ignored the cataclysmic changes which distinguished them, or denied the entrance of new and decisive factors into the evolution of Western society.

The period intervening between these two transitional eras is what we call the Middle Ages. It is the millennium from the fifth to the fifteenth century ; from the fall of the Roman Empire in the West to the fall of the Roman Empire in the East ; from the triumph of Christianity over classical paganism to the revolt of Protestantism against Catholic Christianity. It is the thousand years which saw the rise, the mighty reign, and the decline of the papal monarchy ; which witnessed the dominance of Feudalism and chivalry, whereby the cosmopolitan commonwealth of later Rome was transmuted into the new integration of the modern state-system ; which beheld, and indeed achieved, the education and evangelisation of the bar-barians whose ignorant and demoniac hordes at first over-whelmed both Latin culture and the Catholic faith ; which, finally, effected the fusion of Roman and Teuton into a single homogeneous society.

No precise date, of course, marks either the beginning or the end of this mediæval millennium. Both at the com-mencement and the termination one age merged into the next with the same imperceptible gradation as the seasons of the year pass each into its successor. Those who study the

Middle Ages have to start their investigations long before
the fifth century in order that they may understand what
was that world of pagan antiquity which by some subtle
alchemy was transformed into the world of the papal
hierarchy. Similarly they have to carry their researches
far beyond the limits of the fifteenth century in order that
they may trace mediæval institutions and ideas which
persisted for many generations after the circumstances
that engendered them had passed away—many of which,
indeed, are extant still. For purposes of study, in fact,
mediæval history resolves itself into three periods. First
there is that of the transition from the ancient: this should
be traced from, at latest, the principate of Diocletian, and
should be regarded as complete only in the pontificate of
Gregory the Great; the years covered by this initial phase
are thus roughly A.D. 300–600. Secondly, there are the
seven centuries from Gregory the Great to Boniface VIII,
the true heart of the Middle Ages, A.D. 600–1300.
Finally, there is the period of transition from the mediæval
to the modern, which may be taken as falling within the
two hundred years A.D. 1300–1500. Let us proceed to
note a few of the characteristic features of each of these
three in turn.

III

Gibbon, at the close of his great work, attributes the
fall of the Roman Empire to the bishops and the barbarians. He had grounds for this attribution, but there
was a third cause which he tends to underestimate, viz.,
internal decay. Those, indeed, who seek to explain the
catastrophe which brought to ruin the noblest polity that
up to that time the genius of man had constructed have

first and foremost to examine the fabric of the Empire itself, and to discover the fatal flaws which existed in both its foundations and its framework. Having done this they may follow Gibbon in noting how both the spirit of the Christian Church and its episcopal organisation were incompatible with the polytheistic and autocratic empire of the Cæsars, and in tracing the process of the Teutonic invasions which ultimately broke the defensive frontiers of the weakened Roman dominion and flooded the provinces with barbarian hordes.

The Roman Empire developed from a city-state by a process of almost miraculous expansion. True, it was built up through conquest, and was constructed by means of the military efficiency, indomitable courage, and patriotic devotion of its incomparable legions. But no mere aptitude for war can account for its continuance ; for the fact that it cemented the subject peoples into an organic polity, winning their allegiance and even their enthusiastic devotion ; for the marvellous tranquillity which it gave to the Western world during a space of some four hundred years—a tranquillity undisturbed by insurrection, almost unbroken by attack from without. The permanence of the Roman Empire, its most remarkable feature, was due not so much to its belligerent might as to its genius in the art of government. It evolved a superb and equitable system of law ; it threw open the privileges of its citizenship to its multitudinous provincials ; it allowed them a large measure of local autonomy ; it established peace, maintained order, developed economic resources, and rendered possible a prosperity without precedent. Although shadows have to be inserted into the over-radiant picture of the age of the Antonines as painted by Gibbon, it is still in the main true to say that " if a man were called to fix the period in the history of the world during which the condition of the human race was most happy and prosperous, he would, without hesitation, name that which elapsed from the death of Domitian to the accession of Commodus," *i.e.*, A.D. 96–180.

But even in this Golden Age of Roman imperialism grave defects in the constitution of the State and in the structure of society manifested themselves. In the next century (A.D. 180–284) of bad rulers, military insurrections, civil wars, popular disorders, plagues, pestilences, and famines, these defects became glaringly evident as radical and irremediable flaws, fatal to the well-being and even to the continuance of the body politic. What were they ? Six may be singled out as most conspicuous. First, the Empire included within its far-flung bounds peoples so various in race and in civilisation that it was impossible to weld them into unity ; in particular, Celt-Ivernian, Latin, Greek, Oriental constituted four groups whose differences precluded complete fusion. Secondly, with a constitutional hypocrisy strange in a people so practical and so brave, the Romans refused to face the fact that the Empire was not a republic ; they persisted in regarding the emperor as a mere composite official elected jointly and severally by the Senate—Cæsar Augustus, imperator, consul, censor, tribune, pontifex maximus, etc., etc.—and consequently they made no rules for the succession ; hence, with increasing frequency and in growing violence, the death of a princeps precipitated conflicts of factions, furious rivalries, internecine civil wars, horrible assassinations.[1] Thirdly, the economic foundations of the Roman dominion were unsound ; nearly half the population were

---

[1] Between A.D. 211 and 284 there were twenty-three emperors, of whom twenty were murdered.

slaves, productive industry was despised as servile, taxation pressed with extinguishing severity upon the middle class, the cities were infested with a lazy proletariat fed with doles, agriculture languished on gigantic *latifundia*. Fourthly, economic unsoundness was matched by a growing moral depravity ; the character of the Romans was not able to stand the strain of early prosperity and power ; the austere virtues of the fathers of the State gave place in their degenerate descendants to pride, cruelty, extravagance, self-indulgence, and lust ; a debilitated bureaucracy had to face the tremendous problems of a world in transition. Fifthly, ignorance of science, and especially of hygiene and medicine, rendered the Romans helpless in the presence of devastating pestilences which made their permanent abodes in the fetid slums of the great cities, and issued thence with increasing frequency to ravage the Empire. Hence the population diminished not merely relatively as compared with the barbarians beyond the borders, but absolutely with accelerating rapidity. The horrors of pestilential death, moreover, began to haunt the spirits of the survivors, and to oppress them with the sense of an adverse and inevitable fate. Finally, religious disintegration set in ; the Romans lost faith in the gods on whose divine aid their fathers had trusted in building up the State, and whose worship formed an integral part of the structure of the constitution. In vain did Neoplatonic philosophers strive by rationalist interpretations to bring the incredible within the limits of belief; the brains of paganism were out.

It was in these circumstances of dissolution and decline that the Christian Church developed its doctrine and organisation within the Empire, and that the barbarians began to make their destructive raids across its frontiers.

The one accelerated the religious disintegration of Rome, both by introducing a cult hostile to the civic gods, and by dissociating worship from politics and allying it with ethics. The other shattered the defences of the Empire, destroyed its administrative system, and brought its rotting social structure in ruins to the ground. A few words concerning each of the two must suffice.

The Christian Church rose as heir to the Jewish tradition: Christ came as the Messiah promised to Israel. As developed by St Paul, it claimed further to fulfil the aspirations of the Gentiles: it revealed the Deity whom the heathen had ignorantly sought. The Roman Empire at first regarded the activities of the apostles and evangelists without disfavour or alarm. The Christians seemed harmless and innocent, even if eccentric and superstitious. The magistrates treated them indulgently, and protected them from the inexplicable fury of the Jews. But a change of attitude on the part of the imperial authorities soon took place; they speedily discovered that the new religion was not so innocuous as it had at first seemed to be. It was exclusive and intolerant, denunciatory of the other religions of the Empire, unwilling to take its licensed place as a lowly member of the numerous company of cults, assertive of supremacy and monopoly; it was unpatriotic, showing no enthusiasm for the polity of Rome, withdrawing its votaries from the service of the State, forbidding them to offer symbolic incense at the shrine of the deified Cæsar; it was anti-social, proclaiming the imminent end of the age, holding aloof from secular concerns, shunning theatres and games, shrinking from convivial intercourse, abstaining from commerce and marriage, devoting itself to the inauguration of a new order of things; it was dangerous, for its members formed themselves into churches under

24

the authoritative control of bishops, churches grouped themselves into archiepiscopal federations, and these again became associated and linked together under metropolitans and patriarchs, and thus the Christian community grew to be an *imperium in imperio*, aloof from and antagonistic to the State.   Hence arose the great persecutions—the effort of the State to suppress doctrines subversive of its genius and to eradicate a parasitic growth which threatened its very existence.   The persecutions failed, and deserved to fail.   For in the Church and not in the Empire was life and the promise of life.   All the same the triumph of the communion of saints over the might and majesty of imperial Rome was so remarkable an event that it remains one of the most absorbing of historical problems.   The full explanation of the miracle lies, perhaps, in realms beyond the sphere of the historian.   Yet even he on his low plane of mundane sequences can see four facts which go far to solve the mystery.   First, Christianity was, as a faith, incomparably superior to its rivals, whether they were the old theologies of Rome or the newer and more popular Oriental cults ; it satisfied the religious sense as none of them did, with its revelation of an incarnation, its proclamation of an atonement, its offer of redemption, and its promise of eternal life.   Secondly, it provided a more rational explanation of man and the universe than did any of the current philosophies, rendering more intelligible the mystery of existence, sundering the veil of scepticism and despair.   Thirdly, it set before the eyes of a world sated with bestiality and blood a new and lofty ethical ideal : the old gods were non-moral ; the cults were often frankly immoral ; Christianity came to raise a standard of exalted purity, it showed the ideal already realised in the life of the Perfect Man, and it possessed a power which enabled it to cleanse and transform the debasement of the vilest mortal into the same immaculate sanctity. Finally, the Church had in its organisation—its bishops and presbyters, its synods and councils, its missionaries and evangelists, its monks and anchorites—a social structure of such immense stability and strength that it was able to withstand the most violent shocks of all its foes. The most formidable of the long series of assaults made by the decadent Empire upon the growing Church was that delivered during the reign of Diocletian at the beginning of the fourth century. The completeness of its failure was, without question, one of the causes which led Diocletian's successor, the Emperor Constantine, to make peace with the invincible hierarchy and to recognise Christianity as a lawful religion (A.D. 313). Within eighty years Christianity had secured the suppression of paganism, and had established itself as the only lawful religion of the Empire.

The triumph of Christianity within the Roman Empire synchronised almost exactly with the breaking of the Roman frontiers by the barbarians. The Visigoths crossed the Danube in 375; the Vandals, Alans, and Sueves rushed the frozen Rhine on the first day of 406; Rome itself was sacked in 410. The two centuries which followed these cardinal events were centuries of rapid transition. The barbarians spread themselves over all the Roman provinces of the West, extinguishing the imperial power. Vandals in Africa, Visigoths in Spain, Ostrogoths and Lombards in Italy, Franks and Burgundians in Gaul, Angles and Saxons in Britain—such were some of the settlements which displaced the central administration of the Cæsars. In the East, however, the Roman Empire continued to maintain itself, strong in its homogeneous populations, secure in its command of the sea, and impregnably seated in its new fortress-capital at Constantinople. Meantime the Church pursued its victorious career. In Byzantium and the Orient, it is true, although all the peoples became nominally Christian, the hierarchy remained subservient to the emperor, and the Church continued to be what Constantine made it, a department of the State. In the West, however, a very different condition of things developed. There the imperial authority passed away, and the sole heir to the tradition of Rome was the Catholic episcopate. To the bishop of the Eternal City in particular fell the work of perpetuating the rule of the vanished Cæsars. He took their ancient title of Pontifex Maximus, and with more than their divine authority assumed their task of bringing the lost provinces of the West once again into obedience to the sceptre of Rome. He sent out missionary preachers and monastic embassies, and with these ghostly armies renewed the triumphs of the legions. One by one the barbarian chieftains who had settled in Gaul, Britain, Spain, Italy, were subdued to the obedience of the Cross and brought beneath the sway of the papal monarchy. Greatest and most successful of all the early Popes was Gregory I (590–604). Through his agency the Jutish kingdom of Kent, the Visigothic kingdom of Spain, the Lombard kingdom of Italy, all were brought into communion with the Roman see. From Gregory I may be dated the establishment of the papal monarchy, and hence the beginning of the Middle Ages proper.

IV

The seven centuries of the Middle Ages proper extended, as we have already noted, from the pontificate of Gregory the Great to that of Boniface VIII (d. 1303). Their outstanding characteristic throughout the wide extent of Christendom was the uncontested dominance of the Church. The strength of the Church, by means of which it was enabled without effort to retain its ascendancy, was its hold over the minds and consciences of the community at large. Orientals sated with sensuous cults ; Greeks weary of the uncertainties of philosophy ; Latins disillusioned by the collapse of their Empire ; Celt-Ivernians eager to escape from the barbarities of their crude paganism—all sought and found in the sublime morality, the intelligible theology, the organic vitality, and the mild beneficence of Christianity the satisfaction of their deeper needs. They accepted the faith of the Cross as expounded by their clergy as their guide not only in matters celestial, but also in matters appertaining to the brief probationary term of earthly existence : it controlled their politics, regulated their industry and commerce, ordered their social relations, monopolised their education, inspired their literature and art. Heresies were almost unknown, and such as fitfully arose were easily suppressed : the older rivals to the orthodox faith, such as Arianism, had died down, and not till quite the end of this central mediæval period did those formidable precursors of Protestantism, the heresies of the Albigenses and the Lollards, make their appearance.

But, although the Church was comparatively untroubled by heresy, she was rent by the most deplorable and irreparable of all her schisms, viz., the schism of East from West, of Greek Christianity from Latin Christianity. The process of the severance was slow : not till 1054 was it completed amid a tempest of mutual anathemas and excommunications. But it was a process which began early, and it was due to causes which were operative from the very first. There was a radical difference of genius between the Greek and the Latin. They were divided not only by language, but by a fundamental antagonism of ideas. The one was metaphysical, speculative, disputatious, æsthetic, ritualistic, emotional ; the other was legal, practical, authoritarian, averse from controversy, ready for compromise, eager for conquest, zealous in missionary enterprise, masterly in organisation and government. While, therefore, the patriarchs of Antioch and Alexandria, Constantinople and Jerusalem involved themselves in fratricidal conflicts with one another, and remained subservient to the imperial yoke, the Bishop of Rome, sole patriarch of the Occident, " alien from their mutations and unrest," advanced by slow, undeviating steps toward the papal primacy. His was the see founded (it was believed) by Peter and confirmed by Paul, nurtured by the blood of the martyrs, preserved from error by an unbroken apostolic tradition ; his the mother Church of the converted barbarians, and he the heir of the sovereignty of the Western Cæsars. The claims of the Papacy were maintained, and the triumphant establishment of its monarchy hastened, by the devoted labours of an army of monks, organised from the sixth century onward under the rule of St Benedict. By the seventh century the dominion of the Bishop of Rome was as wide as that of the Emperor Honorius had been at the end of the fourth ; moreover, " regions Cæsar never knew," beyond the Danube and the Rhine, and across the Irish Sea, were being brought beneath the ghostly sway of Cæsar's apostolic successor. The political superiority which the Pope still recognised as vested in the Byzantine emperor was becoming a mere empty suzerainty.

The development of the dominant Christendom—in the East under the Emperor, in the West under the Pope— was suddenly and disastrously interrupted in both Orient

29

and Occident, during the course of that seventh century, by the unheralded assault of a new foe of the same order as Christendom itself, viz., a theocratic monarchy. Mahomet—or Muhammad, as he is now generally and more correctly called—lived during the years 570–632. During the last ten of these years he formulated his simple creed, and organised the nomads of Arabia into the fanatical army of the faithful. Immediately after the death of the Prophet, Islam launched itself upon divided Christendom ; overran and permanently annexed Syria, Egypt, and North Africa ; conquered the bulk of Spain ; and was checked only at Constantinople (717) and on the field of Tours in Gaul (732). Not until the end of the eighth century had the first energy of Islam spent itself ; not until the days when Haroun-al-Raschid ruled in Bagdad, and Charlemagne in Aix-la-Chapelle, was a balance of power achieved. In A.D. 800, however, something of stability seemed to have been recovered. The conquests of the Crescent had been completed, and the empire of the caliphs had begun to disintegrate ; the emirate of Cordova had repudiated the authority of Bagdad, so that Spain formed a separate Moslem state. On the other hand, the Franks whose swords had saved Western Christendom at Tours had established a hegemony over almost all the Catholic world, and their king, Charles the Great, or Charlemagne, had been called upon by the Pope to resume the title and power of Roman Emperor. The coronation of Charles as Cæsar Augustus on Christmas Day A.D. 800 involved on the part of the Pope the formal repudiation of his antique dependence upon the Byzantine ruler. Thus the schism of Christendom was deepened, and Charlemagne found himself (to his annoyance and regret) in conflict with his compeer at Constantinople. In these circumstances political equilibrium was secured and peace maintained by a couple of unnatural alliances. The Byzantine Cæsar fostered the revolt of the Emir of Cordova against the Commander of the Faithful ; while Haroun-al-Raschid on his part sent friendly elephants to Charlemagne, entrusted him with the keys of the holy places in Jerusalem, and recognised him as protector of pious pilgrims. Almost the whole of the known world was at the opening of the ninth century divided into these four states, thus grouped into two alliances ; in the Christian West the only important power that lay outside was the English kingdom of Mercia, which had just then been brought to the height of its power by King Offa (*d.* A.D. 796).

The novel tranquillity which the strong and wise rule of Charlemagne secured throughout his extensive empire seemed to promise a return to long-vanished conditions of material prosperity and intellectual advance. The restoration of the *Pax Romana* was a prelude to a remark-able renaissance of Latin culture. The Latin language recovered something of its pristine purity ; schools were founded ; literary men were encouraged ; the Church was reformed ; the law was humanised. It was possible for men to believe that the painful episodes of barbarian incursions and infidel onslaughts were over, and that the pacific sway of the Eternal City was about to be resumed under the joint authority of the Holy Father and his anointed Emperor. But, alas! the Carolingian dawn was premature. New bands of marauders, terrible in military might, ferocious in hostility to Christendom, untouched by any reverence for the name or civilisation of Rome, were about to hurl themselves upon the devoted West. First, from their Scandinavian strongholds came the Vikings to plunder and to slay. The great Charles himself before he

died (814) had seen the sails of their warships off the
Frisian coast, and had heard how their pagan hosts had
ravaged the monasteries and bishoprics of Northern
England. Under his weaker successors, Louis the Pious
and Charles the Fat, the Christian empire was devastated
by them from end to end, and the reviving Latin culture
ruthlessly stamped out. Secondly, and simultaneously,
the Magyars—a Turanian people akin to the Huns, the
Avars, the Bulgars, and the Turks—advanced up the
Danube, planting themselves in Hungary and reaching as
far as Italy and Burgundy in their raids. Thirdly, Saracen
pirates, released from restraint by the break-up of the
caliphate, wasted all the coasts of the Mediterranean.
Finally, the Slavs from beyond the Oder and the Vistula
crept westward toward the Elbe and the Rhine, penetrating
and percolating wherever they found Teutonic resistance
weak. If any part of the Middle Ages deserves the name
of ' dark ' it is the two centuries A.D. 800–1000 which
intervened between the coronation of Charlemagne and
the conversion of the Magyar king Stephen. During the
longer portion of that distressful period central government
entirely collapsed ; the forces of Christendom were disin-
tegrated, and there was none to whom an abbey plundered
or a town besieged could look for protection or redress.
Each locality was driven to organise its own defence, or
to prepare for perdition. In these circumstances of dire
necessity Feudalism, which was primarily a military system,
sprang up spontaneously, and by its efficiency achieved
the salvation of Europe. Its strength lay in its walled
castles and its panoplied knights ; the massive fortifi-
cations of the one provided islands of secure refuge amid
the floods of invasion ; the serried hosts of the other after
a terrific struggle put a term to the tide of pagan depre-

dation. By the millennial year of the Christian era the horror of darkness was past; Feudalism had done its great work; the Northmen had become civilised members of the Christian community; the Magyars had made their submission to the Papacy; the Saracen pirates were being met and checked on their own element; the encroachments of the Slavs were effectually prevented by a barrier of military marks. Thus the eleventh century opened with a brightness and a hopefulness unknown for many generations.

The three hundred years A.D. 1000-1300 were undoubtedly the culmination and crown of the Middle Ages. It was in this period that the papal monarchy, under Gregory VII (1073-85) and Innocent III (1198-1216), reached the height of its magnificence and power. Under the suzerainty of the Papacy Western Europe was obviously and consciously a unit. Its episcopate, its monastic orders, its chivalry, its schools and its new universities, its Latin literature and its canon law—all were cosmopolitan, and all took their tone from Rome. The great enterprise of the period, viz., the Crusades, was also a cosmopolitan adventure, the effort of Christendom as a whole to defeat Islam with its own weapons of sword and flame, the attempt to recover for the Cross the regions too long usurped by the Crescent, and to restore to the service of the Church the Holy Land where Christ had lived and taught. This strange enterprise, which evoked the wildest enthusiasm throughout the still half-barbaric West, was accompanied by many other symptoms of reviving vitality, rising spirit, and renewed activity. New monastic orders—Cluniac, Cistercian, Carthusian—requickened the flagging zeal of the ancient Benedictine rule. Communities of a still more novel kind, orders of friars—Franciscan, Dominican, Carmelite—carried the beneficence or the orthodoxy of the

Church among the outcast and the lost. The imagination of the faithful awoke; the dream of Gothic architecture stirred their souls, and Europe put on her glorious white robe of cathedral and abbey churches. The climax of this great epoch of mediæval splendour was reached when the princely Innocent III called the Lateran Council in 1215. It was attended by five hundred bishops and by eight hundred abbots and priors. During a session of less than three weeks, with high enthusiasm and striking unanimity, it passed seventy decrees or canons, many of them of first importance, for the comfort of the Church and the welfare of the world. The century which opened with the pontificate of Innocent III saw before its close that mirror of mediæval kingship, the reign of St Louis of France; it saw also the mighty labours of St Thomas Aquinas, who raised in his marvellous *Summa* the flawless temple of mediæval thought; it saw, too, as it ended, the incomparable Dante pondering those themes, sublime and profound, which make his *Divine Comedy* the most perfect of all embodiments of the spirit of the Middle Ages at its best. But contemporary with Dante was Pope Boniface VIII, under whom the papal monarchy reached at once the summit of its pretension and the depth of its degradation. At the splendid jubilee of 1300, when the devout of all Christendom flocked in their myriads to the shrines of the Apostles, the haughty pontiff seemed to touch a height of power such as Innocent III had never reached. But by that time the foundations of pontifical autocracy had been undermined, and only three years later, when the hosts of pious pilgrims had dispersed, and the Pope was left lonely among his enemies at Anagni, the authority which had controlled the Middle Ages was defied and overthrown.

V

The dramatic humiliation of Pope Boniface VIII at Anagni in 1303 by the agents of Philip IV of France was merely a striking manifestation to the world of the fact that for a long time forces antagonistic to mediæval Christendom had been sapping the bases of the papal monarchy. The thirteenth century had been full of presages of change. The Papacy itself had become involved in mortal conflict with its creature, the Holy Roman Empire, and in the course of the struggle had prostituted its spiritual powers to the basest ends of secular ascendancy. The unity of Christendom, shattered by this suicidal schism, had been further rent by the growth of national particularism in England, Scotland, France, Spain, Germany, and Italy : the form of the modern state-system had started to shape itself in embryo. A new intellectual ferment had begun to portend the close of the ages of faith ; a new social unrest had commenced to threaten the existence of the feudal order. In the fourteenth century the new influence became dominant, and from the fall of Boniface VIII we may date the definite transition from mediæval to modern times.

What were the causes of this subtle but irresistible change ? They were many and various ; but the following stand out as eminent. First, the Crusades had brought the semi-barbarians of the West into contact with the more highly cultivated denizens of the East. The rude knights of chivalry had found to their amazement that the infidels against whom they were launched were not only soldiers equal to themselves in valour, but were also men of a culture far superior to their own. Fanatical hostility had given place to respect and even friendship, and not a few

Crusaders had accepted Islam as a purer faith than the debased Catholicism of their day. A new tolerance, a new scepticism, a new eclecticism, had resulted from this intermingling of East and West : the leader of the sixth Crusade is credited (or debited) with the remark that Moses, Christ, and Mahomet were all equally impostors. Secondly, as a result of the Crusades and of the establishment of the Christian kingdom of Jerusalem, commerce between Asia and Europe was immensely developed. New trade routes were opened up ; Christian seamen secured the command of the Mediterranean ; in Italy, Germany, France, the Netherlands, and England, towns and cities rose in importance, and a wealthy merchant class began to challenge the monopolies of nobles and of priests. Thirdly, by way of Syria, Egypt, Sicily, and Spain, the learning of the Arabs—mainly the treasured remnants of the heritage of classical antiquity—began to reach the scholars of the Christian West. Mathematics, astronomy, physics, chemistry, logic, philosophy, medicine—all were infused with a new vitality as the speculations and discoveries of ancient Hellenic sages and recent Arabian savants came to be known. In particular the recovery of the lost works of Aristotle, with the commentaries thereon of Avicenna and Averroes, marked the opening of a new era in European thought. It was from the fusion of Aristotelian philosophy with Augustinian theology that Scholasticism, the supreme achievement of the mediæval mind, was developed. Scholasticism, at any rate in its dominant Thomistic form, was orthodox enough ; but the mental gymnastics and moral contortions which it encouraged undoubtedly trained the nascent intellect of Christendom for its approaching revolt against ecclesiastical authority. Last of all came the general classical revival, due in part to the migration of

Greek scholars from the doomed Byzantine empire. There was not, of course, as used to be supposed, any sudden stampede or descent of parchment-laden *literati* consequent upon the fall of Constantinople in 1453. The movement, indeed, was terminating rather than beginning in the middle of the fifteenth century. For more than three generations it had been in process, as the Ottoman Turks forced their relentless path toward the coveted capital. By way of Southern Italy, where Greek was still a spoken language, the ancient culture had penetrated the mediæval world, bringing back the pagan spirit and the Hellenic view of life. But the classical revival was only in part Byzantine in origin. It was primarily a spontaneous uprising of the secular genius of the West itself. So early as the Council of Constance (1415) the diligent search for antique manuscripts had begun, and the monastic libraries of Europe were being ransacked, with amazing results, by scholars eager to recover the forgotten treasures of pre-Christian Rome.

The advent of the modern spirit—secular, rationalistic, individual, adventurous, curious, anti-clerical, and often anti-Christian—was marked by a change of attitude toward the universe and man. No longer was Nature regarded as inherently evil, or the descendants of Eve as essentially corrupt. No more were asceticism, self-abnegation, penance, withdrawal from the world, mortification of the flesh, conflict with the Devil, felt to be the ways of sanity and sanctity. The monasteries began to languish for lack of inmates. The study of scholastic philosophy and theology declined as the youth of Europe turned their awakened minds to the reading of romances, the writing of lyrics, the pursuit of science. The recovery of the geographies of Eratosthenes and Ptolemy; the invention of printing, which placed knowledge within the reach of the growing laity of the middle class ; improvements in shipping and in the instruments of navigation, opened the way for Vasco da Gama and Columbus to make their adventurous voyages. New oceans and unsuspected continents were brought within the ken of wondering Christendom, and the cosmography of the mediæval Church was shown to be false and even absurd. Soon the astronomical revelations of Copernicus demonstrated the fact that the Ptolemaic conception of the universe, dominant throughout the Middle Ages, was hopelessly wrong, and that the earth, so far from being the centre of all things, was but an insignificant planet revolving round a minor star. The reduction of man to stellar insignificance, and the discovery of the infinite abysses of space, exploded all the axioms and postulates of mediæval thought, and shook the very foundations of the established theology. Unnumbered and enormous heresies began to display themselves throughout Christendom. For the first time in her long history the Catholic Church— weakened by the Babylonish Captivity of the Papacy, torn by the Great Schism, paralysed by corruptions which the Conciliar Movement was powerless to reform, bewildered by the rationalism of the Renaissance—was unable to meet them and stamp them out. In vain did new orders of preachers restate and defend Catholic dogma ; in vain did the papal Inquisition organise itself to burn the pollution out ; in vain did crusades and dragonnades endeavour to drown in blood the monstrous brood of devilish phantasies which haunted the souls of the sectaries. All that denunciation, Inquisition, and massacre accomplished was to inflame dissent from the Church into a passion of implacable hatred, and to

38

obliterate the memory of a millennium of beneficence in the more recent recollection of bloody persecution. The way for the new schism of the Protestant Reformation was made straight.

VI

The Renaissance, with its new representation of life, and the Reformation, with its irremediable disruption of Catholic Christendom, marked the end of the Middle Ages in Western Europe. The thousand years thus terminated had displayed many notable features. They had been dominated by religion ; the powers of the world-to-come had been supreme ; God and the Devil, angels and demons, the saved and the damned, had been more real and potent than persons visible to the mortal eye. The epoch had been characterised by an extreme credulity which no miracle could shock, and no marvel of magic shake. No idea of any order in nature, or any conception of the sequence of cause and effect, awoke a scientific scepticism in the mediæval mind, or led the faithful to doubt the efficacy of relics and rituals. Movement of all sorts had been slow ; stability great ; pain, peril, and death had been constant companions ; life had, as a rule, been hard and short. Yet, in spite of all, the Middle Ages had had elements of singular charm, irresistible fascination, incontestable greatness. In particular they had been eminent for their corporate consciousness, for their sense of community, for the way in which their representative men— the builders of their cathedrals, the formulators of their creeds, the framers of their ideals—had been content to remain anonymous, sinking their individuality in the general life. Christendom had been a reality ; and among its members the greatest realists had been those who proclaimed it, with all its imperfections, as the ideal City of God.

It was necessary and inevitable that the Middle Ages should pass away. They were a time of tutelage, and the growing intellect of Europe could no longer remain subject to authorities whose spirit was alien from the genius of the modern world. But although they passed away, they had not been vain or fruitless. On the contrary, they had been rich and full ; and they left a priceless heritage to succeeding ages. If we are asked what their main contributions were, perhaps we may answer: in *religion*, the truth that the things of the Spirit are of supreme importance; in *philosophy*, that there is an infinite disparity between appearance and reality, between the substance and its accidents ; that the ideal is the real, and that the perfect is the true ; in *science*, that phenomena are but manifestations of occult powers ; in *art*, that the supreme forms of beauty are those that reveal purity, truth, and limitless aspiration ; in *literature*, that the language of the people is the proper vehicle for thought and emotion ; in *education*, that the true aim of all training is to fit a man, not to earn his own living, but to serve his fellows and to worship his Maker ; in *society*, that all men are equal in the sight of the Highest, and that the humblest creature has an infinite worth ; in *economics*, that work is a source of dignity and not of degradation, and that justice should determine wages, prices, and all the industrial relations of man to man ; in *politics*, that all tribes and nations are members of a greater community, that the source of every valid human authority is divine, and that power is a trust for which a solemn account will one day have to be rendered before the judgment-seat of God.

TO MODERN CIVILISATION

These are contributions to modern civilisation by no means negligible in value, and most of them are purely mediæval, free from all admixture of elements drawn from the civilisation of pagan antiquity. It will be the task of the remaining lectures of this course to expand this theme, and to trace the streams of influence one by one. I hope, however, that even this superficial introductory sketch has made clear the truth that the Middle Ages, with all their barbarism and crudity, were not a mere hiatus in the progress of Western civilisation, but an integral and essential part of the evolution of the modern world.

F. J. C. Hearnshaw

II

THE RELIGIOUS CONTRIBUTION OF THE MIDDLE AGES

HORACE WALPOLE quotes a story of a Florentine ambassador in the time of the Commonwealth
who wrote to his Court : " Some say the Protector
is dead, others say he is not : for my part I believe neither
the one nor t'other."[1] It is at least tempting to apply the
mot by substituting for the body of the Lord Protector
the spirit of the Middle Ages. And certainly in regard
to the formative influences of our later age the historical
student may well tread warily where masters disagree.
From Freeman we learn that "in our own history, above all,
every step in advance has been at the same time a step
backward. It has often been shown how our latest constitution is, amidst all external differences, essentially the
same as our earliest, how every struggle for right and
freedom from the thirteenth century onwards has simply
been a struggle for recovering something old."[2] Looking
from a different angle, Lord Acton tells us that " the
modern age did not proceed from the mediæval by normal
succession, with outward tokens of legitimate descent.
Unheralded, it founded a new order of things, under a
law of innovation, sapping the ancient reign of continuity.
. . . It was an awakening of new life ; the world revolved

[1] *Letters*, ed. Toynbee, iii, 262 (Clarendon Press, 1904).
[2] *Historical Essays*, Fourth Series, p. 253 (Macmillan, 1892).

42

CONTRIBUTIONS TO MODERN CIVILISATION

in a different orbit, determined by influences unknown before."[1]   Yet he also adds the saving caution that " we can found no philosophy on the observation of four hundred years, excluding three thousand."[2]

These considerations may serve for warning or encouragement according to the temper of the student as he turns to the subject of the religious contribution of the Middle Ages to our modern civilisation, whatever that somewhat elusive expression may be interpreted to mean. Peculiar difficulties attach to any estimate at a time when theories of civilisation are under revision, and when the bases of religious beliefs and practices, no less than of political institutions, have had to submit to the shock of a great war, and are still being tried by the " hot spirit drawn out of the alembick of hell " in a sense far more terrible than any conceived of by Edmund Burke.   An investigation that is to be fruitful must at any rate in intention be fair ; but in the study alike of theological and political development and of morals and opinions nearly every step has been attended in the past oftentimes by misconception, not infrequently by prejudice.   In our own day to say of any one that he has a mediæval mind will seldom be the language of courtesy, still less of admiration ; and we have need rather forcibly to remind ourselves that a declaration of war against ecclesiastical obscurantism is not even in a modern publicist an irrefragable evidence of the attainment of sweetness and light.

It is said that one of the maxims which Lord Acton impressed upon his pupils at the first opportunity is that " history is the true demonstration of religion,"[3] and Lord

<hr />

[1] *The Study of History*, pp. 8, 9 (Macmillan, 1896).   [2] *Ibid.*, p. 31.
[3] *Letters of Lord Acton to Mary Gladstone.* Introductory Memoir by Herbert Paul, p. lx (Macmillan, 1913).

Bryce in a notable passage has given us a striking illustration from Acton himself : " He spoke for six or seven minutes only ; but he spoke like a man inspired, seeming as if, from some mountain summit high in air, he saw beneath him the far-winding path of human progress from dim Cimmerian shores of prehistoric shadow into the fuller yet broken and fitful light of the modern time. The eloquence was splendid, but greater than the eloquence was the penetrating vision which discerned through all events and in all ages the play of those moral forces, now creating, now destroying, always transmuting, which had moulded and remoulded institutions, and had given to the human spirit its ceaselessly-changing forms of energy. It was as if the whole landscape of history had been suddenly lit up by a burst of sunlight." [1]

There are lights and shadows in the picture of the Middle Ages, as of other times. If we turn to a general European history like that of Lavisse and Rambaud [2] we shall see in its main divisions some of the reasons, though not all. The first volume outlines eight centuries from the fourth to the eleventh and is called *Origins*; the second deals with a century and three-quarters (1095–1270) under the title *Feudal Europe. The Crusades*; the triptych or trilogy is completed by a volume carrying the narrative to 1492 and styled *The Formation of Great States.* The next instalment covers less than seventy years (1492–1559) of *Renaissance and Reform*, while the fifth, from 1559–1648, is a melancholy if inevitable sequel of the Re-formation— *The Wars of Religion.* It is a far cry from the Edict of Milan (313) or the capture of Rome by Alaric (410) to the

---

[1] *Studies in Contemporary Biography*, pp. 396–7 (Macmillan, 1903).
[2] *Histoire Générale du IVe Siècle à nos Jours.* Twelve volumes (Paris : Armand Colin, 1893–1904).

Reformation or to the Peace of Westphalia (1648), and much may be expected to have happened in twelve or thirteen centuries. But the point which suggests itself to our notice is the interpenetration of the ecclesiastical and secular policies, the apparent leavening of the Church by the World. Yet at the outset of our inquiry a caution is necessary. There are no water-tight compartments in History, however readily we allow ourselves to abstract 'epochs' for convenience and dignify them by the title of 'special periods.' We are accustomed to speak of 'The Dark Ages,' 'The Ages of Faith,' sometimes of an 'Age of Reason.' The wise student verifies the contents of his parcel of records as well as the label. It has been, and in some quarters it still is, as common as it is false to represent the life of the Christian society as that of an ideal family within, though sorely tried from without, down to the time of the Edict of Milan, and to attribute to the fourth century with the beginnings of secular associations and patronage the cause of all later troubles. But the conflict or reconciliation of what may be called the two Loyalties begins in Galilee and Judæa, not in Greece or Italy; in the first century, not in any later age. "The separation" of the Church "from the world," says Archbishop Trench, "exists as much for the world's sake as for the Church's own, that so there may be for the world a City of Refuge, an abiding witness in the midst of it for a higher life than its own; which life, higher though it be, may yet be the portion, and on the simplest terms, of every one who will claim his share in it."[1] In one sense the observation is a platitude somewhat unhistorically expressed; in another, and that in which it is most likely to be interpreted, it is profoundly misleading, a relic of the Old Testament rather

[1] *Lectures on Medieval Church History*, p. 9 (Macmillan, 1879).

than of the New. The prayer of the Master for His disciples is not that they should be taken out of the world, but that they should be kept from the evil one. They are to be sheep, it may be, in the midst of wolves, but also, in a changed figure, to be the salt of the earth, the leaven working secretly in the lump; they are to render to Cæsar the things that are Cæsar's and to God the things that are God's; to fulfil all righteousness; to emulate the humility of the publican, the charity of the Good Samaritans of the world, not to imitate the self-satisfied Pharisees or even the priests and Levites of the Temple of the Most High. And if the student be tempted, as he will be, to attribute the decay of Christian ideals to association with ' the State,' he will do well to reflect that there are warnings against the corruptions of the world in the pages of New Testament writers at a time when certainly the infant Church cannot be accused either of assimilation to the State or of association with it.

You may see the same false antithesis when you are told that the sieges and battles and sufferings of the Crusades do not properly find a place in a Church history at all,[1] as though the Church were concerned only with men's ends while the means to attain them and the secular activities amid which they are pursued remained outside its purview. No doubt a series of dark pictures can be drawn in relation to manners and morals from Jerome's description[2] of the scented, bejewelled exquisites among the younger Roman ecclesiastics of the fourth century, to the priests of Strassburg carousing in taverns c. 1299–1306, with their long hair and gold-laced coats, their swords and their boots of red, yellow, and green[3]; from

---

[1] *Lectures on Medieval Church History*, p. 139 (Macmillan, 1879).
[2] *Ep.* xxii, " Ad Eustochium "; *cf.* the famous *Ep.* lii, " Ad Nepotianum."
[3] Martene et Durand, *Thesaurus Novus*, iv, 529–556 (Paris, 1717).

the rhetorical invectives of Salvian of Marseilles[1] against social standards in the fifth century to the record of visitations like that of Cardinal Morton of the Abbey of St Albans[2] in the fifteenth. We can paint if we wish in darker colours still scenes from the history of the Crusades, of persecutions like that of the Albigenses, or the like. We may summarise them as Ranke does in the first chapter of his *History of the Popes*, finding the strange combinations of piety and cruelty " eloquently illustrative of those times and of that politico-religious government."[3] For those to whom religion is an intractable element, a surd in the calculation by which they seek to resolve human history into its component parts, the " Tantum religio potuit suadere malorum " of Lucretius may seem to find at length an appropriate conclusion in " Écrasez l'infâme."

It is of course no answer to inquire whether the crimes committed in the name of Liberty be not greater than those perpetrated under the sanctions of Religion, since unless we adopt a purely naturalistic standpoint the latter would in any case be more heinous. A writer who will not be suspected of clericalism observes in regard to a later period that " it became painfully clear how great a mistake it was to suppose the clergy tainted with some special curse of cruelty. Then, as usually, for good or for evil, they were on about the same moral level with an immense number of laymen, and were not much more than the incarnation of the average darkness of the hour."[4] The historian's function is not to extenuate facts but to endeavour to state them truly, and few it is to be hoped will derive much comfort

---

[1] Salvian, *De Gubernatione Dei*, iii, 9, and Lib. vii, *passim*.
[2] *Cf.* Reg. Morton, i, ff. 22b–23b.
[3] (Bell, 1913.) Vol. i, pp. 25–6.
[4] *Voltaire*, p. 229 (Macmillan, 1897).

from Lord Morley's *apologia* for the clergy of eighteenth-century France. But truthfulness of statement depends on an effort to include all relevant factors and to display them in a just proportion. There is an element of truth in all these transcripts from life, but they are not the whole story nor from every part of the field. The treasure is in earthen vessels; but there is a treasure to be found none the less by those who neither choose by the view nor turn aside after husks and garbage.

It is a commonplace of political philosophers that the root-conception of mediæval theory is the organic unity of all mankind[1]; but further this organic unity has a spiritual basis, since all mankind derives its origin from a single Creator, owes obedience to a single Ruler—God Himself. As the course of the Middle Ages proceeds you may see the working of other conceptions, as for example when the formula for the manumission of a bondman by Robert Mascall, the Carmelite Bishop of Hereford (1404–16), opens with the words " Whereas from the beginning nature created all men freely or free, and afterward the law of nations (*ius gencium*) subjected some of them to the yoke of servitude, we therefore judge that it would be a pious act and one deservedly to be rewarded by God to restore some of those, whose deserts require it, to their pristine liberty "[2]; but the fundamental idea is unchanged. And in consequence, as it has been said, "Christendom, which in destiny is identical with Mankind, is set before us as a single, universal Community, founded and governed by God Himself."[3] But in the realm of human affairs God governs

[1] See Gierke, *Political Theories of the Middle Age*, edited by F. W. Maitland, pp. 9 ff. (Cambridge University Press, 1900).
[2] Contained in Edmund de Lacy's Register, f. 1b (Canterbury and York Society, 1918).
[3] Gierke, *op. cit.*, p. 10, *cf.* p. 18 f.

by human instruments, and the relation of these instruments to God and to one another and to the rest of mankind was one of the supreme problems for mediæval thinkers. As will be evident, it was a religious problem as well as a political one : its solution was of almost immeasurable practical importance ; and if we approach it with some greater measure of hopefulness, for we have not as yet fully solved it, that is because we have the experience of the Middle Ages behind us. Is the relation of the spiritual and the temporal, the ecclesiastical and the secular powers, to be one of co-ordination or is the one to be subordinate to the other, and, if so, which is higher, which lower, and upon what grounds is the solution adopted to be defended ? Let us look at the situation in the East as well as in the West.

It is from many points of view unfortunate, though it has been perhaps inevitable, that to us the story of the Middle Ages presents itself as that of Western civilisation, or, as Dr Poole has preferred to put it, " The history of the middle ages is the history of the Latin church."[1] Yet the survival of the Eastern Empire from the fourth to the fifteenth century is a factor in European history that we do ill to neglect. Byzantine Hellenism has for many nothing that is attractive, much that is repellent ; but it remains Hellenism even if marred and in a state of suspended development. And the history of non-Western Christianity illustrates one solution of the relations of Church and State of which we are bound to take account, whether or not we approve it, for it has been seen still in use for

[1] *Illustrations of the History of Medieval Thought*, p. 2 (Williams and Norgate, 1884). To this work the present writer owes unmeasured gratitude for stimulus many years ago to read the authorities quoted and for constant guidance in doing so.

good or for evil down to our own day, and as an inheritance
from the Middle Ages. We cannot stay to trace the
course of its history ; but look at it at two moments in its
development. For twenty years of unceasing conflict at
the opening of the ninth century Theodore of Studium,
following in the steps of John Damascene, claims for the
Church in face of the Iconoclastic emperors the right of
complete independence of decision in matters of faith.
In the secular sphere princes have complete authority ;
but it belongs not to them to decide upon celestial and
divine dogmas confided to the Apostles and their successors.
No Presbyterian ever upheld the ' Crown Rights ' of the
Redeemer more strenuously than this militant abbot
against time-serving usurpers of the Patriarchal throne
and the secular arm of Leo the Armenian, which broke
his body but not his spirit. Yet it has its limitations of
charity, then as now, this spiritual *intransigeance*. The
Emperor Michael II, having liberated the prisoners, proposes a conference between the Iconoclasts and the Orthodox.
But Theodore, while expressing his wish that the Emperor
would deem him worthy to see his sacred person, to listen
to the entrancing utterance of his august mouth learned in
divine things, replies that any conference with heretics is
forbidden by apostolic precept,[1] and dies in exile a martyr
to conviction, who as so often has failed to learn the beati-
tude which belongs to the makers of peace. After all,
even to those of us who are not episcopal chancellors there
is illumination to be gained from the study of what actually
happened in the long run with regard to ' images,' whether
in East or West. But ten centuries later than Theodore
the essential characteristic of the Orthodox Church as seen

[1] *Ep.* ii, 86 (Migne, *Patrologia Græca*, xcix, c. 1329). The whole letter
is singularly illuminating.

in Russia appears to De Maistre to be the complete submission of the clergy to the civil power, the union in the same hands of spiritual and temporal sovereignty.[1] " I am Pope," said Tsar Alexander I to Napoleon ; " it is very much more convenient (*bien plus commode*)." We have there in its full development one theory of the relation of the two powers : it is logical, coherent, and it may be doubted whether in practice it has proved itself altogether Erastian in the sense in which we abuse that term of abuse. And at least the *societas perfecta* of Jesuit theory receives in both its forms an unexpected simplification as the ecclesiastical and temporal autocrat of all the Russias exchanges confidences with the imperial heir of the royal dictum " L'État, c'est Moi." The world had to wait more than half a century longer before it heard from other lips, not less commanding, the utterance of even fuller significance " La tradizione son' Io."[2]

Let us turn then to the West. We shall not, as every one knows, escape from the influence of Hellenic thought, though its results in combination with other strains may be different. In the agony of the fifth century—at the opening, as some would say, of the Middle Ages—Augustine of Hippo bequeathed to later days the great treatise *De Civitate Dei*, a much celebrated legacy whose magnificence seems still for many who write about it unspoiled by familiarity. Yet it was the book selected by preference, so we are told, to be read to him at his dinner-table by Charlemagne, in whose reign Dr R. L. Poole has seen

[1] *Cf.* C. Latreille, *Joseph de Maistre et la Papauté*, p. 19 (Hachette, 1906).

[2] The attribution to Pius IX was accepted by Lord Acton in his article on " The Vatican Council " (*North British Review*, Oct. 1870), reprinted in *The History of Freedom and other Essays* (Macmillan, 1907). Whether it would have satisfied the canons of E. Fournier's provoking but fascinating work, *L'Esprit dans l'Histoire* (Paris, Dentu, 1883), is another matter.

MEDIÆVAL CONTRIBUTIONS

" the dividing line between ancient and medieval history . . . not only by virtue of its political facts but also because it begins the age of the education of the northern races, fitting them in time to rule the world as the Romans had done before them." [1] What that education might mean the non-Christian races saw on the one hand in the Emperor's efforts to " compel them to come in," not by the appeal of the philanthropy of Christ, but by the less gentle inducements of the sword and the block, on the other in the history of the Crusades. It would be absurd to make Augustine responsible for the excesses of his readers, but it is almost impossible to overestimate the extent of his influence : it seems sometimes so constant and so universal as to make it legitimate at least to suspect its presence even when unacknowledged.

For Augustine there are two kinds of human society or association, and two only—two citizenships or modes of living, a heavenly and an earthly, with different ends attainable by different means. But the conception implied in the first and last chapters of the fourteenth book was almost inevitably replaced by the conception of two States, and therewith came difficulties of a very serious kind, since the ordinary mind tends to think of States in terms of institutions. The student whether of Augustine or of the thinkers of the Middle Ages will need again and again to be on his guard against the persistent if subconscious tendency to interpret their language in terms of the modern antithesis of Church and State, and the view of each which that antithesis implies; and he will find this the more difficult because the Empire and the Papacy, the Emperor and the Pope, will seem to him two great factors in the political and religious situation in the Middle Ages, exactly corresponding with

[1] *Medieval Thought*, p. 15.

that antithesis. He must ask himself not simply what was their history, what did they do, but for what, in the view of mediæval thinkers, did they stand? Of this he will learn much from Gierke's *Political Theories of the Middle Age*, splendidly edited by F. W. Maitland, Dr Poole's *Illustrations of the History of Medieval Thought*, Dr Figgis' *From Gerson to Grotius* and other works, and Bishop Robertson's *Regnum Dei*. But if he would fully realise how much trouble the matter gave to mediæval thinkers from many points of view he must study for himself that truly painful compilation, the *Monarchia* of Melchior Goldast[1] in the seventeenth century, and that, as he will ruefully find, is far more than an *Opus Nonaginta Dierum*, if we may misapply the title of the treatise by William of Ockham which one of the volumes contains.

" The State is not in the Church, the Church is in the State : . . . above the Emperor there is God alone, who made the Emperor ": so says Optatus of Milevum in the fifth century.[2] " The spiritual power," answers Hugh of St Victor in the twelfth, " is superior to the secular in antiquity, dignity and usefulness."[3] " God ought to obey the Devil,"[4] if Wyclif be not libelled in the fourteenth, while Luther, like Gerard of York, puts the secular ruler in the place of the Ignatian bishop and solemnly burns the Canon Law. But if in the opening years of the eleventh century there had been realised the dream of the Emperor Otto III and Pope Sylvester II of an Empire and a Papacy, such as in a

---

[1] *Monarchia S. Romani Imperii* (Hanoviæ, 1612–13).

[2] *Optati Milevitani Libri VII*, ed. Ziwsa " Corp. Script. Eccl. Lat.," xxvi (Vindobonæ, 1883), iii, 3 : " Non enim respublica est in ecclesia, sed ecclesia in republica, id est in imperio Romano " (p. 74) ; " Cum super imperatorem non sit nisi solus deus, qui fecit imperatorem " (*ibid.*, p. 75).

[3] *Cf. De Sacram.*, . . . ii, 2 throughout (Migne, *P. L.*, clxxvi, c. 415 ff.).

[4] *Cf.* Reg. Courteney, f. 25.

modified form Nicolas of Cusa yearned for centuries later,
wherein the two powers ordained of God should exercise
an universal rule in amity and concord side by side, the
continent of Europe might have witnessed an experiment
which would have made the later ideals of Gregory VII,
Innocent III, and Boniface VIII on the one hand or those
of Dante in the *De Monarchia* or Marsiglio of Padua in the
Defensor Pacis on the other appear superfluous, if not
un-Christian. True, the Donation of Constantine and the
pseudo-Isidorian Decretals were ready to hand for anyone
who cared to use them, and had been so for more than
two centuries before Hildebrand ; but they would probably
have remained in decent obscurity, or been summarily
ejected from the *Concordance of Discordant Canons*, had not
political circumstances arisen in which they could be
prayed in aid of a theory of the Church's universal jurisdiction which was clearly, as it would seem, not based
upon them, but for which they were quoted with probably
much less of conscious dishonesty than has often been
assumed by controversialists. Origins are a notoriously
difficult subject, and assertion has been known to take the
place of evidence in the pedigrees of institutions and
customs as well as of men. Few of us, perhaps, would
accept without hesitation Newman's statement in the
treatise on Development which was his last gift to the
Church of England that " first local disturbances gave rise
to Bishops, and next ecumenical disturbances gave rise to
Popes," [1] even though supported in part by the authority
of St Jerome. Still less readily, probably, shall we assent
when we hear : " Who does not know that [kings] had their

[1] (Oxford : Parker, 1845), p. 167. *Cf.* Hier. *in Ep. ad Titum*, i, 5, and
the use made of it by Wyclif, *De Potestate Pape*, cap. iv, quoting from
Decretum, Pars Iᵃ dist. 95, c. 5.

beginning from those who, being ignorant of God, by pride, by acts of brigandage, perfidy, homicide, and finally by almost every species of crime, at the instigation of the prince of the world, that is the Devil, by blind cupidity and intolerable presumption affected to exercise dominion over their peers, namely, over men ? " The introduction of the reference to supernatural agency, even though it be diabolical, forbids us to discern in this full-blooded rhetoric an anticipation of Bolshevist propaganda—it is taken of course from the well-known letter[1] of Gregory VII; and by a polite fiction of considerable pragmatic value the balance can readily be adjusted. Regard the Pope's theory in the spirit once more of De Maistre, and say that " it is from the Pope that sovereignty descends on crowned heads, and it is he who gives them that consecrated character which commands respect and obedience," [2] and all is simple and straightforward. The organic unity is preserved and the Spiritual Power reigns supreme. The only difficulty is to find a period in which the facts really corresponded with the theory. And two observations may be made. It need not trouble us in theory that for some seven centuries at any rate of the Middle Ages there were two opposed Empires of East and West—a condition of affairs very different from the original plan of Diocletian; and in this regard the student may derive considerable amusement from reading side by side the Alexiad of Anna Comnena and the Letters of Gregory VII. In theory there was still only one Empire, though in reference to this again modern interpretation will not easily square with mediæval theory. The Empire of Charlemagne

---

[1] *Epp.* viii, 21, to Herman of Metz in 1081 (Jaffé, *Mon. Greg.*, p. 457, Berlin, 1865). *Cf.* iv, 2, in 1076, to the same (*ibid.*, p. 243).

[2] Latreille, *op. cit.*, p. 11, and the second book of *Du Pape*, esp. c. 5.

we are accustomed to hear was not a new creation of the Pope nor a legitimate succession to the Empire of the West : it was a transfer in more or less dubious circumstances, by a person to whom it did not belong to a person to whom it belonged still less, of the Eastern Empire seated at Constantinople. And the Holy Roman Empire which bulks so large and for so long in mediæval history is a succession to neither, but a German invention of which one of the wittiest of Frenchmen has written the epitaph and one of the most erudite of English political thinkers has articulated the skeleton. And secondly, it is impossible not to be struck with the continental character of this mediæval theorising : this is as true in reading William of Ockham as in the case of the other works collected by Goldast. Neither English sovereigns nor the English people were wanting generally in deference to the see of Rome in the Middle Ages ; but the attitude of William the Conqueror to Gregory VII's demand for homage finds an echo in the sense of intolerable outrage to national feeling with which the chroniclers record John's surrender of his crown to Innocent III ; and therefrom followed consequences of which papal statesmen seem always to have failed to appreciate the significance.

There are few investigations more fascinating, if more elusive, than that of the power of ideas to mould facts as well as to account for them. From some writers one would judge that the Hildebrandine idea of the Papacy presented itself to the world as a strange and monstrous portent in the eleventh century. It would seem to them not less original perhaps in its development, but at any rate less catastrophic, if they would consider on the one hand the conception of the Christian State which underlies the Code of Justinian, a monarch for whom orthodoxy was a political duty,[1] or the fact that in the Eastern Empire at the beginning of the eighth century Baptism was the gate to citizenship for men of every race [2]; or on the other hand the circumstances of the pontificate, and some of the utterances of Gregory the Great more than two centuries earlier, and the very curious little disquisition by Agobard of Lyons in the ninth century on the two rules—ecclesiastical and secular. We have spoken of the influence of Augustine, but there are others to be taken into account. If you seek to build as mediæval thinkers did your political and religious theory upon bases so discordant as the Holy Scriptures, Aristotle, and the Civil Law, you may expect results as strange as some seem desirous of achieving in our own day on the foundations of Rousseau, Karl Marx, Herbert Spencer, and Count Tolstoy.

The modern student who sets himself to examine the mediæval exegesis of Scripture will at least recognise the reason for Lord Acton's differentiation of the modern age. Columbus, Machiavelli, Erasmus, Luther, Copernicus are his examples of the men who stand between us and the Middle Ages.[3] In a very well-known passage Dr Figgis has described the changed position. " It would require," he says, " an intellectual revolution—quite inconceivable in magnitude—to induce us to regard it as an argument for the Papal power, that the sun is superior to the moon, or that S. Peter gave two swords to Christ; that the Pope is like Sinai, the source of the oracles of God, and is

---

[1] A convenient summary, though only a summary, of the effects of this view upon Justinian's legislation will be found in W. G. Holmes, *The Age of Justinian and Theodora*, vol. ii, cc. xiv, xv (London : G. Bell & Sons, 2nd edit., 1912).

[2] *Cf.* Lavisse et Rambaud, *Hist. Gén.*, i, 201.

[3] *Study of History*, p. 8.

57

superior to all kings and princes, because Mount Sinai is higher than all other hills (which it is not) ; that when Daniel speaks of beasts, the writer means that tyranny is the origin of earthly power ; that the command to feed my sheep, and the committal of the keys to S. Peter gave to the Papacy the absolute political sovereignty of the world ; or on the other side that Adam was the first king, and Cain the first priest, that the text forbidding murder proves immediately the Divine origin of secular lordship, that unction is not indelible save in France, but there it is so because the oil is provided by an angel." [1]   These things have served at least to enliven the dreariness for the modern reader of many a mediæval disquisition sometimes of great value, usually of great length ; and one may be allowed to add to the list for the delight which it caused when first read to one who has lived under the prosaic *régime* of the Third Republic the reason why the crown of France may be worn neither by a workman nor a woman : viz., that the lilies " toil not, neither do they spin." It is easy to be contemptuous, but it is a sure bar to understanding ; and in appropriateness of exegesis the modern observer may possibly think that there is little to choose on either side for some centuries before and after the Reformation. However this may be, it is at least significant that the attempt to interpret and to apply the Scriptures with due regard to their proper setting should have been deferred, though with some exceptions, until to our lasting impoverishment they are, apart from public services and professional studies, rapidly ceasing to be read at all.

No one now reads Boethius, though there are still a few

[1] *From Gerson to Grotius,* pp. 23–4 (Cambridge University Press, 2nd edit., 1916).

who are believed to find consolation in philosophy. He announced, we remember, his intention of translating into Latin every work of Aristotle within his reach. Of the influence of Aristotle's *Politics* upon Thomas Aquinas in the thirteenth century all students have heard; but have you ever examined a succession of great political and theological treatises of the Middle Ages in the West to see what would be left of them if you excised all traces of Aristotle? The result is so startling as to suggest that the whole course of Western history, civil, philosophical, scientific, religious, might have been changed had his works as we now possess them been known in Latin from say four hundred years after the death of Boethius in 525. It is no mere affectation of the pedant which makes Wyclif begin his treatise on the power of the Pope with Aristotle's fourfold distinction of power as active, passive, purposively controlled or accidentally acquired (the illustration of the last is medical skill).[1] He adopts the method because it was natural to his age. Holy Scripture for him includes all truth but it does not provide a dialectic, and though it may be true that he is Platonist rather than Aristotelian and that his conclusions owe more to reflection on the Scriptures and on Augustine than to any other influences, such Platonism as he may have learnt from Augustine would not have given either to him or to his age what was wanted for their expression. To Dr Poole "the fundamental principle of" Wyclif's "Doctrine of Lordship justifies its author's title to be considered in no partial sense the father of modern Christianity"[2]—a judgment with which some of us would venture strongly to disagree; but just as you can most easily read the handwriting of some people by determining

[1] *De Potestate Pape*, cap. i, "Wyclif Society," pp. 2–4 (Trübner, 1907).
[2] *Op. cit.*, p. 306.

the angle from which they wrote, so you can more readily understand the thought of a systematic writer of the Middle Ages if you can imagine anew the framework in which in the process of thinking new ideas struggled for expression. And the inquiry as to the latest writer for whom a text from Scripture and a text from Aristotle, when not discordant, had equal validity as an argument *in pari materia* would yield more useful results than the quest for the latest ecclesiastic who wore a wig.

A lecturer who enters upon the subject of the Civil Law, especially if he live in the parts of Britain south of the Tweed and be a clerk in orders, will nowadays order himself more lowly and reverently than has always been the fashion. One is sorely tempted in the terms of the stately preface to Bacon's *Maxims of the Law* to try to estimate the political bearings of the differences between the Roman civil law and the laws of England, but one observation cannot be omitted, at any rate, because of its direct bearing upon the present subject. The maxim that the pleasure of the ruler has the force of law is regarded with just disapprobation by many who do not know that it comes from the *Digest*[1]; for that reason the fact is often overlooked that it is based on a theory that the source of rule is to be found in the will of the people. And however strange the transformations which it sustained in the hands of mediæval writers and those of the modern age the idea of popular sovereignty which is therein contained is one of the many for which we owe a debt to the Middle Ages which preserved though they did not create it.

What is the real legacy of the Middle Ages in Western

[1] "Quod principi placuit legis habet vigorem," l. 1, *Dig.*, i, 4. See the interesting discussion in Gierke, *op. cit.*, pp. 37 ff, 147.

Europe to our modern day on the political side so far as it affects or is affected by religious conceptions ? Professor Tout, in a notable and striking passage, has illustrated the efforts both of Pope and Emperor each in his own way to establish God's Kingdom upon earth. Beside Hildebrand he sets the noblest of the House of Hohenstaufen, Frederick Barbarossa, " the most imposing, the most heroic, and the most brilliant of the long line of German princes, who strove to realise the impracticable but glorious political ideal of the Middle Ages." [1] And yet, one may venture to think, if our inheritance is still the vision of a *Civitas Dei* which those ages learnt from Augustine and Augustine from the New Testament, we shall not take from them the conception of its possible realisation either through an universal Empire—a world-domination German, French, Latin, British, Mongolian, or Slav, wherein religious activities might probably be either ordered by a Minister of Public Worship or peremptorily excluded, nor through an universal Papacy, the earthly embodiment of that Divine Wisdom by whom kings reign and princes decree justice. We shall seek it rather through the development of that national consciousness among the several races of the civilised world which then rendered impossible the achievement of the ideal of the mediæval Popes and on the other hand fostered a national expression of religion which we are gradually learning to regard as involving, not the negation of that unity among Christians for which their Master prayed, but an enrichment of the life of the One Body " fitly framed and knit together through that which every joint supplieth."

Clearly this view will not pass unchallenged. Lord Acton, for example, would have rejected such a conclusion;

[1] *The Empire and the Papacy*, p. 247 (Rivingtons, 1909).

and there are many indeed to whom such a statement will seem a bewildering confusion of the issues raised by the facts of what is called the 'religious situation' in the several nations of Western Europe, even if we take no wider outlook. As so often, the mental constructions of one epoch are the prisons of the next until the power of some new idea avails to burst the bonds which men forge for themselves from age to age. The formation of great states rendered improbable the continued recognition anywhere of the Holy Roman Empire as being still in theory what it had never been in fact, the *Civitas Dei*. The forces political, intellectual, religious, which made themselves felt in the century from 1450 to 1550, but of whose presence we may find indications a century earlier, served to disintegrate the mediæval conception of the Catholic Church. An attempt was made, is still made, to substitute for it one less vulnerable if more elusive, because *ex hypothesi* invisible, though neither was that idea again wholly new. But its unity was marred from the outset by the fierce claim of the several Churches to exclude from it all others of whose principles and practice they disapproved, and those who were themselves, like the Pilgrim Fathers, the victims of intolerance could not always show a subsequent record free from the stain of persecution; while in theology the new scholasticism proved for many generations even more burdensome than the old.

Let us look a little closer. On the political side we should all reject the abominable doctrine expressed in the words *Cuius regio eius religio*—the theory that the ruler has the right to determine the religion of his subjects, an inheritance not from the Middle Ages but from the Reformation period of which you may find an exemplification in the Peace of Augsburg in the sixteenth century or in some of the consequences of the Peace of Westphalia in the seventeenth. On the other hand, whether we agree or disagree with Lord Acton's famous essay on "The Protestant Theory of Persecution," [1] the student will find himself obliged to conclude that in the history of the struggle for religious toleration the prime movers have seldom been found among the official representatives of organised Christianity, Catholic or Protestant. He may also infer without sacrifice of historical truth that that toleration which is actually guaranteed by every enlightened state is the product not of indifference but, as a matter of fact, of the Christian conscience of the majority of its citizens. And within the expansive limits of that toleration so painfully won our later age has seen the signs of a new *rapprochement*, a consciousness of shame at our unhappy divisions, a recognition of a unity in diversity which at one time seemed impossible, and still to some is an idle dream. From the sense of an underlying unity has come a new conception of a visible Church, the realisation of which may indeed be far distant but which has possibilities that men are at least ready to explore. The Reformation is seen as a stage in the drama of Western Christendom, an episode of enormous importance necessary to the development of the action, but not the whole, one which indeed cannot be understood by blotting out twelve centuries of Christian history. And those who turn with reawakened curiosity to the Middle Ages will assuredly not return unrewarded. Where will you find a nobler expression of the true ideal of the new commonwealth which we are seeking to build than in Marsiglio's adoption of Aristotle's definition [2] of the

[1] *The Rambler,* March 1862, reprinted in *The History of Freedom* (Macmillan, 1907).
[2] *Politics,* i, 1 ; Mars., *Def. Pacis,* i, 4 (Goldast, *Monarch.,* ii, 157).

rationale of the State " in order that men may live well " and his explication of " living well " as " having leisure for liberal tasks, such as are those of the virtues of the soul as well of thought as of action " ?

If it be suggested that we have been dwelling too much upon the political side of mediæval thought in our search for religious contributions to our modern civilisation, it must be remembered that, humanly speaking, if ever the kingdom of the world is to become the Kingdom of our Lord and of His Christ it will be because the visible Church of which we dream is not a City of Refuge but the embodiment of Christian citizenship because of Christian discipleship. You cannot divorce the politics and the religion of the true citizen without detriment to the State, any more than you can build a common life on a basis of self-interest, however much enlightened. It is often argued that religious men are unpractical, but it may be questioned whether the stricture sounds well in the mouth of people who are endeavouring to teach what by a new barbarism is called Civics, in which we may recognise some of the maxims of Christian conduct divorced from the Christian motive. Again, the mediæval aspirations after a life of evangelical poverty, which are found so beautiful to read even by many who frankly admit that they could never themselves attempt to rise to their level, represent a reaction against the impoverishment of Christian ideals, the degradation of Christian practice observable in the life of the mediæval Church. But those aspirations are themselves part of that life. As we study them in Arnold of Brescia, in the Rule of St Francis of Assisi or the works of Franciscans like Archbishop Peckham or of Dominicans like Tauler, to take only a few instances, or as we trace the later history of the Spiritual Franciscans, we may possibly feel the same

64

superiority or the same sadness in noting where on the
practical side their doctrine fails, and why, as we might
in reading Mr George Jacob Holyoake's history of the
early stages of the Co-operative Movement.[1] But study
their implications and see whether you may not find in
them some of the principles for which our modern age is
still seeking. " The whole social economy of the Franciscans," says a modern exponent of it, " proceeded from
the ideal of service having for its motive the evangelical
law of love. . . . So far the Franciscan social ideal is that
of a perfect democracy ; of a society in which all the members are on an equality of comradeship, whatever be the
accident of their place or position, and in which all, whether
rulers or governed, are subject to the same law of personal
service. But where the Franciscan democracy differs
from the ordinary political democracy is, in the first place,
that with the Franciscan equality is generated in voluntary
assumption of common duties and responsibilities and not
in the assertion of individual rights. The Franciscan
begins at the other end from that generally taken by the
political democrat. He starts practically from the idea
that he himself owes a duty to his neighbour rather than
that his neighbour owes a duty to him ; he is more concerned to curb his own arrogance and selfishness than to
curb that of others ; he is more willing to submit to the
will of another than to claim another's submission to his
will. In short, the ideal Franciscan society is akin to that
democracy of spirit which exists in the personal relations
of all true men." [2] It is strange to contrast such an ideal,
which to many will seem no unfair representation of that

[1] *The History of Co-operation* (Trübner, 1875, 1879), revised and completed (T. Fisher Unwin, 1906).
[2] Fr Cuthbert, O.S.F.C., *The Romanticism of St Francis*, pp. 64–5
(Longmans, 1915).

spirit of St Francis himself which lives on from the Middle Ages in the freshness of an eternal spring, with the language of Gregory VII as to the origin of secular governments or with a definition of the purpose of the laws that was still being taught in England within living memory—that they were intended "to preserve the rich in their possessions and to restrain the vicious poor."

Once more, of course, a caution is necessary. The casual student will learn, shall we say, from Lord Acton's works that the Whig theory of the Revolution may be found in the works of St Thomas Aquinas, written at the time when Simon de Montfort summoned the Commons,[1] or that the doctrines of the sovereignty of the nation, representative government, the superiority of the legislature over the executive, and the liberty of conscience were worked out by Marsiglio of Padua, who lived at the same time as Edward II.[2] These facts are dear to students of politics, if unknown to politicians who do not study. But it would be the wildest absurdity to suppose that the theologians and jurists of the Middle Ages were generally in favour of liberty of conscience any more than of representative government ; or that such an injunction met with universal approval as is found in the Decretals that " secular judges who with damnable presumption compel ecclesiastical persons to pay debts are to be restrained from such temerity by ecclesiastical censure through the ordinaries of the places." [3] And the fact that in a bygone age an idea is tentatively sketched out, or even seriously

---

[1] This much misquoted statement occurs in the remarkable address to the members of the Bridgnorth Institution in 1877 on " The History of Freedom in Christianity," printed in *The History of Freedom* (see pp. 36–7).

[2] *Ibid.*, p. 37.

[3] Quoted by Figgis, *From Gerson to Grotius*, p. 260, from the Sext., ii, 2, 2.

put forward, which seems to some the acme of ' modernity,' is no ground in itself for claiming that we receive it by legitimate succession or for denying the originality of its presentation in our own day. Dr Poole with justice has claimed Marsiglio as one of "that rarest class of *doctrinaires* whom future ages may rightly look back upon as prophets,"[1] but in their own day they were as a rule rather solitary figures, and even where they attracted followers they had usually few successors. It is a striking and curious fact, but it is no more, that William of Ockham should have argued in the fourteenth century for the inclusion not merely of laymen but of women in the general councils of the Church, where the wisdom, goodness, or power of women should be necessary for the treatment of the Faith.[2] And even the suggestion of the Invincible Doctor, perhaps not intended to be taken very seriously, though he puts it forward with gravity, must yield place to the rich variety of novelties in the tractate *Of the Recovery of the Holy Land* by the Norman advocate Pierre du Bois. Dr Figgis calls it " a mine of reforming ideas," though we may well think that some of them would have startled the Fathers of the Reformation. " Disendowment or the Church, and of the monasteries, absolute authority for the secular State, women's enfranchisement, mixed education, are all advanced with the one object of increasing the power of the French king, who is to be made Emperor and to rule at Constantinople. International Arbitration was to decrease the horrors of war, and educated women were to be sent to the Holy Land in order to marry and convert both the Saracens and the priests of the Orthodox Church, and also

[1] *Op. cit.*, p. 275.
[2] " Propter unitatem fidei . . . quae omnest angit et in qua non masculus nec femina " (*Dialogus*, c. 85 *ad fin.* Goldast, *Mon.*, ii, 605).

to become trained nurses and teachers. . . . The whole spirit of the book is secular and modern. Bishop Stubbs was wont to declare that everything was in it, including the new woman."[1]

It is required of the Bishops of the Church of England by the thirty-fourth and thirty-fifth canons of 1603, under pain of two years' suspension from the power of ordaining, that they admit none to holy orders save after examination and being such as are able as a minimum qualification to render an account of their faith in Latin. The requirement was certainly enforced as late as the time of Archbishop Tenison, and though it may not be a discipline of which the restoration is nowadays much wished, at any rate by ordination candidates, it is certain that much loss has come to clerks as well as to laymen from the fact that they cannot as a rule read with any facility the ecclesiastical Latin of the Middle Ages. In view of this disability, it is worth while to insist upon the fact that any student can now read a considerable part at least if he will of the *Summa* of St Thomas Aquinas in an admirable English translation. This fact is the more important because in the minds of many the philosophy of the Middle Ages means nothing more than is expressed by a vague reference to the Schoolmen regarded as protagonists of a series of wearisome logomachies, the inventors of antitheses of knowledge falsely so called. Thus to regard it is to stultify reason and to misread history. We may as easily eliminate from the doctrinal content of the theology of the undivided Church the influence of ancient philosophy on, let us say, the Christian Gnostics of Alexandria, as treat the Nomin-

---

[1] Figgis, *op. cit.* pp. 31–2. There are few works of equal compass from which the student may derive so much amusement as Langlois' edition of the *De Recuperatione Terræ Sanctæ* (Paris : Picard, 1891).

alists and Realists of the West with their quest for truth in forms borrowed from Platonist and Aristotelian sources, acutely studied if imperfectly known, as mere triflers. The sanity of the nobler minds of the Middle Ages is seen in other fields of religious interest besides politics. Mr Taylor in his useful if discursive work on *The Mediæval Mind* has spoken of those who in the twelfth century cultivated logic and metaphysics with the desire to know more active in them than the fear of hell.[1] " By doubting," says Abelard in his *Sic et Non,* "we are led to inquire ; by inquiry we perceive the truth." [2] After all, one may suppose that logic is not always the enemy of truth—was it not deemed a requisite for a degree in medicine at Salerno ?—though theologians have perhaps been more prone than other men to take refuge in language such as St Bernard allowed himself with regard to Abelard : " Would not a mouth which says such things more justly be beaten with bludgeons than refuted with reasons ?" [3]

One who has spent more time than he cares to remember in turning pages of manuscripts of Rabanus Maurus in search for other things may be excused if in what follows he shows that, like Rabanus, according to Mr Taylor, " the operations of his mind " are " predominantly Carolingian, which is to say that ninety-nine per cent. of the contents of " what he has to say " consists of material extracted from prior writers." [4] To Rabanus " the foundation, the state, and the perfection of wisdom is knowledge of the Holy Scriptures."[5] Philosophy, in the view of the

---

[1] i, 247 (Macmillan, 1911).

[2] " Dubitando ad inquisitionem venimus : inquirendo veritatem percipimus " (*P. L.,* clxxviii, c. 1349).

[3] *Ep. de Erroribus Abælardi,* v, § 11. *Cf.* Dr Rashdall's comment in his *Idea of Atonement,* p. 359, note 4 (Macmillan, 1919).

[4] Taylor, *op. cit.,* i, 222. [5] Rabanus, *Cler. Inst.,* iii, 2 (*P. L.,* cvii, c. 379).

early Middle Ages, is a part of secular riches, even if, as Alcuin taught, it be the only part which has never left its possessor miserable.[1] But just as Alcuin insists on a religious purpose in all education, Rabanus holds that the clergy ought to learn logic and " have its laws in constant meditation, so that subtly they may discern the wiles of heretics and confute their poisoned sayings with the conclusions of the syllogism."[2] But if we have papal authority for the statement that God is not tied by the rules of grammar, it was no less certain that the time would arrive when the freedom of inquiry allowed in the philosophical schools would extend into the domain of theology. For our present purpose it is irrelevant to consider whether such excursions were officially regarded as orthodox or the reverse. If it be contended that the attitude of ecclesiastical authority in all ages has seldom been found to be a mean between excessive rigorism and a no less dangerous credulity, it would not be unfair to extend the stricture to the official exponents of philosophy and of natural science. What is important for us to remember is that, with whatever necessary qualifications, the demand for a rational theology is a legacy handed on from some of the greatest minds of the Middle Ages : true, it did not originate with them, but still less is it a new discovery of our own day. And the liberty of prophesying would always be dearly bought at the price of the liberty of thinking.

Of course the attempted solutions are conditioned in every age by the circumstances of the time ; and there will inevitably be periods of reaction. Those who have read Dr Poole's delightful chapter on John of Salisbury will remember its closing reflections on the

[1] Taylor, *op. cit.*, i, 216.

[2] *Ibid.*, i, 222. Rabanus, *Cler. Inst.*, iii, 20 (*P. L.*, cvii, c. 397), reading " dicta veneficata."

attempt at the opening of the thirteenth century to proscribe
the Physics and Metaphysics of Aristotle; and it is very
easy for us who live in an age when Greek has not as yet
been again forgotten to be unjust to the Latin West. But
this in itself makes it the more necessary that we should
not treat the Eastern Church as though it had no history
with which we need concern ourselves. Its dogmatic
controversies, extending into the Middle Ages, have an
importance which the development of modern philosophical
theology may yet bring into higher relief. And it is
surely not unworthy of remark, though it is often forgotten,
that the one Creed of the universal Church is an Eastern
creed. M. Lavisse, in a striking picture of the East and
the West, recalls the contrast familiar to every student
between the spirit of the philosopher and that of the jurist.
" The Pope is a theologian making laws, whilst a philosopher survives in every Eastern theologian." [1] " Hæreti-
corum patriarchæ philosophi," jibes the lawyer Tertullian [2];
and it is significant that the one Western philosopher of
the early Middle Ages whose philosophy of religion,
though evolved among Christian associations, has sometimes been regarded as capable of sustaining without impoverishment the removal of its Christian elements was
a disciple of Hellenic learning. William of Malmesbury [3]
tells us that he was stabbed to death with the points of
their pens by his English pupils—a pungent warning of
the dangers of attempting to teach the unimaginative ;
but whether this be true or not it is a fact that, as Dr Poole
says, " the voice of orthodoxy on all sides was directed against
Johannes Scotus, the belated disciple of Plato, and the last

[1] *Hist. Gén.*, i, 172.
[2] *Adv. Hermogenem*, 8 *ad fin.*, a work which it is none the less good
for philosophers (and others) to read.
[3] *Gesta Pontif.*, v, §240 (Rolls Series), " garfiis foratus."

representative of the Greek spirit in the west."[1] Orthodox
or not, he anticipated the fundamental principle of Descartes,
Cogito, ergo sum, though that too, as Dr Poole has pointed out,
is to be found like so much else already in St Augustine.[2]

We must leave it to others to estimate the specific
debt of modern philosophy, so far as such an expression
has a meaning, to those great masters of the Middle Ages
who dared to think when originality had a spice of danger
which might prove a salutary tonic in our own day. But
there is a class of thinkers—perhaps we should say one type
of mind—regarded in all ages with dislike by the philosopher and with suspicion by the theologian, though
having affinities with both. Few words have been used
to cover so great a variety of disparate and even incoherent
beliefs as Mysticism. It is as difficult to find a common
term between different schools of mystics, Neoplatonist,
Christian, Mohammedan, Persian, and others, with endless
combinations of one or more strains, as it is among the
early Gnostics. In the exposition of the Aristotelian
philosophy by successive Christian interpreters such, for
example only, as the Franciscan Alexander of Hales and
the Dominicans Albertus Magnus and St Thomas may be
found a progressive attempt to express within the four
corners of orthodoxy ultimate truths as to the nature of
God, of the world, of man regarded from the standpoint
of philosophy as well as of Revelation,[3] by a union through
which each is found to be the proper complement and
interpretation of the other. In a sense it would be true to
say that the type of scholasticism represented by Aquinas is
the supreme triumph of human reason in the Middle Ages.
But there is another way of approach with which we are

[1] Poole, *op. cit.*, p. 52.   [2] *Ibid.*, p. 65, note 18.
[3] Taylor, *op. cit.*, ii, 393–4.

now concerned. Look at it in the twelfth century as you see it in Hugh of St Victor and his followers. A Platonist at heart, even if in some things he follows Aristotle, Hugh found his real source of inspiration in the extraordinary, and in some ways fascinating, Neoplatonist work on the Celestial Hierarchy which was preserved among the supposed writings of Dionysius the Areopagite, a belief in the genuineness of which was sufficient to work miracles in France in the days of St Louis. All true mysticism, so far as one can judge, is concerned with the approach of the soul to God. But in Hugh and his followers, unlike many later schools to which the same title of mystics is applied, this approach is the crown of an intellectual process which it transcends : it is not a substitute for it. In all this approach involves the surrender of the will ; but seldom if ever in Hugh, or in any of the mystics whose influence has been lasting, has it involved the negation of the reason. The Christian mysticism of the Middle and later ages (which the Dean of St Paul's, it may safely be said, has induced hundreds to study) is widely sundered perhaps in many of its forms from their ordinary modes of thinking or apprehension. Its attraction has lain probably on its ethical side rather than in its philosophical implications, often very imperfectly understood ; and the attraction of different mystics for different types of student has certainly varied largely according to their temperament. It has been claimed, justly or unjustly, for Tauler and his school in the fourteenth century that they gave to the German nation a philosophical terminology.[1] But what is more likely to interest most readers is the ideal of living set forth in the Sermons and the criticism of the ideal of poverty of the Spiritual Franciscans, his

---

[1] C. Schmidt, *Johannes Tauler von Strassburg*, p. 79 (Hamburg, 1841), hard to procure and hard to read, but worth the trouble.

73

substitution for the renunciation of all earthly wealth of that poorness of spirit which appropriates nothing but holds all in trust. On the other hand, the self-mortification by almost incredible bodily austerities described in the life of Henry Suso belongs in the last resort to the sphere of morbid psychology rather than of religion. In its exaggerated form there may seem little to choose between the Servitor as he describes his way of life and St Simeon Stylites as not he himself but Tennyson pictures him ; but in the underlying motive a real difference can be distinguished, for the basis of Suso's actions is neither the averting of wrath nor the acquirement of merit, but, however pitifully misinterpreted, that which is the basis of all true mysticism—the love of God, shown in his case in the passionate yearning to share in the sufferings of his suffering Lord. And those who would see this love for God exhibited on its truer, fuller side should study it in Dame Julian of Norwich or in the joyful spirit of the works of the Hermit of Hampole, Richard Rolle, though even in the latter may be found that distrust of natural human love which is alien to the spirit of the Gospel but quite consonant with much of the teaching alike of the Early Fathers of the Church and of mediæval theology.

Dr Inge says of William Law's book, *The Grounds and Reasons of Christian Regeneration*, that he knows " no better summary of the theology and ethics of Christian mysticism," [1] and those who are led by his account of it to study it and other works will see that, while Law's theology is his own and in its exposition he is profoundly influenced by the seventeenth-century German mystic whom we call Jacob Behmen, there is not a little in the thought which is common to earlier mystics in the Middle Ages ; and in many of

[1] *Studies of English Mystics*, pp. 152-3 (John Murray, 1906).

74

them, one may venture to think, much that breathes the very spirit of the Johannine theology. And so again if there are parts of Meister Eckhart's sermons which seem to link him with Christian Gnosticism, there are others where he is speaking of intelligence, will, and love in a way that makes us wonder whether he would have regarded Mr McTaggart as a master or a misguided disciple.

It is not a question of establishing a legitimate descent in this or like cases, any more than between the ideals of Tauler's Friends of God or the Brethren of the Common Life at Deventer, whose story was so beautifully illustrated by Thomas à Kempis, and those of any organised body that is to be seen in our own day. But there is, as Abelard knew, "something divine in every noble thought,"[1] and the kernel remains though the husk may perish. We do not condemn the doctrine of the Inner Light or of the spark within the soul because the Beghards of Alsace in the thirteenth century and later abolished the distinction between the Creator and the created or claiming as Brethren of the Free Spirit an antinomian freedom erred concerning the Faith. There are certain tendencies of the human spirit which are reproduced from age to age. "L'histoire ne se répète jamais, mais les hommes se ressemblent toujours "—a fact to which testimony is borne alike by the long continuance of Montanism and by the upholders of the Eternal Gospel attributed to Joachim of Floris and many a strange eccentricity of individuals or of communities of our own time. If in some of these things we are the heirs of the Middle Ages, by none of them, let us remember, are those ages represented in any more than a minor degree. If even the sermons of Bernard of Clairvaux on the Song of Songs, following a method of interpretation which goes

[1] Poole, *op. cit.*, p. 170.

75

back to Origen, cannot reconcile many to an exegesis which, historically regarded, they would pronounce to have been profoundly mischievous, yet in the same century we may trace the growth of a demand for a more historical treatment of Scripture.

Look yet deeper. Thousands and tens of thousands, even though they may not know of the obligation, still find comfort and inspiration for their devotions in language drawn from mediæval sacramentaries, Gregorian, Leonian, Mozarabic, from the Breviaries of Rome and of Sarum, from Augustine or Alcuin or even from Anselm and Aquinas. Still the *Fioretti* of Francis of Assisi appeal with the quaint simplicity of the fourteenth century to many who would understand as little of the learned disputations of the world in which the book was written as St Francis himself would have done a century earlier. And still the *Imitation of Christ*— whether it be written by À Kempis or by Hilton matters little to its readers—speaks to conscience and kindles love with a power which no later work has ever rivalled.

Of the religious inspiration of the Art of the Middle Ages others must be left to speak : it would furnish material for many lectures. Who has not felt it—in our own great Abbey of Westminster, in many of the great cathedrals of England or of France, in some parish church which has escaped restoration by a miracle or more miraculously survived it ? He understands little of the Middle Ages who has not studied

> This that never ends,
> Still climbing, luring fancy still to climb,
> As full of morals half-divined as life,
> Graceful, grotesque, with ever new surprise
> Of hazardous caprices sure to please,
> Heavy as nightmare, airy-light as fern,
> Imagination's very self in stone !

But of one debt less generally recognised, perhaps, but of even wider significance something must be said. It is in regard to the hymns which we sing. Even if we set aside as too early to be included with fairness those associated with the names of St Ambrose, of Sedulius or Prudentius, of Synesius of Cyrene or the earliest hymns of the Eastern Church there remains an astonishing collection. John Mason Neale's hymn " The day is past and over " is from the Late Evening Service of the Orthodox Church, and goes back to the sixth century. From the eighth are derived " Come, ye faithful, raise the strain Of triumphant gladness " and " The Day of Resurrection," both by St John of Damascus, and from the ninth " Stars of the morning so gloriously bright " by St Joseph the Hymnographer. But the mediæval hymns of the West have naturally possessed a greater attraction for translators. From Venantius Fortunatus, Bishop of Poitiers in the sixth century, we inherit " The royal banners forward go " and " Sing, my tongue, the glorious battle," both first sung as relics of the Cross were borne from Tours to Poitiers, and the " Salve, festa dies," " Hail, festal day! " which many have taken in hand to translate. " Jesu the Father's only Son " is perhaps of the same age. In the following century Ireland gives us " Draw nigh and take the Body of the Lord," and not much later are " Jesu, our Hope, our heart's Desire " and " Blessed City, heavenly Salem," with its second part, the " Angularis fundamentum Lapis Christus missus est," on which are based " Christ is made the sure Foundation " and " Christ is our corner-stone." To St Theodulph of Orleans (*c.* 820) we owe " All glory, laud, and honour," and possibly to Rabanus Maurus, Archbishop of Maintz in the same century, the " Veni Creator Spiritus," so familiar to us in Bishop

77

Cosin's seventeenth-century version, " Come, Holy Ghost, our souls inspire " ; while from St Gall in Switzerland we have " The strain upraise of joy and praise, Alleluia ! " At Canterbury in the tenth century you might have heard the canons singing " Conditor alme siderum, Æterna lux credentium "—" Creator of the starry height." To the same period belongs "Hark ! a thrilling voice is sounding," a great Advent hymn, and little later are two hymns still more famous—" Alleluia, song of sweetness " (" Alleluia, dulce carmen "), and " Sing Alleluia forth in duteous praise," of whose history in both cases the best-known facts are associated with the disuse of the ' Alleluia ' they proclaim, according to a curious ecclesiastical perversity not unobservable in other connexions. Dr Walter Frere, of the Community of the Resurrection, to whose magnificent historical edition of *Hymns Ancient and Modern* [1] all students of the subject, and not least the present writer, owe unstinted gratitude, recalls to mind in regard to this the mediæval custom of burying the ' Alleluia ' at Septuagesima in a coffin with full funeral ceremonies— a custom which is said to have lasted until the fifteenth century. To St Fulbert of Chartres, who died in 1028, is due " Ye choirs of new Jerusalem," and to the same century belongs the famous poem formerly attributed to St Bernard but now assigned to a Benedictine abbess, which has given us three hymns—" Jesu, dulcis memoria," rendered as " Jesu, the very thought is sweet," or " Jesu, the very thought of Thee " ; " Jesu, dulcedo cordium," " Jesu, the joy of loving hearts " ; and " Jesu, Rex admirabilis," " O Jesu, King most wonderful." To Bernard of Morlas or Cluny in the twelfth century belongs with better right the great poem of over

[1] (London : William Clowes & Sons, Ltd., 1909.)

78

3000 lines from which are derived " Brief life is here our
portion," " The world is very evil," " For thee, O dear,
dear country," and " Jerusalem the golden." Equally
well known, and perhaps even more popular, is " O Quanta,
qualia sunt illa sabbata," " O what the joy and the glory
must be," which comes from the collection of hymns made
by Abelard for Héloïse in 1129. As one hears people singing the " Pange lingua," " Of the glorious Body telling,"
with its second part " Tantum ergo," " Therefore we,
before Him bending "; the " Verbum supernum pro-
diens," " The Heavenly Word proceeding forth," with its
second part " O salutaris hostia," " O saving Victim ";
or the " Adoro te devote, latens deitas," " Thee we
adore, O hidden Saviour, Thee," one sometimes wonders
how much we have learnt in our day and in our own experience of the blending of reason with faith and faith with
reason which was taught by the great scholastic who wrote
those hymns—St Thomas of Aquinum in the thirteenth
century. To the greatest Pope of that century, Innocent
III, are assigned, though not with certainty, " Veni Sancte
Spiritus," " Come, Thou Holy Spirit, come," and " Stabat
mater dolorosa," " At the Cross her station keeping."
And it may help us to understand a little more of the spirit
of the Middle Ages that the author of the " Dies iræ,"
" Day of wrath ! O Day of mourning ! " should have
been Thomas of Celano, the friend and biographer of St
Francis. Our list of debts to the Middle Ages might be
largely extended, but we may close it with the mention of
three from the collection assigned to Thomas à Kempis.
" O Love, how deep ! how broad ! how high ! " (" O
Amor quam ecstaticus ! "); " If there be that skills to
reckon All the number of the blest " (" Quisquis valet
numerare "); and " Light's abode, celestial Salem."

Jerusalem luminosa! It is the brighter side, the undying hope of the Christian's faith. In passing from the Middle Ages to the period of the Reformation men did not change their Hell but only their view of its occupants. And though in the preaching of our day the emphasis has shifted almost immeasurably, as some of us can recognise whose memories go back perhaps no more than thirty years, the number is probably growing rather than decreasing of those who would understand what Carlyle meant when in his lecture on " The Hero as Poet " he says that " Dante, the Italian man, was sent into our world to embody musically the Religion of the Middle Ages, the Religion of our Modern Europe, its Inner Life," even though Carlyle's modern Europe is now eighty years behind us.

An historian of Italian name writing in a great French history has found himself able to give to Dante rather less than ten scattered lines which tell us that he was a Florentine, a scholastic, that he attacked Boniface VIII, wrote the *De Monarchia*, and in the *Divine Comedy* prepared the cult of antiquity for the Renaissance that was to come. So much for the modern historian on what Carlyle calls " the most remarkable of all modern Books," the "mystic Song, at once of one of the greatest human souls, and of the highest tuing that Europe had hitherto realised for itself." And yet the last two cantos of the *Paradiso* are, one might suppose, the most characteristic expression of the Middle Ages, on more sides than one, that can anywhere be found. Cicero, Vergil, St Paul, St Augustine of Hippo, St Thomas of Aquinum—many have read them since, even perhaps understood them better ; but what makes the *Divine Comedy* different from a *Sic et Non* is the poet himself; and as the poet is often the true historian, even though here

80

and there his blunder may evoke a footnote of learned superiority, so we may venture to think he is often and again the true theologian. Not that Dante's theology is more or less complete than that of the Fathers or of the writers of the Reformation: it is different in kind; and there is another side which few perhaps save the mystics could grasp from the days of Augustine to the nineteenth century. " God has ordained that the Pauline aspect of Christianity, and the Pauline nomenclature, should for the last three hundred years at least mould almost exclusively the thoughts of His church: but we must not forget, that St John's thoughts, and St John's words, are equally inspired with those of St Paul." So wrote Charles Kingsley in his preface to Miss Winkworth's edition of Tauler's *History and Life*.[1] And as men in our own time turn from a Paulinism, distorted, misinterpreted, perhaps sometimes outgrown, from the cramping fetters of Augustinianism or an etiolating modernism which leaves the mind unsatisfied and the soul unfed, to the Christ whom Paul preached, they may learn with Dante from the questionings of St John to understand the cords that draw them to the Divine Wisdom, the Incarnate Word whom Paul also knew. And perhaps, too, they may find something more. For if the Middle Ages open with the dream of the City of God, it is certain that our modern age which has inherited the dream is tending toward a struggle for results more utilitarian, but likely to be less satisfying. And the last canto of the *Paradiso* may still have its lesson; for its end is the vision of the Light Eternal and a will wholly guided, moved, and turned at length by the Love that moves the sun and the other stars.

CLAUDE JENKINS

[1] Republished 1905 (London : H. R. Allenson).

III

PHILOSOPHY

THE inquiry which I propose to undertake I have formulated in the following question. Is there any dominating concept in our modern mind, giving it a definite and characteristic direction in the search for truth, warping it perhaps with a distinctive bias, which it does not derive from ancient Greece, and which it would not possess had it not lived through the dominating concepts of the mediæval period ? I hope it will be possible to suggest, not merely a vague and general, but a precise answer.

The method I must follow in such an inquiry is different from that of the historian who, studying original records and documents, endeavours to discover the origin and trace the development of the ideas which have materialised in institutions. It is different also from that of the student of the history of philosophy who, studying the connected narratives, attempts to give an inventory of, or make a classified catalogue of, the philosophical output of a period and appreciate its value. My method is to look at history in its grand outlines and, disregarding minutiæ and details, to endeavour to discover and lay bare the concepts which dominate the mentality of a period, concepts which find expression in its art, religion, philosophy, political and social institutions. The history of any period can only be interpreted, it seems to me, when we are able to discover and understand the concepts of reality which determine

82

its philosophy. For example, during the first centuries of the Christian era the pure Greek philosophy still lived and developed side by side with the Christian concepts which were becoming increasingly dominant. There was, that is to say, not only an influence of Greek philosophy on Christian doctrine ; there was also a contrast and competition between them. We have recently had our attention called to this in the very valuable work of Dean Inge on the philosophy of Plotinus. I mention this work not merely because it illustrates the method I propose, nor on account of its high value as a contribution to history and to philosophy, but because it affords me a starting-point for the philosophical reflection I am about to follow. The great service which it appears to me Dean Inge has rendered to contemporary philosophy is that in his lucid exposition of the history of that last period of the ancient philosophy, the neoplatonic, he has brought out with incisive clearness the nature of the dominating concept in the mentality of the Greek world. It was the concept of a reality purely intelligible, eternal and perfect, a world of fixed forms, change being unreal and time the moving image of eternity. The philosophical, apart from the historical, value of Dean Inge's work is due in great measure to the fact that he has not only expounded that concept with sympathetic appreciation, but he has let it take hold of him. Proclaiming himself a Platonist, he has thrown down a challenge to the modern world in his rejection of the idea of progress. This idea is so deeply rooted in our modern thought, so intimate a part of our science, politics, and religion, particularly since the principle of evolution has become generally accepted, that to challenge it is, in effect, to challenge the intellectual soundness of the concept on which modern civilisation rests. In contrast with the philosophy of ancient Greece, particularly in its final period, the dominating concept in our philosophy to-day is the reality of change. We may be said to have turned away from the contemplation of things *sub specie æternitatis*, and to be absorbed in the problems of activity, evolution, and relativity.

I do not defend the idea of progress in so far as it can be taken to mean the attainment by the modern world of a higher plane of existence as judged by its ethical, social, political, or religious standards, nor do I think there exists any criterion by which the standards themselves can be judged, but I do hold that the modern world is dominated by the concept of reality as activity, and the philosophy which seems to me effectively interpretative in our world to-day is not Platonism, a philosophy of unchanging forms, but a philosophy of change, based on a new concept of time and history.

It is to me a significant fact that Bergson, who has given such forcible expression to this dominating concept of modern thought, the reality of change, had his interest in the philosophical problem awakened, and the direction of his speculation directed, by the study of Plotinus. The effect of that study on Bergson was, however, so he has told us, to convince him that the last and greatest effort of the ancient philosophy ended in failure, that if philosophy is to succeed it must seek out and follow a new way. The concept of change as fundamentally real, of time as the very stuff of reality, is the direct opposite of the Platonic theory of the eternal forms. Identifying myself with the philosophy of change, regarding it as what is most characteristic of the modern spirit, I proceed to inquire what there is in the dominating concept of the mediæval mind which may have served to give birth to it.

84

History is continuous. When we view it from within there are no transitions, no breaks in its flow. When we view it externally, however, it appears as a stream of events in which we mark off very sharply the beginnings and ends of periods. In the history of philosophy the old Greek period comes definitely to an end and the modern period has a definite beginning. The two events are separated by an intervening period which we describe vaguely as the middle age or mediæval period and which, whatever value we assign to it, in regard to philosophy, when compared with the Greek and the modern periods, appears emphatically negative. The middle age seems to separate the old philosophy from the new, and not in any respect to supply a connecting link. This negative character of the mediæval philosophy is the more pronounced by reason of the quite definite events which we are accustomed to assign as marking the end of the old and the beginning of the new. Greek philosophy, which had developed continuously for more than a thousand years, died a violent death when Justinian closed the schools of Athens in the year 529, and modern philosophy was literally born, and began a new life, when Descartes published the *Discours de la Méthode* in the year 1637. In the two centuries which immediately preceded this new birth Europe had witnessed the renascence of classical learning, the reformation in religion, and the rise of the natural sciences, but philosophy, as we recognise it to-day, in its special problems, its principles, and its methods, began with Descartes. In the true sense he is its father. A period, therefore, of over a thousand years separates ancient and modern philosophy.

Two opposite and conflicting views are held to-day with regard to the philosophy of this middle period. Increasing knowledge has toned down sharp historical judgments and blunted the incisiveness of verdicts. Nevertheless, there are many who still take the view that in the Middle Ages philosophy, in the only true meaning of the word, did not and could not exist. Throughout the whole period, according to this view, there is desolation. Philosophy could not exist by reason of the repressive legislation of religion exercising authority over the reason. It was a period, we are told, when the human mind was in bondage, when reason was suppressed and human life in consequence became degraded and sunk in superstition. Gibbon is in large measure responsible for this view, and has given forcible expression to it. Following his account of the suppression of the schools of Athens by Justinian, he says :

> The Gothic arms were less fatal to the Schools of Athens than the establishment of a new religion, whose ministers superseded the exercise of reason, resolved every question by an article of faith, and condemned the infidel or sceptic to eternal flames. In many a volume of laborious controversy they exposed the weakness of the understanding and the corruption of the heart, insulted human nature in the sages of antiquity, and proscribed the spirit of philosophical inquiry, so repugnant to the doctrine, or at least to the temper, of an humble believer.[1]

The irony of the passage has lost its bite, but the view it represents survives. A student presenting himself for an Honours Degree in philosophy in this university is required to know the history of ancient philosophy and the history of modern philosophy, from Descartes to Kant, and must have special knowledge of the books of those periods, but mediæval philosophy is no part of the course. Were anyone to offer a thesis in it he would probably be referred to the department of history or theology.

On the other hand, there are many who can claim to be representative exponents of modern thought who hold that

---

[1] *Decline and Fall,* chap. xi.

the mediæval period, and more particularly the later part of that period to which the scholastic philosophy belongs, was that in which philosophy in its true meaning, both as a formal science of reasoning and as a material science of metaphysic, ontology, and theology, attained its zenith. In the Catholic universities and seminaries, philosophy, quite distinct from dogmatic theology, is the subject of a long and laborious discipline, and the history and text-books deal exclusively with the schoolmen.

Now both these views—the view that philosophy in the Middle Ages was non-existent and the view that only then did philosophy exist—have some truth, for each follows a perfectly consistent definition of the particular nature of philosophy and of its content or subject-matter. But there is a third view which rests on a wholly different and profounder meaning of philosophy. This is the view that the concept which found expression in the mediæval period, which determined the direction of its thought, the bias in its mentality, and the character of its social and political institutions, is a philosophy. Philosophy is not, that is to say, a special principle or a special method which one may accept and another reject; it is an activity of the mind, inherent in the human spirit, its life. In this meaning philosophy does not exist at one time and not exist at another, for the absence of any particular principle or method is the presence of another, and therefore the very negation of the principle of one philosophy is itself the affirmation of another. In every period of history the expression of the life of the period is to be interpreted by the concept which determines the mentality of the period. The idea of an historical revelation and its expression in the institution of an authoritative Church is based on a concept of philosophy.

MEDIÆVAL CONTRIBUTIONS

The three great periods into which the history of Western civilisation is divided, the Greek, the mediæval, the modern, are distinguished by their philosophy. In each there is a characteristic outward expression of a concept of the nature of reality, and it dominates the mentality and directs the activity. The dominating concept of the Greek mind is the sovereign supremacy of reason as interpretative of life and nature. The dominating concept of the mediæval mind is history as the revelation of meaning and purpose—history as the divine event. The dominating concept of the modern mind is the infallibility of the experimental method, and this is not a mere reassertion of the principle of reason; it is a new thing, giving its characteristic bent to the modern mind.

From this standpoint the view of Gibbon that the new religion, in whose interest the schools of Athens were closed, destroyed philosophy, is seen to be, not false, but based on a complete misconception of what philosophy really is. The new religion rested on a pure concept of philosophy. The special character and the particular form of expression which distinguished it outwardly from the religions it supplanted were adventitious, but the concept on which it depended was a new concept, and it was that underlying and supporting concept which dominated the mediæval mind. We may trace its origin to Hellenistic and Judæistic sources, but as we find it embodied in Christian doctrine, it is a new concept, giving a bent or bias to the human mind, causing it to express itself in forms of activity wholly new, and it is this concept which gives its characteristic feature to the thought of the Middle Ages.

" God who at sundry times and in divers manners spake in time past unto the fathers by the prophets hath in these last days spoken unto us by his Son, whom he hath appointed heir of all things, by whom also he made the worlds." If we suppress in these words, as we easily can, the special application, which the writer intends and is about to make explicitly, to the life and death of Jesus of Nazareth, we may read in them the pure concept of philosophy which they express. Stripped of all special reference, that concept is the concept of history itself revealing reality. It is something much profounder than an appeal to the belief in the significance of facts supported by the evidence of records. It is the concept that history is purpose and reveals purpose. The notion of gods or of one supreme God was a general notion. The idea that the gods interested themselves in human affairs and occasionally made known their will in particular revelations was quite familiar. Homer had conceived the Trojan War as having its reflection, and also its deeper causes, in the conflicts of the gods. Herodotus had conceived history on the analogy of a great drama. Thucydides had made history point a political moral. The Hebrew chroniclers had presented history as the expression of the favour or anger of a divine ruler. But here there is a totally different concept—a concept which finds its embodiment in the Kingdom of Heaven, the City of God, the Universal Church—the concept of historical revelation.

It seems to me that we owe this concept to the Apostle Paul. If we look at Christianity as a philosophy, it is clear that the founder, Jesus himself, belongs to a different category from that in which we place the philosophers. Paul was essentially a philosopher. It is universally acknowledged that he rationalised the new religion to which he was converted, his mind ready prepared in the Greek and Hebrew learning. In my view Paul did much more than this, and he should be ranked with the great philosophers, with those who, like Plato, like Descartes, like Kant, have given expression to new concepts—concepts which have transformed and reformed the mode of our mentality. There are no doubt other channels by which philosophy entered into the beliefs of the new religion, but it seems to me that Christianity owes its dominating concept, and that which specially stamps it as a philosophy, as something more than a mere rule of life, to the Apostle Paul. Only consider what Christianity would have been without it ! There is an instructive parallel in Mohammedanism. Undoubtedly there is a philosophical concept of the nature of reality underlying alike the gospel of Mohammed and the gospel of Jesus, and it is quite a fair comparison to consider the preachers of those gospels and the founders of those new religions as representing those concepts. Each proclaims himself a prophet sent by God and divinely inspired to reveal to men a new way of life. But compare the religions. Where in Mohammedanism do we find anything like the profound concept which comes to expression in Christianity in the words " the fulness of time " ? The Jesus whom Paul preached was not a prophet who might have appeared at any time and whose message was indifferent to his particular age. Paul has a completely new concept of history. History is reality manifested or self-revealing. Without this Pauline concept Christianity might have been a Sermon on the Mount—a beautiful, possibly a realisable, ideal of life —it would not have been to mankind a new concept of reality dominating its whole mentality.

The mediæval mind was dominated, then, by a concept which, I maintain, was a pure concept of philosophy, and it found expression in its characteristic institutions, and especially in that of an authoritative Church. What, then, was the character of that dominating concept ? It cannot be denied that, judged by the philosophy which preceded it and the philosophy which succeeded it, it presents to us a distinctly negative character. The reason is plain. It holds within it an inherent contradiction. Throughout the whole period of mediæval philosophy we find two factors in continual opposition, a principle of reason and a principle of faith. The whole philosophic effort is an attempt to reconcile them, to justify authority by an appeal to reason in the interest of faith. It ended in failure. It was bound to do so, for the only principle the philosopher could invoke to reconcile the contradiction was the principle of reason of the Greek philosophy, and this principle was itself one of the opposing factors. It is this inherent contradiction in the mediæval mind which gives to its philosophy throughout the whole period that negative character which it assumes even in its most enlightened exponents. *Credo quia impossibile*, *Credo ut intelligam*—these are its watchwords. The Pauline doctrine of justification by faith is the embodiment of the contradiction. The faith to which Paul appealed was not intuition or any form of the mind reconcilable with reason. It was an irrational and an anti-rational principle, and this was the tragedy so far as philosophy is concerned.

I maintain, then, that despite the negative character of mediæval philosophy and the inherent contradiction with which it had to struggle, despite the fact also that one of the conflicting principles was the principle of reason itself, particularly in the form in which it had found expression in Greek philosophy, the fundamental concept which dominated the thought and activity of the whole mediæval period was not anti-philosophical, but a pure concept of philosophy, the concept of history revealing reality.

MEDIÆVAL CONTRIBUTIONS

I want now to direct attention to another significant fact and one which is vital for the appreciation of what I contend is the essentially modern concept, the concept that reality is change. Every dominating concept creates in the mind a bias or inclination giving rise to a mode of mentality. We are wholly unconscious of this bias in our own thinking, and only with difficulty become conscious of it if we compare the mentality of one historical period with that of another. An illustration will perhaps make my meaning clear. There is a well-known story of the early days of the Royal Society which relates that some one appealed to the members to explain why, when a living fish is placed in a bowl of water, the weight is not increased, whereas it is if the fish be dead. It is said that several ingenious explanations were put forward by members of the Society, and that Charles II came to hear about it. He was curious to see the experiment, and it then appeared that the weight was increased just the same whether the fish was alive or dead. Now a story like this makes an immediate appeal to the modern mind. We have a natural bias or bent which makes us in the search for truth depend primarily, and rely absolutely, on the experimental method. If we transport ourselves in imagination into the Middle Ages, however, and try to look at nature as the mediæval mind conceived it, we see at once that such a story would make no appeal at all. For the mediæval mind the unseen world was full of occult forces, it was peopled with malignant and beneficent spirit agents, the scientific workers were the alchemists and astrologers, a suspect and uncanny folk, and successful experiment depended on the terms the experimenter was on with those spirit agents and forces. The mind naturally directed its attention rather to the experimenter than to the experiment; it was his control of natural occult influences

92

which was supposed to determine the event. But now, if we transport ourselves in imagination to ancient Greece, say to Athens in the fourth century B.C., we feel very differently. The Greek mentality seems so like our own that we can easily suppose the story of the Royal Society adapted to the imagery of the time, and told, let us say, by Aristophanes as having occurred at the Phrontisterion of Socrates described in *The Clouds*. Yet if we reflect we shall see that this too is quite impossible. To the Greek mentality the story would be pointless and its moral irrelevant— but for a different reason. The Greek mentality had a bias which directed the mind from the principle to the fact, and not *vice versa*. It would have been natural to the Greek philosopher to decide the principle first as the Fellows of the Royal Society are said to have done, and they would not necessarily or immediately have been disconcerted by the failure of the experiment. I doubt if it would have seemed relevant to the Greek to make the experiment; I am sure it would not have seemed the primary condition to satisfy. It was not because it did not happen to occur to Aristotle to make experiments like those which Galileo made on the inclined plane, and from the leaning tower of Pisa, that Aristotle did not forestall by nearly two thousand years Galileo's discoveries. It never could have occurred to Aristotle to investigate nature in that order, for the bent or bias of his mentality would not allow his mind to take that direction. The Greeks were, indeed, pre-eminently mathematicians, but mathematics indicates an entirely different direction of thought from that of modern experimental philosophy. I can quite well imagine, for example, that a Greek might have discovered Einstein's principle of relativity. It is exactly the kind of theory which would have appealed with special force to the

Greek mind. I am quite sure, however, that if a Greek philosopher had formulated the principle it would not have occurred to him as the first condition of recommending its acceptance that he should be able to devise some means by which it could be brought to an experimental test. That direction of Einstein's thought is peculiarly modern. I do not mean that the ancients did not experiment. I do not forget Archimedes and his practical devices. What I refer to is the unqualified confidence which the modern mind has in experiment. No better instance of it can be given than the principle of relativity to which I have referred. This originated in a single experiment, the famous experiment of Michelson and Morley, the result of which was disconcerting, and which appeared also irrational and paradoxical in the highest degree; but the experiment as a test of truth was never challenged. The experiment was repeated indeed, but only to test the conditions, not the authority, of the experiment.

The mediæval mind presents a complete contrast to the modern mind in this respect. Take as an example the mediæval attitude toward a doctrine like that of the Real Presence, which filled so preponderating and central a place in the popular imagination as to the nature of the Christian scheme of redemption and the Christian cosmogony generally. I do not refer, of course, to the doctrine itself as a religious dogma, or to its inner meaning or truth, or to any philosophical problem it raises. I refer only to the imagery in which the doctrine presented itself to the mediæval mind. Over and over again we find this taking definite materialistic shape and giving rise to tales of wonderful appearances, tales which claim to verify the actual fact of miracle in its grosser as apart from its spiritual meaning. To us such claims would immediately challenge laboratory tests. Why did they not to the mediæval mind ? Surely not on account of sacrilege; to suppose this is to miss the whole point of their claim to be evidence. The reason is that the mediæval mind did not work that way.

A story is told of St Thomas Aquinas which illustrates very markedly the difference between the mediæval and the modern mind in regard to what we call evidence. In 1271 (three years before he died) Aquinas was appointed to the chair of theology at Naples, and the following anecdote, which I quote from Mr O'Neill's introduction to his *Things New and Old in St Thomas Aquinas*, relates to this time. Romanus, to whom Aquinas had but recently resigned the chair of theology at Paris, appeared to him and told him that he was dead and now in heaven ! Aquinas immediately asked : " Do acquired habits remain to us in heaven ? " Romanus replied that God absorbed all his thoughts. Aquinas then asked: " Do you see Him immediately or by means of some similitude ? " To appreciate the mentality thus disclosed, compare the story with any of the modern stories of communications with the dead, with the famous " Honolulu " story in *Raymond*, for example. (The medium professing to be the vehicle of Raymond's communication uttered the word chosen as a test, there being a practical certainty of the entire absence of collusion.) What strikes us at once is how in the one case the questions directly concern what the inquirer is eager to know, and reveal an underlying assurance that the answers will themselves provide the evidence or verification. In the other case, the information sought is always trivial, intended only to afford evidence. Modern psychical research is entirely absorbed in the evidential character of alleged communications, and has no use for, and does not look for, intrinsic value in their content. This difference

95

is not to be explained by saying that the Middle Ages were a period of faith while our modern age is a period of doubt. Faith and doubt are not characteristics of periods. It is a difference in the mental bias, and this bias is formed by the dominating philosophical concept.

What, then, was the dominating concept which determined the mentality of the Middle Ages ? It found expression in the Christian idea of divine revelation, of a fore-ordained Redeemer, and of an authoritative Church supported by Scripture and tradition. All this, however, was its imaginative clothing, its embodiment. Let us strip off the particular religious beliefs and the particular application to historical personages and events, and we find a concept of history, distinct from the ancient concepts, Greek or Semitic, and distinct from and in marked contrast to our modern concept. It is the concept of the whole course of universal human history, not as directed by God, not as ruled or overruled by divine providence, but as the real work itself which God is in process of accomplishing. The history to which Paul appealed, and which he intel-lectualised, was the history recorded in the Hebrew Scriptures. But that is accidental, or at any rate adven-titious. Paul knows no other; for him, the Hebrew record is the authentic account of human history from the Crea-tion up to times present. The Jews are the central interest indeed, but in the same way in which in mediæval cosmology Jerusalem is the centre of the earth, as in Greek cosmology Delphi had been. For Paul, the first man is Adam, through whom came death, and the second Adam is Jesus Christ, through whom has come eternal life. But it is no longer the concept of a creator God, who has made man and let him go his way, at times repenting that he has made him, and even despairing of him. We can take away from the concept its entire mythological embodiment, and then we see that it is a new concept of history itself. History is the real thing. Not only is purpose revealed in history, but history is the embodiment of purpose.

It is this concept which makes the mediæval mind present to us so striking a contrast to the old Greek mind and to the modern mind. In the Greeks we have the domination of mathematical concepts, in the moderns we have the domination of scientific concepts; separating these, and presenting the contrast of a direct negation, we have in the mediæval mind the domination of spiritistic concepts. It affects every domain, not art, religion, and ethics merely, but scientific conceptions.

Every physicist is familiar with the very modern hypothesis known as 'Clerk Maxwell's demon.' The famous professor once gave a striking illustration of the way in which a law of nature might conceivably be reversed in its direction; for example, how heat might be made to flow from a cool to a hot body in contradiction to the law of degradation of energy. He supposed that there might be a demon who, without adding to, or taking anything from, the sources of energy, that is, without creating or destroying physical energy, would simply open or shut a door in the path of an individual molecule. The notion of a demon producing real effects without performing actual work is strange and fantastic to us only because the imagery is unusual, a mixture of mediæval and modern conceptions of the nature of causal agency. To the mediæval mind the notion of a demon would have been commonplace. The whole universe was full of such forces, often conceived as playing fantastic and mischievous tricks. Not only the material world but the mental world, human life and history, was the stage and drama of spirit forces. We smile at what we call the naïve and childish ignorance displayed in the notion. To us it is not only pre-scientific, but anti-scientific. This is to fail to understand the mentality. It is a view of nature which follows from the dominating concept that in history reality is revealing itself as an embodiment of universal purpose.

When we endeavour to discover, following the same method, what is the dominating concept in our modern period, and inquire further what is the warp or bias it is giving to our mentality, we meet at the outset a formidable difficulty to which we must at least be respectful. We are ourselves subject to the warping influence of the dominating concepts of our own time, and the very principle we invoke warns us that we may ourselves each individually be prejudiced by our own particular predilections and be following our own warped judgment when professing and believing that we are interpreting the modern mind. With this caution kept continually before us, we may proceed. There is, then, characteristic of the modern mind, by universal agreement, the experimental method. This is not what psychologists name the principle of trial and error, nor is it the utilitarian bent in human intellectual nature which enables it to profit by the practical devices which it may invent or discover. It finds expression in the notions of law in the natural world, and of the unity and uniformity of nature. As a method it depends on the concept that the behaviour of anything under specified conditions follows from and reveals the whole nature of the thing, and that consequently sufficient knowledge of the history of anything enables us to predict absolutely how the thing will behave under all conditions. We do not usually attribute this concept to any particular philosopher's insight or to any individual scientific worker's discovery. We see its origin in the gradual rise and development of positive science, and it appears to be not so much a discovery as an emancipation of the mind. We describe the experimental method as the direct interrogation of reality, and the employment of it seems natural to an enlightened age. It does not seem to us to rest on any concept of reality, and so far from appearing to warp our mentality it seems to indicate simple freedom from every kind of warp. Yet reflection will show that beneath this expression of the modern mind there is a distinctive concept, and to me at least (I am obliged to speak diffidently, for there are many and discordant voices) it is a new concept of time and history.

In speaking of a dominating concept finding expression in the modern mind, I am not able to point to any definite formulation of a concept of reality which may be said to be at once recognisable beneath the diverse forms of the modern problem. These concepts do not spring up before us and present themselves " in questionable shape." What I have in mind is a tendency rather than a form, a concept vague at first but which gradually assumes a definite shape as we watch its emergence through an historical development. The experimental method, indeed, is in its nature and origin directly associated by us with a materialistic, or at least with a definitely mechanistic, concept of reality. The first form which modern philosophy assumed when it took shape in the Cartesian system was that of a rigid mechanism. But it contained from the first a principle destined to alter completely that aspect. It is only when we look at the course of philosophical speculation from Descartes to times present as one continuous unfolding, or development, or living

evolution that we are able to discover the true nature of
the concept which is dominating it. It is then seen that
the whole tendency of modern thought is to pass from
a static to a dynamic standpoint. Externally it is easily
explicable by the order in which the natural sciences have
had attention concentrated on them and have consequently
perfected their methods. First in order to receive attention are the mathematical and physical sciences dealing
primarily and essentially with spatial relations and generally
with space. It was inevitable that it should be so, first
because the new science is closely associated with the
renascence of the old learning, and secondly because it is
the astronomical discovery, the Copernican revolution,
which has overthrown the mediæval cosmology. In the
first formulation all reality is conceived in terms of extension and movement, and movement is conceived as a fixed
quantity and purely mechanical. This determined also
the sciences of the organism and of the mind, physiology
and psychology, which slowly differentiated themselves.
Science remained dominated by the concept of reality as
fundamentally spatial. Not till two hundred years after
Descartes, not until quite close to our present era, did time
begin to supplant space as the essential form of what is
fundamentally real. It is only in Darwin and with the rise
of the biological sciences that time and history begin to
· present the central metaphysical problem. But it is not
a kaleidoscopic change; it is a continuous development,
quite definite and distinctive in its tendency and direction.
One and the same principle is at work from Galileo to
Einstein, from Descartes to Bergson. A concept of
activity, a concept of reality as creation, a concept of change
as real, a concept of life as involving the fundamental
reality of time and history, is the dominating concept of

the modern mind. One could illustrate it abundantly, but I must be content to indicate it. In every one of the sciences we have seen a complete revolution in method and standpoint. It is premature, perhaps, to say that chemists and physicists have now at last abandoned the search for a primordial stuff, but it no longer counts or serves as a necessary hypothetical basis of the universe. It is energy, not stuff, which is interpretative in science. The atoms of modern physics and chemistry are only in name identical with the atoms of the old theory of Democritus, or even with the modern theory of Dalton.

The essential doctrine of the philosophy of change is that stability, shape, repetition, in nature, the spatial articulation of reality, are derivative and not original. Space is relative to the intellect, and intellect is a mode of activity the particular function of which is spatialisation. The 'real' things which our intellect apprehends are not shapes cut out in a solid matrix, but 'actions' virtual or carried out, just as for physical science mass is not the continuous solid, but a function of the trajectories of moving particles. The concept which underlies this philosophy is that history is reality, that the past is present. It is what Bergson has named the true duration. I define, then, the dominating concept of modern thought as the identity of history and reality, the concept of history not as the record of the non-existent past, but as the past existing in a creative present.

I now come to the question with which I opened. Am I able to answer it? I have tried to show in what the essence of the mediæval concept consisted. We may describe it as an anthropocentric concept of history. History is not merely interpretative of human life. It is human life realising its purpose. Now in modern thought I have maintained that the dominating concept is history, but it is no longer anthropocentric, it is no longer the realisation of purpose. It is the concept of history as present creative activity. Let us put aside the meaning of history as record, as what has been but is not, and think of history as the essence of what lives, or rather of life. A living thing is its history, and its past is present in its life and continually creating. This is a new concept; there is nothing resembling it in the old Greek speculation. It is, as I tried to indicate in the beginning, the antithesis of it. Should we have ever reached it, then, had not modern philosophy had as its task not merely to recover the continuity of ancient philosophy but also to solve the inherent contradiction which the mediæval concept presented to it ?

To give precision and definiteness to this reflection I will give an historical reference which may illustrate my meaning better than argument. Benedetto Croce has raised to notoriety a neglected philosopher who lived in Naples at the beginning of the eighteenth century— Giambattista Vico. He was professor of rhetoric in the university of his city, and famous in his day for his erudition, particularly for his knowledge of the old Italian learning. The Cartesian philosophy was then enjoying its full influence, and the intellectual society of Naples was filled with adherents and enthusiastic followers of the ' new science.' By the Cartesian philosophy must be understood not the new method, but the new mechanistic system of the vortex movements. Vico vigorously opposed it, but from an altogether different standpoint from that of Locke and Newton in England and Voltaire in France, and by very different arguments. He had no kind of sympathy for these writers if he was acquainted with their works. His book, now held in honour as one of the classics of Italian philosophy, was named *The New Science*. The title was ironical; it was directed at the Cartesian philosophy. Your new science, he said in effect, is very old stuff. It is nothing but the old mechanism revived. It is not new, it is only the old arguments and the old ideas of Democritus and Epicurus tricked out in a modern dress, and it is as dead as they are. There is a new science, but that science is not mechanism, it is history. By a science of history Vico revealed in his work the consciousness of a new principle and a new method. For material he had the historical records sacred and profane, and he made a strange mixture of them. He had also the science of language, that is, philology, and the various forms of æsthetic expression. From this material he formed his science of the activity of the human spirit and the development of its expression. The work, despite its flashes of insight, is full of strange notions and fantastic theories built on Greek and Hebrew legends accepted uncritically, but the idea was fruitful and pointed a new direction. Francesco de Sanctis, the Neapolitan patriot and historian of Italian literature, acknowledged his indebtedness to it, and Croce and Gentile in their philosophy to-day are continually referring to Vico and insisting, almost with reverence, that he is to be regarded as the first who pointed out the true subject-matter and method of modern philosophy. If we follow Croce in holding that the dominating concept in contemporary philosophy is a new meaning of history, a meaning which identifies it with philosophy as pure interpretation of present fact, then we shall see plainly that this concept does not come to us from the Greek philosophy, for it stands in strong contrast to the mathematical mechanism which dominated the Greek mind, and it is not, like the mediæval concept, a philosophy of history. It is a new concept, which is in very truth a synthesis of the Greek and the mediæval concepts, the concept that philosophy is history.

What, then, is the concept of the modern period which dominates our mentality and which gives us the bias or warp, of which we may easily become conscious, to trust implicitly and unhesitatingly the experimental method ? It is not, like the mediæval concept, the idea of purpose accomplishing itself in the unfolding of human history. Neither is it the idea of a force or agency, natural or supernatural, expressing itself in and through, and in despite of, a recalcitrant material. Were it only the notion of some matter which has a history, matter the nature of which is independent of and indifferent to its history, whence would the experimental method derive its cogency ? The experimental method is rational only if the thing we conceive is identical with its history. It sounds paradoxical only because we do not at once realise the implications of our ordinary reasoning methods. If there is a stuff unchanged and unaffected by, and indifferent to, what it is doing when we experiment to observe it, why should any amount of experimenting inform us what it is ?

The modern concept is, then, the idea of an activity, real in the sense in which life and consciousness are real, continually creating new, unforeseeable forms, and limiting and circumscribing itself in the forms it is creating. This is what we now call the vitalistic concept. I do not claim that it is accepted unchallenged or that it is unchallengeable. I do claim that it has supplanted and is supplanting the old mechanism in every domain of modern life. It is especially remarkable in physical science where the whole tendency is toward dynamism. The essence of this concept is that

104

the reality of the world is exhausted in its history—history is not what the world has been, but what it is, there is no core which abides and which in some unexplained and inexplicable way gives rise in time to moving shadows, images of itself.

In what sense, then, can we say that we owe this modern concept to the philosophy of the Middle Ages? The concept itself supplies the answer. If present fact is history, then the present mentality of our Western civilisation is its continuous life. The history of philosophy is not the record of the thoughts which individual men at various times have had about the universe; it is the unity of all thinking in the universal consciousness. Our modern concept is then seen to arise in the process, and as the product of the process, of the life of thought itself. To discover it and to understand it we have to penetrate the forms of the mentality of the great periods. It follows also that there is no finality. The modern concept is not emancipation from superstition and mythology. It is change and it is growth, but also it is changing and growing. It presents to us, indeed, a definite form, but it is creating new form. The more deeply we comprehend the dominating concepts of the Greek and mediæval periods, the more we understand our own mentality.

H. WILDON CARR

IV

SCIENCE

IT is the common opinion that science, in the usual modern sense, was almost entirely absent in the Middle Ages, and there is much to be said for this verdict. Our scientific system is often regarded as 'essentially an outgrowth of classical antiquity. Such a view contains but a partial truth, and is due to the circumstance that for four hundred years there has been a widespread educational attempt to represent our entire civilisation as the continuation of that of Greece and Rome.

Not until the nineteenth century did anyone begin to doubt this estimate. The brothers Grimm were among the first in the field. They proved that folk-belief had been largely untouched by the great classical models on which we had sought to shape our political and philosophical systems. Next the archæologists demonstrated a whole series of civilisations passing in majestic procession through the ages, a series of which Greece and Rome were but members, and not even the most ancient nor the longest lasting. Then the anthropologists and the psychologists brought their contribution, and showed how much men of all races and civilisations had in common, independent of the classical culture. And now, coming to the proper subject of our discussion, during the last generation or two there has arisen a school of mediævalists who are applying a critical spirit to the very copious mediæval records, and

are gradually reconstructing for us a picture of the life of
the time, so that we are coming to understand better what
our ancestors of the Middle Ages really believed and
thought, and whence and how they derived their beliefs
and thoughts.   However we may define science, it is surely
a fact that in mediæval times men had their beliefs and
thoughts on the nature of the external universe, and had
their own attitude toward phenomena.   This attitude
we shall describe by the word *science* in the pages which
follow.   Its consideration is an integral part of the history
of science, a study which is bound to consider the periods
of disintegration and deterioration as well as those of
reconstruction and advance.

Yet in most histories of science the Middle Ages are
substantially omitted and the narrative passes almost direct
from Greek to modern times.   For this state of affairs
mediæval scholars are partly responsible.   In the synthesis of
the life of the period, which it is their function to construct,
the detailed examination of the mediæval attitude toward
phenomena has had longest to wait.   It is, indeed, only in
very recent times that a serious attempt has been made
toward a comprehensive examination of mediæval science.
This has been largely a task of the twentieth century and
is still very incomplete.

In scrutinising the results of this work it will be well to
make a preliminary examination of the terms we are using.
An accurate examination of these terms will lead us some
way into our survey of mediæval science.   What then do
we mean by the terms *science* and *Middle Ages* ?

The word science is of course derived from *scientia*,
knowledge, a common term of scholastic philosophy, but
there are many kinds of knowledge that we should not
now call science.   Most kinds of knowledge, indeed, are

clearly *not* science. That kind, for instance, that we call ' knowledge of the world ' is not science. May science be described as accurate and organised knowledge ? I think not, or at least not adequately, though this definition is often used. There is much accurate and organised knowledge that is not science. The election agent, for instance, makes out lists of people who will vote this way or that, and his knowledge is most certainly organised and often wonderfully accurate, but he is not therefore a man of science. The milkman knows accurately how much the law will allow him to dilute his milk, and he has doubtless an organisation to defend his action, if needed, but his knowledge is not scientific. What knowledge, then, is it that we call scientific ? At once such people occur to our minds as the chemist, the biologist, and the mathematician. But why should these be called men of science and the title be denied to the equally industrious and more ' knowing ' election agent and milkman ? I think the answer is that the professor's knowledge is progressive, that his science is *knowledge-making* rather than knowledge *per se*. The adjective formed from science, we may note, is not *sciential* or *sciencic* as it should be on the simple etymological rule, but *scientific*, which means literally *knowledge-making*, and I seriously doubt if the title *science* should be applied to any knowledge as such, but should not rather be reserved for the *process which makes knowledge*. Science, in fact, is a process, a method; it is not a subject, as a few schoolmasters and many parents of school-children vainly imagine. Science, the method, may be applied to anything, a language, a school of art, chemicals, religion, a group of plants, a period of history, and it is an error to suppose that it has only to do with horrible smells, diseases, and methods of killing an enemy. Science, then, is the process of

108

making knowledge. It must be admitted at once that in discussing ' mediæval science ' we shall encounter little of the *knowledge-making* process. It is rather with knowledge as such, or supposed knowledge of nature, that we shall have to deal.

Let us now turn to the definition of our other term, the Middle Ages. The delimitation of periods is a constant difficulty of historians. It is a problem which all will admit cannot be finally solved, for the human mind does not confine itself within exact secular limits, and the periods of the historian are but a *memoria technica* on which to build a more detailed statement of movements and peoples. The Middle Ages would therefore be differently defined according as we should be dealing with politics, with literature, with art, or with science. Yet the historian of mediæval ' science ' is perhaps more fortunate than his colleagues in that the principles on which his period is separated from those which precede and those which follow it are relatively clear-cut and simple.

We may first consider the *terminus a quo* of the mediæval attitude toward the external world, applying our test of science as the progress of making knowledge. *The Middle Ages begin for science at that period when the ancients ceased to make knowledge.* Now, ancient science can be clearly traced as an active process up to the second half of the second century of the Christian era. Galen, one of the very greatest and most creative biologists of all time, died A.D. 201. Ptolemy, one of the greatest of the cosmographers, was his contemporary. After Galen and Ptolemy Greek science flags. Some scientific writings survive from the succeeding generations. Several of these, such as the works of Oribasius (A.D. 325–403), are very laborious. Others, such as that of Nemesius (*c.* 390), show considerable philosophical grasp with some conception of the limits of contemporary knowledge. Both groups exhibit much power of organised arrangement, with some sense of the nature of experiment, yet with very little capacity or desire themselves to appeal to experience.

As time goes on the ancient scientific inspiration dwindles. Mathematics holds out the longest, but with the mathematician Theon of Alexandria, at the end of the fourth century, we part altogether with the impulse of the science of antiquity. Stoicism and Neoplatonism too, the chief systems of thought of the late Empire, are dying and are giving place to that great philosophical and religious movement the repercussion of which is felt right through the Middle Ages and down to our own time. The standpoint of its great protagonists, Tertullian (155–222), Lactantius (260–340), and, above all, St Jerome (340–420) and St Augustine (354–430), is outside the department with which we have here to deal, but it was assuredly not conducive to the exact study and record of phenomena.

The work of the physician Vindician (c. 400), the friend, countryman, and convert of St Augustine, represents an expiring flicker of Greek science. More degraded are the medical works of the provincial Christians, Sextus Placitus (c. 400) the Galatian, and Marcellus Empiricus (c. 420) the Gaul. The tradition of Greek scientific method was now utterly gone, and we may fix the commencement of the Middle Ages for science at the end of the fourth or the beginning of the fifth century.

The *terminus ad quem* of mediæval science is, perhaps, less easy to determine. Mediævalisation, in our view, was a slow process under the action of which the human mind, without consciously increasing the stock of phenomenal knowledge, sank slowly into an increasing ineptitude, but at a certain point reached the nadir and tended again upward. The point of lowest degradation of the human intellect was probably about the tenth century. After this may be discerned a slow ascent. Later, in the thirteenth and fourteenth centuries, we encounter considerable extension of natural knowledge. There is still, however, no widespread acceptance of the ancient view that knowledge may be indefinitely extendible, an essential element in any effective doctrine of progress. In this scholastic period at last appear a very few such forward-looking minds as that of Bacon (1214–1294), but these are as yet very rare and exceptional. When at last we get to the fifteenth century we encounter a larger number of forward-looking thinkers, but they are still isolated. Not until the sixteenth century is any effort made, at once organised and conscious, to translate into action this new-born hope in the future.

If we have to name a year for the end-point of mediæval science we would select 1543, when appeared two fundamental modern works based on the experimental method, the *De fabrica corporis humani* of the Belgian Andreas Vesalius and the *De revolutionibus orbium cœlestium* of the Pole Nicholas Copernicus. It is true that for many generations after the time of Vesalius and Copernicus the characteristic doctrines of the science of the Middle Ages were almost universally taught in the schools and diffused by literature, and are, for instance, displayed in the writings of Shakespeare. But the ideas on which the works of Vesalius and Copernicus had been based gain, from now on, an ever wider hearing. It is also true that for generations before 1543 there was a dawning consciousness of the inadequacy of the mediæval cosmic system. But that year saw for the first time two published and authoritative works that formally rejected the old view and supplied a new one.

For science, then, 1543 is the natural *terminus ad quem* of the Middle Ages.

Now, since the human mind turned on its upward course about the tenth century, and since the process was accelerated during the great scholastic period of the thirteenth century and again at the Revival of Learning of the fourteenth and fifteenth centuries, it may be asked, why should we not choose one or other of these dates as the end-point of the scientific Middle Ages ? The thirteenth century, the great epoch of consolidation of Catholic philosophy, has been selected as one of exceptional enlightenment, and has been specially exalted by those who lay great emphasis on the continuing *rôle* of the Church in the development of the intellectual system of our modern world. There are, therefore, some who would place the division in the thirteenth rather than the sixteenth century. There are yet others, biased perhaps by the literary training of the classics, who would place the cleavage a little later, say in the second half of the fourteenth and the first half of the fifteenth century. They would make the Revival of Learning, and especially of Greek letters, the basis of the differentiation between mediæval and modern. For them the fall of Constantinople at the hands of the Turks in 1453 forms a convenient separation.

Yet to make the great division in the tenth, in the thirteenth, or in the fifteenth century would be, to my mind, a philosophical and historical error, because, with very few exceptions, the point of view of the eleventh-century encyclopædist, of the thirteenth-century scholastic, and of the fifteenth-century scholar was formally and essentially an effort to return to the past. It was the literature and language of antiquity, the antiquity of the Fathers, of the philosophers, or of the poets, that these men sought more or less vainly to revive. Both the clerical and the classical education of our day still bear the trace of these backward-gazing standpoints. It would surely be unjust to deny that there are elements both in our clerical and in our classical education that do not partake of this character ; but much of the form in which such studies have been cast is due to a desire to imitate rather than to build. The great Catholic scholastics believed that they were mainly reconstructing the philosophy of Aristotle; whether they were right or wrong is beside the point for our purpose. Imitation rather than origination was the characteristic mental attitude also of the most enthusiastic scholars during the period that we call the Revival of Learning. Even the process by which they recovered the ancient texts, though it may rightly be regarded as containing scientific elements, had for its motive the imitation of the past by the present, rather than the modern archæological aim of the mental reconstruction of the past with the object of understanding the present. What is true of the literary studies of the Renaissance is just as true of the scientific studies of the period. The recovery of the Greek texts, even if it enlarged the mental horizon, chained men's minds more closely than ever to the past.

There is a point, however, at which the gaze of those interested in phenomena, of the physicists, and especially of the physicians, is at last turned away from the past and toward the future. What the philosophical basis of this change may be can hardly be discussed here. I would but briefly state my own belief that the essential bases are the hope in mankind, and its corollary the idea of progress, with which is bound up the idea of the indefinite extendibility of knowledge ; and I would further claim that this idea is not unconnected with the disturbance in the religious outlook of the period. We may at least say of the two great works that appeared in 1543 that they present a new thing in the thought of the time, they are consciously creative, and their authors are aware of a break with the past and are looking to the future for the development and vindication of their views. The work of Copernicus, though it appeared in 1543, had been prepared many years before. It is therefore much the more conservative of the two. But when the proof-sheets were brought to the old man as he lay on his death-bed, he must, I think, have been sufficiently aware that times had changed since he first penned those pages. He must have felt that his outlook in his seventieth year had greatly changed from that of the class-rooms of Bologna and Padua where, as a young man, he discussed with a group of brilliant fellow-students the problems of heaven and earth. Very different is the history of the second of these two great early works of modern science. Vesalius when he produced his magnificently printed and illustrated *Anatomy* was a vigorous young man of twenty-eight. He was in full revolt against tradition, and he saw the situation clearly and saw it whole. He parts definitely with the Middle Ages, and has no use for ancient knowledge save when he can demonstrate it to be in accord with anatomical details as he sees them before him. He is every inch a modern.

Thus for effective purposes we may place the limits of mediæval science between the years 400 and 1543. This vast stretch of time is divided by an event of the highest importance for the history of the human intellect. Between the beginning of the tenth and the end of the twelfth century there was a remarkable outburst of intellectual activity in Western Islam. This movement reacted with great effect on Latin Europe, and especially on its scientific views, by means of works translated from Arabic which gradually reached Christendom. In the light of this great

114

intellectual event we may divide our scientific Middle Ages into three parts, an *earlier* Dark Age, an *intermediate* Age of Arabic Infiltration and Translation, and a *later* Scholastic Age. During these three periods the general principles of science hardly change, but the difference in presentment of the material is such that the student of mediæval science is seldom in doubt into which category to place any document that may come into his hands.

The task of the first mediæval period was the conveyance of the remains of the ancient wisdom to later ages. During the closing centuries of the classical decline the literature that was to be conveyed had been delimited and translated into the only language common to the learned West. We may briefly discuss this classical heritage.

The work of Plato that is least attractive and most obscure to the modern mind fitted in well with the prevalent views of the Neoplatonists. The commentary on the *Timæus* prepared by Chalcidius in the third century from a translation of Apuleius in the second presents the basis of views held throughout the entire Middle Ages on the nature of the universe and of man. Thus the *Timæus* became one of the most influential of all the works of antiquity, and especially it carried the central dogma of mediæval science, the doctrine of the macrocosm and microcosm.

Of Aristotle there survived only the *Categories* and the *De interpretatione*, translated in the sixth century by Boethius (480-524). A Greek introduction to the *Categories* had been prepared by Porphyry in the second century, and this also was rendered into Latin by Boethius. Thus the only Aristotelian writings known to the Dark Age of science were the logical works, and these determined the main extra-theological interest for many centuries. It is a world-misfortune that Boethius did not see his way to prepare versions of those works of the Peripatetic school that displayed powers of observation. Had a translation of Aristotle's *Historia animalium* or *De generatione animalium* survived, or had a Latin version of the works of Theophrastus on plants reached the earlier Middle Ages, the whole mental history of the race might have been different. Boethius repaired the omission, to some small extent, by handing on certain mathematical treatises of his own compilation, the *De institutione arithmetica*, the *De institutione musica*, and the (doubtful) *Geometrica*. These works preserved throughout the darkest centuries some fragment of mathematical knowledge. Thanks to them we can at least say that during the long degradation of the human intellect, mathematics, the science last to sink with the fall of the Greek intellect, was not dragged down quite so low as the other departments of knowledge. The main gift of Boethius to the world, his *De consolatione philosophiæ*, which preserved some classical taste and feeling, lies outside our field.

A somewhat similar service to that of Boethius was rendered by his approximate contemporaries, Martianus Capella (*c.* 500) and Macrobius (395–423). The former, in his *Satyricon*, a work of far less literary value than the masterpiece of Boethius, provided the Dark Age with a complete encyclopædia. The work is divided into nine books. The first two contain an allegory, in heavy and clumsy style, of the marriage of the god Mercury to the nymph Philology. Of the last seven books of the work, each contains an account of one of the ' Liberal Arts,' grammar, dialectic, rhetoric, geometry, arithmetic, astronomy, and music, a classification of studies that was retained throughout the Middle Ages. The section on astronomy has a passage containing a heliocentric view of the universe that had

116

been familiar to certain earlier Greek astronomers. The passage gave rise to no comment in the Middle Ages, but it may have drawn the attention of Copernicus, who quotes Capella. In other respects the cosmology of Capella, like that of Chalcidius, is Neoplatonic, as is also that of Macrobius, whose commentary on the *Somnium Scipionis* of Cicero gave rise to some of the most prevalent cosmological conceptions of the first mediæval period.

In addition to the cosmography, mathematics, and astronomy that could be gleaned from such writings as these, the Dark Age inherited a group of scientific and medical works from the period of classical decline. The most important was the *Natural History* of Pliny, which deeply influenced the early encyclopædists. Very curious and characteristic is a group of later pseudepigrapha bearing the names of Dioscorides, Hippocrates, and Apuleius, the history of which has not yet been fully investigated. They were probably all prepared between the fourth and sixth centuries. Manuscripts of the pseudo-Apuleian treatise *On the Virtues of Herbs* are often beautifully illustrated by miniatures, and examples from every century from the sixth to the sixteenth have come down to us, showing the most extraordinary constancy of tradition. The Dark Age inherited also certain medical works in translation from Greek. These were prepared between the fifth and eighth centuries, and included treatises of Hippocrates, Dioscorides, Galen, Oribasius, Alexander of Tralles, and Paul of Ægina. A very curious medical survival of this period is a work on embryology for the use of women, translated by the sixth-century Moschion from a work of the second-century Soranus.

This material, then, was the basis of the mediæval scientific heritage. Traces of much of it are encountered

in *De institutionibus divinarum et humanarum literarum* of
Cassiodorus (490-585), perhaps the earliest general writer
whose works bear the authentic mediæval stamp. The
scientific heritage, however, is much more fully displayed
in the *Origines* of Isidore of Seville, a late sixth-century
work which formed a cyclopædia of all the sciences in the
form of an explanation of the terms proper to each. For
many centuries Isidore was very widely read, and the series,
Isidore (560-636), Bede (673-735), Alcuin (735-804),
Raban (786-856), who borrow from one another successively,
and all from Pliny, may be said to contain the science of the
Dark Age. The work of these writers is summarised by the
early eleventh-century English writer Byrhtferth (*d. c.* 1020),
whose copious commentary on Bede's scientific work may
be regarded as the final product of Dark Age science.

The only Dark Age writer who deals with cosmological
problems in an original way is Erigena (*c.* 800-*c.* 877).
But his remarkable genius hardly concerned itself with
phenomena, and so we may pass him by, relegating him to
the philosophers. With the somewhat belated Byrhtferth
we part company with the Dark Age and enter upon a new
period, with new forces and new movements at work.

The tenth century and those that follow bring us into
relation with the wisdom of the East. In these centuries
the relation of East and West with which we are nowadays familiar is reversed. In our time most Oriental
races recognise the value of Western culture, and give it
the sincerest form of flattery. The Oriental recognises
that with the Occident are science and learning, power and
organisation and public spirit. But the admitted superiority of the West does not extend to the sphere of religion.
The Oriental who gladly accepts the Occidental as his
judge, his physician, or his teacher wholly repudiates, and

118

perhaps despises, his religion. In the Europe of the tenth, eleventh, and twelfth centuries it was far otherwise. The Westerner knew well that Islam held the learning and science of antiquity. His proficiency in arms and administration had been sufficiently well proved—the Occidental belief in them is enshrined in our Semitic word ' admiral.' There was a longing, too, for the intellectual treasures of the East, but the same fear and repugnance to its religion that the East now feels for Western religion. And the Western experienced obstacles in obtaining the desired Oriental learning analogous to those now encountered by the Eastern in the Occident.

The earliest definitely Oriental influence that we can discern in the department of science is of the nature of infiltration rather than direct translation, and the earliest agents of this process, for reasons which we shall presently discuss, appear to have been Jews who had been under Saracen rule. Such influence can first be traced in two works in the Hebrew language by Sabbatai ben Abraham (913–970), better known as Donnolo, a Jew of Otranto who practised medicine at Rossano in Southern Italy. One of his works is an ' antidotarium,' or book of remedies, and bears slight but definite evidence of Arabic influence. His other can be dated to the year 946, and is on astrology. It unquestionably draws on Arabic sources, and sets forth fully the doctrine of the macrocosm and microcosm. Donnolo learnt Arabic while a prisoner in Saracen hands; he was taught the language by a Bagdadi, and, like Constantine in the next century, he claimed to have studied "the sciences of the Greeks, Arabs, Babylonians, and Indians." He travelled in the Italian peninsula in search of learning and thus must have spread some of his Arabic science.

The first Latin document betraying Oriental influence

of the type traced in Donnolo has only been discovered during the last few years. It is a treatise on astrology to which the name 'Alcandrius' (Alexander) is attached. This work has come down to us in but a single manuscript written about 950 or a little later, probably in Southern France. The repeated use of Hebrew equivalents for the names of constellations and planets, and the occasional use of Hebrew script, leave no doubt that it has passed through Jewish hands.

The existence of these works of Donnolo and 'Alcandrius' enables us to understand the Saracenic influence detected in the mathematical writings of the learned Pope Silvester II (Gerbert, d. 1003), who spent some years in Northern Spain. Gerbert was, perhaps, among the earliest to introduce the Arabic system of numbering which slowly replaced the much clumsier Roman system, with its tiresome use of the abacus for simple mathematical processes. He is also believed to have instigated a translation from the Arabic of a work on the astrolabe.

Hermann the Cripple (1013-1054) spent his life at the Benedictine abbey of Reichenau in Switzerland. He wrote certain mathematical and astrological works which were extensively used in the following century by Bernard Sylvestris. There is no evidence that Hermann could read Arabic, and, since he was unable to travel by reason of his infirmity, it is unlikely that he had any opportunity of learning that language. Yet his writings display much Arabic influence, which was almost certainly conveyed to him by wandering scholars of the type of Donnolo and 'Alcandrius.' Similar evidence of the somewhat belated influence of what we have called the process of Arabic infiltration is exhibited in the lapidary of Marbod of Anjou, Bishop of Rennes (1035-1123), and in the work on the medicinal use of herbs by Odo of Meune, Abbot of Beauprai (Macer Floridus, *d.* 1161).

The Arabic learning that was thus beginning to trickle through to the West in a much corrupted form was, however, by no means an entirely native Saracen product; it was derived ultimately from Greek work. There was, indeed, yet one channel by which the original Greek wisdom might still reach Europe. Communication between the West and the Byzantine East was very little in evidence in the centuries with which we are now concerned, but a Greek tradition still lingered in certain Southern Italian centres, and especially in Sicily. That island had been a part of Magna Græcia, and its dialects bear traces, to this very day, of the Greek spoken there and in Calabria and Apulia until late mediæval times. But the Saracens had begun their attacks on the island as early as the seventh century, and their rule did not cease until the Norman conquest of the eleventh century. The Semitic language of the Saracens left the same impression on the island as did their art and architecture, so that between the tenth and twelfth centuries Sicily is a source of both Greek and Arabic learning for Western Europe.

One seat of learning felt especially early the influence of the Græco-Arabic culture of Sicily and Southern Italy. Salerno, on the Gulf of Naples, possessed something in the nature of a medical school at least as far back as the ninth century. It is clear from surviving manuscripts that, even apart from the Greek language, some traces of ancient Greek medicine lingered widely diffused in Magna Græcia during the centuries that succeeded the downfall of the Western Empire. Such Greek learning as remained was galvanised into life by Saracenic energy in Sicily and Southern Italy, and, with what we now know of the carrying agents of Arabic culture, it is quite easy to understand the popular tradition that attributes the founding of the great medical school of Salerno to the co-operation of a Greek, an Arab, a Latin, and a Jew. The very earliest Salernitan writings that have survived, such as that of Gariopontus (*c.* 1050), are, it is true, free of Arabic influence, but from the end of the eleventh century Salernitan material is full of Semitic words, some of which remain in medical nomenclature to this day.

A very important agent of this early Arabic revival was Constantine the African (*d.* 1087), a native of Carthage, who came to Italy about the middle of the eleventh century. He became a monk at Montecassino, and spent the rest of his life turning current Arabic medical and scientific works into Latin. In his desire for self-exaltation he often conceals his sources, or gives them inaccurately. His knowledge of both the languages which he was treating was far from thorough, and his translations are wretched. But these versions were very influential, and they remained current in the West long after they had been replaced by the better workmanship of such Toledo students as Gerard of Cremona in the twelfth century and Gerard of Sabbioneta in the thirteenth.

The earliest Oriental influences that reached the West had thus been brought by foreign agents or carriers, such as Constantine or Donnolo. But the desire for knowledge could not be satisfied thus. The movement that was soon to give rise to the universities was shaping itself, and the Western student was beginning to become more curious and more desirous of going to the well-springs of Eastern wisdom. Yet there was many a lion in the path.

The main difficulty was one of language. Arabic was the language of Eastern science and letters, and its idiom was utterly different from the speech of the peoples of

Europe. Moreover, its grammar had not yet been reduced to rule in any Latin work, nor could teachers be easily procured. Even in the thirteenth century we find that Bacon, though he clearly perceived the importance of linguistic study and eagerly sought to unlock the literature of foreign tongues, had still not found the key. He had only time to commence laboriously the grammatical apparatus of the Greek and Hebrew languages. He was still without an Arabic grammar. The only way to learn Arabic was to go to an Arabic-speaking country. Yet this was a dangerous and difficult adventure involving hardship, secrecy, and perhaps abjuration of faith. Moreover, to learn the language at all adequately for rendering scientific treatises into Latin meant a stay of years, while the work of translation demanded also some understanding of the subject-matter to be translated. There is good evidence that an effective knowledge of this kind was very rarely attained by Westerns, and probably never until the later twelfth century.

At the period during which Western science begins to draw from Moslem sources there were only two points of contact: these were respectively Spain and Sicily. The conditions in the two were somewhat similar. In the tenth century the Iberian peninsula was Moslem save for the small kingdoms of the Spanish march, Leon, Navarre, and Aragon. Here the grip of Islam had relaxed after a short hold, and this territory remained historically, religiously, racially, and linguistically a part of the Latin West. The Moslem South was ruled from Cordova, which became increasingly Mohammedanised, but at the more northern Toledo the subject population, though speaking an Arabic *patois*, remained largely Christian. It was at Toledo that most of the work of transmission took place.

It is probable that the process was frequently carried on by the intervention of Jewish students. The tenth, eleventh, and twelfth centuries, a time of low degradation of the Latin intellect, was the best period of Jewish learning in Spain. Arabic was the natural linguistic medium of these learned Jews, the works of some of whom, as Ibn Gebirol, disguised in Latin works as Avicebron, and Maimonides, known to the scholastics as Rabbi Moses, were themselves rendered into Latin, and formed part of the Eastern heritage won by the translators during these centuries.

We can fairly picture to ourselves the very details of the actual process, piecing our scene together from a variety of documents. An eccentric and restless European student, dissatisfied with the teaching of Paris, of Bologna, or of Oxford, and attracted by floating stories of the wonders of Arabic learning, arrives at Toledo or Cordova. He has crossed the frontier from the Spanish march, having evaded or bribed the sentries. Perhaps he carries letters from a patron in his native land to an official of the native church. These native dignitaries bear something of the same relation to the governing powers that the Christian *rayahs* in the late Turkish empire bore to the ruling powers. All are in a state of nervous subjection, leagued together by common instinct and common interest. Even after the Moslem retreat, generations must pass before such men can free themselves from the servile inheritance of ignorance. Our student makes his way to the church or monastery and establishes his credentials. His host can converse with him in Latin, but only with difficulty, for their pronunciations differ greatly.

The student has now to be housed with a monastery or family, that he may learn the vernacular of the place. The language that was to develop as Castilian is hardly yet known, for the native Christians have adopted the speech of their conquerors. The vernacular of these Mozarabs is a non-literary *patois* of mixed Arabic and Latin origin. To acquire facility in this is essential before the task of translation can be thought of. Later, in the twelfth century, when the tide had turned and Islam was in retreat, it was occasionally possible for a scholar with a gift for languages, such as Gerard of Cremona (1114–1187), to find a skilled native Christian teacher such as Ibn Ghâlib. But in the tenth or eleventh century Christian learning and Christian society in Spain were subject and depressed. Like many modern peoples similarly placed, these native Christians were attached with the more fanaticism to the religion which held them together, and to the language of their Church. The student of an earlier time could find no effective Christian teacher of literary Arabic, while the very sciences which he sought to acquire were suspect as the mark of the infidel and the oppressor.

The Jews of Spain of that age, however, though equally subject to the Moslem, had entered with greater spirit into the scientific heritage of Islam. While quite ignorant of Latin, with which they had not the same spiritual link as their Christian fellow-subjects, many of them spoke and wrote the language of science, the literary language of the Koran. Our student, now with some command of the vernacular, makes the acquaintance of a Jew of this type, and arranges a series of meetings with him and with a native clerk who has some knowledge of Latin. The work selected for translation might be in Arabic or Hebrew, for many of the most important Arabic works of science had been turned into the latter language. In either event it is improbable that the Christian members of the *séance* could read the Semitic script, or that the Jew could read the Latin. The Jew would then laboriously turn the

Hebrew or Arabic text, sentence by sentence, into the vernacular, and the student, aided by his native assistant, would then translate from the vernacular to Latin. Naturally, in this process many words would be met that could not be rendered either into the vernacular or into the barbarous Latin of the student who had now long been away from any centre of Latin learning. Especial difficulty would be encountered with the technical scientific terms. The meaning of some of these might well be imperfectly known to the Jewish translator himself. Such words would simply be carried over in a transliterated Arabic or Hebrew form into the translation, and the early versions are full of these Semitic expressions. The mediæval astronomical and medical vocabularies abound in Semitic words, some of which, such as 'azure,' 'zero,' 'zenith,' and 'nucha,' have come down to the speech of our own time. The sort of translation which emerged from this process may be imagined. When it is also remembered that to reach the Arabic from the original Greek it had already passed through similar stages, probably with Syriac as an intermediary, it will be understood that the first scientific books that reached the West were a wretched travesty of the Greek originals from which they were ultimately derived.

Men who may be supposed to have worked in such a way as we have pictured are Adelard of Bath (c. 1100), who visited both Spain and Sicily, and who published a compendium of Arabic science—and his pupil John O'Crea, who translated Euclid's *Elements* from the Arabic. To the same group belongs Michael Scot (1175?–1234?), who produced versions or abridgements of the biological works of Aristotle. More scientific in their methods were Robert of Chester (c. 1150), who rendered the Koran into Latin and translated works on alchemy and astronomy

126

and the valuable algebra of Al Khowarizmi, and Alfred the Englishman (*c.* 1220), who rendered the Peripatetic work *On Plants*, and thus preserved for us a fragment of a work of the Aristotelian school that would otherwise be lost. But the greatest of all the translators was Gerard of Cremona (1114–1187), who spent many years at Toledo and obtained a thorough knowledge of Arabic from a native Christian teacher. He and his successor Gerard of Sabbioneta (*c.* 1230) translated into Latin a multitude of works, among them the *Almagest* of Ptolemy on which Regiomontanus began his work in the fifteenth century, and the *Canon* of Avicenna, the most widely read medical treatise that has ever been penned. Contemporary with Gerard of Cremona, and perhaps stimulated by him, were certain native translators, one of whom was Domenico Gonzalez, a Christian who rendered into Latin the *Physica* and the *De cœlo et mundi* of Aristotle, and another Johannes Hispalensis or Avendeath, a converted Jew who translated, among many other works, the pseudo-Aristotelian treatise *Secretum secretorum philosophorum* which greatly influenced Roger Bacon, as well as the astronomical works of Messahalah which long formed the staple popular account of the system of the world. These all worked in Spain. The Sicilian group was less active. The last translator of Sicilian origin, the Jew Farragut (Farradj ben Selim, Moses Farachi, *d.* 1285), was a student at Salerno, and his works were among the latest of any influence that issued from that ancient seat of learning. These later translators are, however, mainly unimportant, and at the end of the twelfth century we may say that the period of translation was rapidly closing.

We have now to turn to the actual material thus conveyed to Latin Christendom. It differed rather in degree than in kind from that of the earlier Dark Age and from that of the Age of Arabian Infiltration. The systems differed in the degree to which the logical conclusions from the premises provided were pushed, and in the degree to which each was influenced by certain theological conceptions.

In the late classical age there had developed the Stoic system of thought, which divided with Neoplatonism all the more philosophical minds of the ancient world. This Stoic philosophy assumed that man's fate was determined by an interplay of forces the nature and character of which were, in theory at least, completely knowable. The microcosm, man, reflected the macrocosm, the great world that lay around him. But how and to what extent did he reflect it ? In seeking to determine these points Stoicism and Neoplatonism and the other philosophical systems of the classical twilight gleaned from many sources material which they passed on in a corrupted state to the Latin world. In a somewhat less imperfect form these materials lingered for centuries in the Byzantine world until, with the great outburst of Islam, they were caught up and elaborated by the Arabic culture. Thus elaborated, they were sent forth a second time to Latin Europe by the process of infiltration and translation.

The astrological conceptions of the Stoics and of the later Christian ages drew both on Plato and on Aristotle. The hylozoism of the *Timæus*, the doctrine that the universe itself and the matter of which it is composed is living, gave a suggestive outline to the hypothesis of the parallelism of macrocosm and microcosm. But the main details of the hypothesis were drawn from Aristotle, whose views of the structure of the universe were the framework on which the whole of mediæval science was built. Especially Aristotle's conception of the stars as living things, of a nature higher and nobler than that of any substance or being in the spheres below, was a clear point of departure from which the influence of the heavenly bodies over human destinies might be developed. The changes undergone by physical bodies on the earth below were held to be controlled by parallel movements in the heavens above.

Aristotelian theory carried the matter farther. It distinguished the perfect, regular, circular motion of the fixed stars from imperfect, irregular, and linear motion, such as that of the planets. The stars moving regularly in a circle controlled the ordered course of nature, the events that proceeded along regular, manifest, and unalterable rounds, such as those of winter and summer, night and day, growth and decay; the erratic planets governed the less ascertainable group of events that comprise the variable elements in the world around and within us, the happenings that make life the uncertain, hopeful, dangerous, happy thing it is. It was to the ascertainment of the factors governing this kaleidoscope of life that astrology set itself.   The broad general happenings were certain, death in the end was sure, and, to the believing Christian, life after it.   But there was a great uncertain zone between the sure and the unsure that might be predicted and perhaps avoided, or, if not avoided, its worst consequences abated.   It was to this process of insurance that the astrologer set himself, and his task remained the same throughout the Middle Ages.   In this hope *savoir afin de prévoir* the mediæval was at one with the modern scientist.   The matter is summarised for us by Chaucer:

> Paraventure in thilke large book,
> Which that men clipe the hevene, y-writen was
> With sterres, whan that he his birthe took,
> That he for love sholde han his deeth, allas !
> For in the sterres, clerer than is glas,

Is written, God woot, whoso koude it rede,
The deeth of every man, withouten drede.

. . . But mennes wittes ben so dulle
That no wight kan wel rede it atte fulle.

The Man of Lawes Tale

There was, however, another relationship which we
cannot fully treat here. In all ages there are two prevalent
types of mind. The religious type sees that the world
cannot be wholly explained and falls back on supernatural
hypotheses. The scientific type prefers to assume that
the laws he is able to trace in regions he knows and understands are but a sample of those which govern the universe
in all its unknown parts also, and that if we knew enough
we should be able to trace law everywhere. The type of
the scientific intellect is Lucretius, who accepts, as a matter
of course, the control of man's fate by a law which includes
even the heavenly bodies. " We must," he says, " give
good account of the things on high, in what way the courses
of sun and moon come to be, and by what force all things
are governed on earth." He will not allow immortality
to the stars, much less to man. All are subject to
the same immutable law of generation and corruption.
Very different is the attitude of St Ambrose, who takes
no interest in aught but final causes, for whom the very
investigation of phenomena seems frivolous and aimless.
" To discuss the nature and position of the earth," he says,
" does not help us in our hope of life to come. It is
enough to know what Scripture says, that ' he hung up
the earth upon nothing ' (Job xxvi, 7). Why, then, argue
whether He hung it up in air or upon water, and raise a
controversy as to how the thin air could sustain the earth,
or why, if upon waters, the earth goes not crashing to the

130

bottom ? . . . Not because the earth is in the middle, as if suspended on an even balance, but because the majesty of God constrains it by the law of His will, does it endure stable upon the unstable and the void." (*Hexaëmeron*, i, 6.)

Between two such extremes the mind of man has always hovered, and thus hovered the mediæval mind. The average man recognises the reign of law in the smaller events of life, but places all his spiritual and mental life in the hands of God. The average scientifically trained man recognises the reign of law in higher matters also, but believes in his own free will, and in another will outside his own that ultimately governs the higher and greater events of his life. Beyond these two stand the religious mystic on the one hand and the materialist on the other; the one for whom all the world is but the projection of the will of a spirit, the other for whom all those elements in our lives which most men assign to spirit are but the workings and interaction of the properties of matter.

In the earlier Middle Ages, as in the earliest Christian centuries, the world was but God's footstool, and all its phenomena were as little worthy of study as Ambrose held them to be. This sums up the general attitude of the fourth and fifth centuries set forth by Augustine, who speaks of " those impostors whom they style mathematicians (*i.e.*, astrologers) . . . who use no sacrifice, nor pray to any spirit for their divinations, which arts Christian and true piety consistently rejects and condemns."[1] By the sixth and seventh centuries, however, the Church has come to terms with astrology, and Isidore regards it, in part at least, as a legitimate science. He distinguishes, however, between *natural* and superstitious astrology. The latter is " that science which is practised by the *mathematici* who

[1] *Confessions*, iv, 4.

read prophecies in the heavens, and who place the twelve constellations as rulers over the members of man's body and soul, and who predict the nativities and dispositions of men by the courses of the stars." [1] Nevertheless Isidore accepts many of the conclusions of astrology. He advises the physicians to study it, ascribes to the moon an influence over plant and animal life and control over the humours of man, while he accepts without question the influence of the dog-star and of comets. He is followed by the other Dark Age scientists, who each accept a little more astrological doctrine, until finally in such a writer as Byrhtferth we get the complete scheme. (See Fig. 1.)

With the advent of the Arabian learning astrology became the central interest, and remained so until the triumph of the experimental method in the sixteenth and seventeenth centuries. We cannot here follow the details of the developed astrological scheme. It is enough for our purpose to have observed that the general material law which it implies had become widely accepted in the Middle Ages, and to have traced its passage from antiquity and from the Orient into the thought of the period of which we are treating.

There was another fundamental theory of mediæval science which, equally with astrology, was inherited from antiquity, and equally with it was reinforced and amplified by the Arabian revival. The doctrine of the four elements was conveyed to the Middle Ages by the Aristotelian writings.

All matter was held to be made up of four essential elements—earth, air, fire, and water. Each of the elements was in its turn compounded of the four ' primary qualities,' heat and cold, moistness and dryness, in binary combination. Thus earth was cold and dry, water cold and moist, air hot and moist, and fire hot and dry. Moreover,

---

[1] *Origines*, iii, 27.

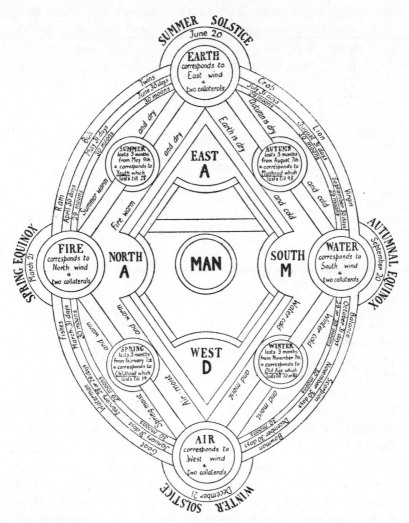

Fig. 1. Scheme showing Relation of Macrocosm and Microcosm,
after Byrhtferth (c. 1000)

each element in the macrocosm corresponded to one of four imaginary 'humours' in the microcosm; thus elemental earth corresponded to 'black bile,' elemental water to 'phlegm,' elemental air to 'red bile,' and elemental fire to 'blood.' (See Fig. 2.) Now, it must not be imagined

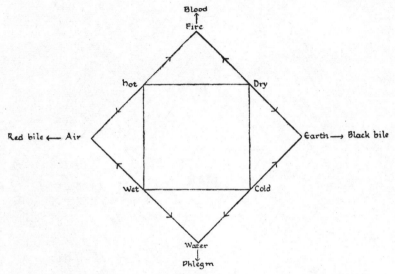

Fig. 2. SCHEME OF THE FOUR QUALITIES, THE FOUR ELEMENTS, AND
THE FOUR HUMOURS

that these elements were the substances that we know by the names of earth, water, air, and fire in this world below. The elements are found here only in combination, that is, in their state of *mistio*, to use the technical mediæval expression. Thus the substance water, though it contains a preponderance of the element water, contains also less amounts of the other three elements; so the substance air is not pure elemental air, but contains only a preponderance of that element intermixed with the others. It was usually admitted, however, that the elements were to be found

134

in a *pure* form in certain regions of the world, though where and how distributed these pure elements might be, was a matter of varying opinion.

The usual view was something like this. Earth, the heaviest, drossiest, and least aspiring of the elements,

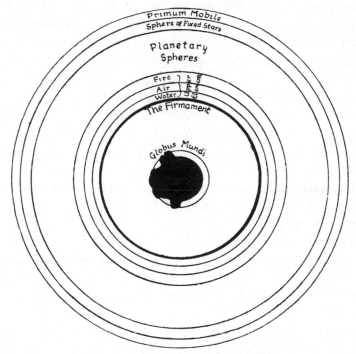

Fig. 3. SCHEME OF THE SPHERES

naturally tended to the centre of the world. It was least likely of all the elements to be found pure because of its drossiness. On its surface floated material water, and above that was the air, also in the material state in which we breathe it. High up in the air, far beyond the reach of men, were the eternal zones of the stars, both fixed and wandering, but just below these spheres, wherein the celestial bodies dwelt, were three concentric zones of the upper and pure elements. These, proceeding outward and in ascending degrees of tenuity, were water, air (sometimes confused with ether), and fire. The watery zone exhibited evidence of its presence by clouds, the waters that God had placed above the firmament. The fiery outermost zone was somehow related to the eternal fire of the heavenly bodies which lay in a series of concentric spheres around it. In these outer concentric spheres moved the planets, each in its own sphere, and beyond them all was the sphere of the fixed stars, surrounded by the outermost zone of all, the sphere of the *primum mobile*. (See Fig. 3.) There was a certain amount of variation in the details of the scheme, but a full and characteristic development of it is provided for us by such a writer as Dante. (See Fig. 4.)

Especial attention was always paid to the relation of the zodiacal signs to the planets. Each zodiacal sign was held to govern or to have special influence on some region of the body, and each of the planets was held to influence a special organ. The actual relations of zodiacal signs, planets, and bodily parts and organs is set forth in such late Latin writers as Firmicus Maternus (*c.* 330) and Avienus (*c.* 380), and in innumerable Greek texts. This belief, conveyed to the Dark Age, but gradually lost during its course, was brought back again to the West by the Arabs. Nothing is commoner in mediæval manuscripts of the scholastic period than a human figure on the various bodily parts of which are placed the signs of the zodiac held to control that part. Common, too, and penetrating even to Books of Hours, are schemes showing the relation of the organs to the seven planets. The whole system thus became intimately interwoven with the conception of the relation of macrocosm and microcosm.

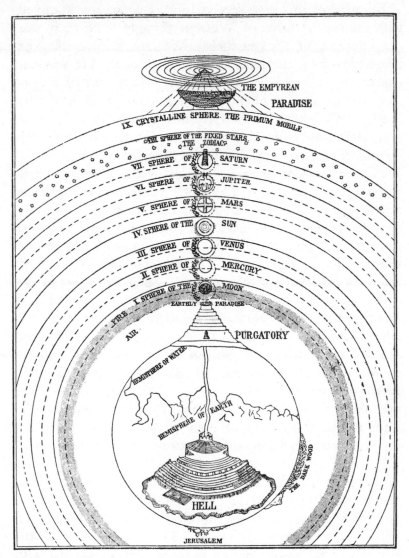

Fig. 4. DANTE'S CONCEPTION OF THE UNIVERSE

Doctrine of this type received into Europe was stamped with the special form of Western thought. Now, it was characteristic of the mediæval Western thinker that he sought always a complete scheme of things. He was not content to separate, as we do, one department of knowledge or one class of phenomena, and consider it in and by itself. Still less would he have held it a virtue to become a specialist, to limit his outlook to one department with the object of increasing the sum of knowledge in it.

His universe, it must be remembered, so far as it was material, was limited. The outer limit was the *primum mobile*, and of all within that he had been provided with a definite scheme. His task, and at first his only task, was to elaborate that scheme in connexion with the moral world. To do this was in the first post-Arabian period the work especially of the mystics. Such writers as Hugh of St Victor (1095–1141), who drew on the earlier and more vague Arabian rumours, Bernard Sylvestris (*c.* 1150), who relied on Hermann the Cripple, and Hildegard (1098–1180), who was influenced by Sylvestris and by other Arabicised writings, all produced most elaborate mystical schemes based on the doctrine of the macrocosm and microcosm. These schemes took into account the form of the world and of man as derived from Arabian accounts, and read into each relationship a spiritual meaning. For such an attitude of mind there could be no ultimate distinction between physical events, moral truths, and spiritual experiences. In their fusion of the internal and external universe these mystics have much in common with the mystics of all ages. The culmination of the process, so far as our period is concerned, is reached with Dante (1265–1321).

But with the thirteenth century new currents of thought

set in. The Arabian science was at last won, the scientific works of Aristotle were becoming accessible and gradually entering the curriculum, the universities were firmly established, and there were the beginnings of a knowledge of Greek. We are now in the high scholastic period. The appointed task of the great teachers of that period, Alexander of Hales (*d.* 1245), Robert Grosseteste (*d.* 1253), Albertus Magnus (1193–1280), and St Thomas Aquinas (1225–1274), was to marshal the new knowledge and to make it more readily accessible. It is remarkable that this process, involving a rapid change and development in the whole mental life of the world, involving, that is to say, progress *in fact*, did not develop a more passionate and more conscious faith in progress in knowledge. Yet there is little or no evidence of direct observation of nature in the great physical encyclopædias of the thirteenth century, such as that of Alexander of Neckam (1157–1217), Vincent de Beauvais (1190–1264), and Bartholomew de Glanvil (*c.* 1260). The mediæval mind was obsessed with the idea of the mortal world as finite, and therefore completely knowable both in space and in time, so that the motive for detailed *research*, in our modern sense of the word, was not present. The task of the writers of these encyclopædias was rather to give a general outline of knowledge in their scheme, to set forth such a survey of the universe as would be in accord with spiritual truth. The frame-work on which this encyclopædic scheme was built was Aristotle, largely as conveyed by the Arab commentator Averroes. Yet it is an amusing reflection on the incompleteness of all philosophical systems that Albert, who perhaps more than any man was responsible for the scholastic world-system, was among the very few mediæval writers who were real observers of nature. It is, after all, in the very essence of the human animal to love the world around it and to watch its creatures. *Naturam expellas furca tamen usque recurret.* Albert, scholastic of the scholastics, drowned in erudition and the most learned man of his time, has left us evidence in his *De vegetabilibus* that the scientific spirit was beginning to awake. As an independent botanical observer he is by no means contemptible, and this element in him marks the new dawn which we trace better in his successors.

Thus the best of the systematisers among the schoolmen were leading on to the direct observation of nature. Contemporary with Albert and Aquinas were several remarkable scholastic writers who form the earliest group with whom the conscious advancement of knowledge was a permanent interest. These men were the first consciously forward-looking scientific thinkers since the fourth century. The earliest of them was the Pole Witelo (*c.* 1250), an acute mathematical investigator, whose work was based on a translation of the Arab Alhazen. Witelo knew something of optics, and was aware of the action of segments of a crystal sphere as lenses.

Contemporary with Witelo was a very remarkable Franciscan group. There is no stranger and more impressive chapter in the whole history of thought than that of the early history of the Franciscans. Within the memory of men who had known the saintly founder of the Order (1181–1226), the 'Penitents of Assisi,' the 'friars minor,' sworn as 'jongleurs of God' to bring Christ cheerfully to the humblest and the meanest, sworn to possess nothing, to earn their bread from day to day by the work of their own hands, or at need by begging, forbidden to lay by store or to accumulate capital, this Order of humble servants of Christ had produced a series of monumental and scholarly intellects, who between them not only initiated what bid fair to be a renaissance of science and letters, but also aided in the formation of the bulwark which long resisted the very movement that thus emanated from the Order itself. To both parties the English Franciscan houses contributed an overwhelming share. To the former, or scientific party, as we may call them, belonged Robert Grosseteste Bishop of Lincoln, John Pecham Archbishop of Canterbury, the elusive Adam Marsh, and, above all, Roger Bacon; to the latter or theological party are attached the names of Alexander of Hales (*d.* 1245), Duns Scotus (1265 ?–1308 ?), and William of Ockham (*d.* 1349).

The primary inspirer of the scientific movement was undoubtedly the great Bishop of Lincoln himself, and its aims are set forth for us by his pupil Roger. " Nobody," says Bacon, " can attain to proficiency in the science of mathematics by the method hitherto known unless he devotes to its study thirty or forty years, as is evident from the case of those who have flourished in those departments of knowledge, such as the Lord Robert of holy memory and Friar Adam Marsh . . . and that is the reason why so few study that science." Again: " There were found some famous men, as Robert Bishop of Lincoln, and Adam Marsh, and some others, who knew how by the power of mathematics to unfold the causes of all things and to give a sufficient explanation of human and divine phenomena; and the assurance of this fact is to be found in the writings of those great men, as, for instance, in their works on the impression [of the elements], on the rainbow and the comets, on the sphere, and on other questions appertaining both to theology and to natural philosophy." The work of this remarkable group of Franciscans at Oxford extended beyond the sciences to language and literature. There was the beginning of a real renaissance of Greek letters which died an early death. But the scientific revival lingered on until recalled to life by a second revival of a later century. It may be convenient to have on record a summary of the scientific achievements of Bacon, the greatest of the Franciscan group and the first man of science in the modern sense.

1. He attempted to set forth a system of natural knowledge far in advance of his time. The basis of that system was observation and experiment. He was clearly the first man in modern Europe of whom this can be said.

2. He was the first man in modern Europe to see the need for the accurate study of foreign and ancient languages. He attempted grammars of Greek and Hebrew along definite scientific lines. He also projected a grammar of Arabic. Moreover, he laid down those lines of textual criticism which have only been developed within the last century.

3. He not only expatiated on the experimental method, but was himself an experimenter. The criteria of priority were not then what they are now, but his writings are important in the development of the following sciences:

(a) *Optics.* His work on this subject was a textbook for the next two centuries. He saw the importance of lenses and concave mirrors, and showed a grasp of mathematical optics. He described a system which is equivalent to a two-lens apparatus, and there is trustworthy evidence that he actually used a compound system of lenses equivalent to a telescope.

(b) *Astronomy* was Bacon's perpetual interest. He spent the best part of twenty years in the construction of astronomical tables. His letter to the Pope in favour of the correction of the calendar, though unsuccessful in his own days, was borrowed and reborrowed, and finally, at third-hand, produced the Gregorian correction.

(c) *Geography.* He was the first geographer of the Middle Ages. He gave a systematic description of Europe, Asia, and part of Africa. He collected first-hand evidence from travellers in all these continents. His arguments as to the size and sphericity of the earth were among those that influenced Columbus.

(d) *Mechanical Science.* Suggestions by him include the automatic propulsion of vehicles and vessels. He records the working out of a plan for a flying-machine.

(e) *Chemistry.* The chemical knowledge of his time was systematised in his tracts. His description of the composition and manufacture of gunpowder is the earliest that has reached us. It is clear that he had worked out for himself some of the chemistry of the subject.

(f) *Mathematics.* His insistence on the supreme value of mathematics as a foundation for education recalls the attitude of Plato. It was an insistence that the method of thought was at least as important as its content.

Summed up, his legacy to thought may be regarded as accuracy of method, criticism of authority, and reliance on experiment—the pillars of modern science.

The interest taken in Roger Bacon's works was continuous. "Friar Thomas Bungay, whom ancient tradition associates with Bacon, was the tenth lector to the friars at Oxford. John Pecham, the eleventh lector, studied mathematics and optics under Bacon, and was first attracted and finally repelled by his astrological theories. William Herbert, who afterward became lector at Oxford, was at Paris about the time of Bacon's death, and diligently collected manuscripts of his works for the friary at Hereford. Before the end of the thirteenth century attempts were made to ' edit ' Bacon by collecting together passages from his writings bearing on the same or kindred subjects. Pierre Dubois recommended the study of his mathematical work at the beginning of the fourteenth century. The large number of manuscripts of his *Perspectiva*, or *Optics*, still existing, some of them ' school copies,' and references to it in disputations at Oxford, show that the work was studied and regarded as authoritative in the fourteenth and fifteenth centuries. But his influence extended beyond the Middle Ages; through Pierre d'Ailly and the *Imago mundi* Bacon reaches out his hand to Columbus; through Paul of Middelburg (1445–1534) and the reform of the calendar to Copernicus." (*A. G. Little.*) Bacon was not an isolated phenomenon, but an important link in the chain of scientific development.

But during the century after Bacon, though his mathematical and philosophical works were still studied in the schools, the greatest advances were rather among the physicians, of whom the last half of the thirteenth and the first half of the fourteenth century exhibit an especially brilliant group. Bologna had possessed a medical school since the twelfth century, and had inherited the learning of Salerno. At Bologna had worked Hugh of Lucca (*d.* 1252 ?) and his son or pupil Theodoric (1206–1298). Here, after Salerno, surgery may be said to have been born again with the practice of Roland of Parma (*c.* 1250), the successor and faithful follower of Roger of Salerno. Here, above all, William of Saliceto (1201–1280) established a

144

practical method of anatomisation which was inherited by Mondino da Luzzi (1276–1328), whose work became the general anatomical text-book of the later Middle Ages.

The medical school of Montpellier was now coming to the fore, and here practised one of the most remarkable personalities of mediæval medicine. Arnald of Villanova (1235–1313) was not only one of the earliest exponents of the Hippocratic method of observing and carefully recording symptoms of actual cases of disease, but he also deeply influenced alchemy. Even more remarkable and more modern in his outlook was the heretical Peter of Abano (1250–1320). He had a knowledge of Greek, but the chief philosophical influence under which he came was that of the Spanish Arab Averroes, whose doctrine of the infinite extension of the universe gave a better background to a progressive outlook than the more prevalent mediæval view. Peter's greatest and best-known work, the *Conciliator*, expresses his mediation between the now commencing humanistic Greek school and the Arabists. Among his views most worth record may be mentioned his statements that the air has weight, that the brain is the source of the nerves and the heart of the vessels—all ideas that in his time were new. He made a remarkably accurate measure of the length of the year as 365 days, 6 hours, 4 minutes.

The second half of the fourteenth century, in part owing to the prevalence of epidemics and notably of the Black Death, shows a distinct falling off in the advance. In medicine the most noteworthy name is that of Guy de Chauliac of Montpellier (1300–1370), perhaps the most influential of all the mediæval surgeons. Outside the ranks of the physicians perhaps the most remarkable figure in fourteenth-century science is the French Jewish philosopher Levi ben Gerson (1288–1344). His work as astronomer

145

was important as illustrating the consciousness of a growing discontent with the Ptolemaic system of the universe. With the fifteenth century discontent with the entire mediæval scientific scheme becomes more obvious, and there is a real attempt to adjust theory by means of experiment. The turning-point is provided by the work of Nicholas of Cusa (1401–1464), who became a cardinal and made a fruitless attempt to reform the calendar. The philosophical basis of his experimental bias is set forth in his book *De docta ignorantia*, which has nothing to do with the absurdity of erudition, as its name might be thought to imply, but concerns itself with acknowledged ignorance, *i.e.*, with the inability of the human mind to conceive the absolute or infinite. His theoretical views led him to a belief that the earth is moving, though he attained to no genuine heliocentric theory. He is a real experimenter, and he records a careful experiment on a growing plant— afterward pirated by the seventeenth-century writer van Helmont—proving that it does absorb something of weight from the air. This is the first biological experiment of modern times, and incidentally the first formal proof that the air has weight.

Beginning with Nicholas of Cusa, we may watch the Middle Ages branch out into the Renaissance period. In philosophy Nicholas reaches out through Pomponazzi and Ramus to Francis Bacon and Descartes; in his conceptions of the nature of matter, through Paracelsus to the dawn of modern chemistry; in astronomy, through Purbach, Regiomontanus, and Paul of Middelburg to Copernicus. By the work of such men as these the whole fabric of the mediæval teaching of the macrocosm was gradually torn to shreds.

The history of the process from this stage onward is

146

CHRONOLOGY OF MEDIÆVAL SCIENCE

THE CLASSICAL TWILIGHT

	Latins	Greeks	Fathers	
		Ptolemy		
		Soranus		
		Galen		
200	Apuleius		Tertullian	200
	Porphyry			
	Chalcidius		Lactantius	
300				300
	Pseudo { -Dioscorides / -Hippocrates / -Apuleius	Oribasius	[Baptism of Constantine]	
	Firmicus Avienus	Nemesius	Ambrose	
	Vindician	Theon	Jerome	
400	Martianus Capella	THE DARK AGE	Augustine	400
	Macrobius			
	Sextus Placitus			
	Marcellus Empiricus			
500	Moschion	Alexander of Tralles		500
	Boethius			
	Cassiodorus			
			Gregory the Great	
600	Isidore	Paul of Ægina		600
700	Bede			700
	Alcuin			
800	Raban			800
	Erigena			
900		AGE OF ARABIAN INFILTRATION		900
		First Arabian Impact		
		Donnolo		
		' Alcandrius '		
	Byrhtferth	Gerbert		
1000	Gariopontus and other early Salernitans	Hermann the Cripple		1000
	Translators	Later Salernitans		
	Constantine		*Transmutors*	
	Adelard			
1100	O'Crea	Marbod	Hugh of St Victor	1100
	Avendeath Gonzalez	Odo of Meune	Bernard Sylvestris	
	Robert of Chester		Hildegard	
	Gerard of Cremona	SCHOLASTIC AGE	Alexander of Neckam	
	Michael Scot	*Experimenters*	Alexander of Hales	
1200	Gerard of Sabbioneta	Witelo Adam Marsh	Albert Aquinas	1200
		Roger Bacon Pecham	Grosseteste Vincent Beauvais	
	Alfred the Englishman	William of Saliceto	Bartholomew de Glanvil	
	Farragut	Theodoric		
1300		Arnald Mondino		1300
		Peter of Abano		
		Levi ben Gerson		
		Guy de Chauliac		
1400		Nicholas of Cusa		1400
		Purbach Regiomontanus		
		Pomponazzi		
		Leonardo		
1500		Paracelsus		1500
		Copernicus		
		Vesalius		

not very complex. Anatomy had been systematically studied in the universities since the thirteenth century. By the end of the fifteenth it was common for artists and physicians to have had some experience of dissection, and the genius of Leonardo was only working on a subject of general study. With the dawn of the sixteenth century anatomy was a recognised subject of investigation as well as of teaching, and the achievement of Vesalius, vast though it was, differed from that of his predecessors in exactness, completeness, and independence, but not in its fundamental character. By 1543 it was as difficult for an anatomist to trace in the lineaments of the viscera the impress of the heavenly bodies as it was for the astronomer to believe that the heavens were foreshadowed in the anatomy of the body of man.

In theology too the vociferous insistence of both religious parties on the divine origin of their doctrines implied an independence of the spiritual from the material universe that would have been incomprehensible to the mystics of the twelfth and thirteenth centuries. The material world had ceased to have its old spiritual significance, and was become the acknowledged dwelling-place of laws, discoverable but not discovered.

As the proof-sheets of the *De revolutionibus orbium cœlestium* fell fluttering to the ground from the dying hand of Copernicus, something more than his great spirit had gone from the world; the whole system of mediæval science was no more.

CHARLES SINGER

V

ART

I

IT has been said—and such epigrams serve to hang a half-truth in the memory—that all the great representative art of the world flows from two sources, Greece and China. The art of China never penetrated into Europe; and therefore, though it was a mediæval art, and the painters of the T'ang and Sung dynasties were during some centuries the greatest in the world, I will make a present of it to the Adversary and confine myself to Europe—nay, to Christendom; since the argument for mediæval art is so great that we can afford to neglect those Persian, Saracenic, and Mughal developments, derivative from Byzantinism or interwoven with it, and to make of them also a present to the Adversary—leaving them as reserves behind the lines of our argument which it will not be necessary to draw upon.

We have a period of a thousand years, from the fifth century to the fifteenth, from Theodoric with his basilicas and mosaics, from Justinian, when architectural creation culminated in the glory of St Sofia, from the purely Byzantine city of Rome between the sixth and ninth centuries, through the giant vitality of the Romanesque period and the mastery of Gothic, to the dispersion of the Greeks and of their 'new' old learning in 1453, and the discovery of America in 1492.

The end of this period was very brilliant. Consider painting, for instance. Before the fall of Constantinople, Duccio, Giotto, Orcagna, Taddeo Gaddi, Masaccio, the Van Eycks were already figures of the past; Van der Weyden was some fifty-three years old, Fra Angelico within two years of his death. Or if you take the later date, 1492, as the close of the Middle Ages, Paolo Uccello and Dierick Bouts were dead, the two Bellinis were over sixty, Crivelli was probably dead, Memlinc and Ghirlandajo had but two years to live, and Benozzo Gozzoli six. Nay, by 1492 Botticelli was already forty-six and Leonardo forty; even Dürer, Michelangelo, and Titian had begun to draw. We owe the art of modern painting to the later centuries of the Middle Ages. That, in the realm of art, is one 'mediæval contribution to modern civilisation.' It is so stupendous that I feel tempted to say " My lecture is now over "; or, at least, following an old custom, to sit down for a moment and take a pinch of snuff.

II

I understand that the historians of the twentieth century have no use for the Renaissance. We have discovered the principle of continuity. Even in natural science there was no renaissance: there was just a beginning, and that beginning came, I understand, in the England of the thirteenth century.

In art also we have, I think, no real use for the word, except to describe a style of architecture—at first Italian—which became really articulate with Alberti in 1460 and Bramante in 1490. There was, it is true, a growing antiquarian enthusiasm in the fifteenth century which

more or less affected all the arts,[1] and revolutionised ornament, so that to the revival of Roman decorative motives
we may also justly apply the word ' Renaissance,' as a
convenient though inaccurate term, like ' Gothic '; but
there was no renaissance or rebirth of art in the fifteenth
century. There was only a continued growth; and that
growth, when it was fully infected by the classical antiquarianism, was quickly smitten with decay, so that in the
first half of the sixteenth century its decline was in full
progress, and the end came while Michelangelo was still
towering to his grave. There remained, of course, the
technical mastery which had been acquired between the
eleventh century and the sixteenth. That skill has never
left us; and at all periods since the thirteenth century it
has therefore been possible for great accomplished artists to
arise.

Victorian writers like John Addington Symonds, while
freely acknowledging the speedy and pitiful collapse,
under the blight of pedantry and pseudo-paganism, of
what they called the Renaissance, exaggerated the importance of this imaginary rebirth by including every
Italian painter of distinction, as far back as the thirteenth-
century Cimabue. In architecture they were more modest,
and dated the Renaissance from Brunellesco's great dome
at Florence (1420), which is partly Byzantine, partly
Gothic, and wholly Brunellesco. They used also to claim
all the later mediæval Italian sculptors, not only Niccola
but Giovanni and Andrea Pisano, Giotto, Orcagna, Ghiberti,
Donatello, Luca della Robbia, Mino da Fiesole. Yet

[1] Painting was never directly affected, because there were no antique
paintings then to be copied—only statues, buildings, and books (cf. B. Beren-
son, *The Venetian Painters of the Renaissance*, 3rd edit., p. 7). Luckily for us,
Pompei was then well hidden under its scoria.

they acknowledged that even enthusiasts for the antique, like Ghiberti and Donatello, never copied it, but remained wholly original and realistic.[1]

The truth is, of course, that art in the Middle Ages had moved on natural lines, and therefore had continued to be traditional, and had never broken with antiquity—as the very word ' Romanesque ' (of which Gothic was a development) should remind us. The earliest Christian art was Græco-Roman; this was followed by the development of Hellenistic art which we call Byzantine, which in turn modified Basilican art into Byzantinesque and Romanesque. In the eleventh century, side by side with Byzantine sculpture and painting in Sicily and Venice, Roman capitals were still carved in Italy and France.[2] As Romanesque passed into Gothic, we find sculpture sometimes obviously inspired by antique Roman models, as in the *Visitation* group at Reims Cathedral, the remarkable little school in Apulia under Frederick II (1240), and in 1260 the sculpture of Niccola Pisano (an artist whose merits have been exaggerated), who himself came

[1] It is characteristic of our false perspective that even in so excellent and modern a history of art as Reinach's *Apollo*, Duccio and Fra Angelico come in a chapter after that on Renaissance architecture.

[2] Not in Italy only, but in France as a whole. Even a district as far north as Burgundy is rich in fluted Corinthian pilasters of the twelfth century. Provence abounds in Roman ornament and Byzantine statuary : it did not become part of France till the fifteenth century, and passed straight from Romanesque to Renaissance. In architecture, it is curious to compare with Brunellesco's dome or with his Pazzi Chapel in Florence (*c.* 1415) such a piece of work as the twelfth-century porch at Notre Dame des Doms, Avignon, which is so classical that it might be mistaken for Roman work ; whereas the Pazzi Chapel is, like the dome, wholly original, and could never be mistaken for Roman. Neither could the earlier Renaissance palaces, or the façade of the Certosa of Pavia (1491), which might be described as flamboyant Romanesque. When Renaissance architecture had freed itself from the mediæval spirit, it speedily lost its character and developed into the Baroque and Jesuit styles at the end of the sixteenth century.

from Apulia.[1] And it was just at this time that there came the great period of Gothic sculpture, an art realistic and original. All the while in the East the autumn glory of Byzantine art had continued, alive but unchanged.

In painting itself, there lay behind the great Italian developments of the thirteenth century a long unbroken tradition of wall-painting, which reaches back to the beginning of the mediæval period,—beside which there runs a similar practice of miniature painting, unequal, uncertain, but alive and full of power. Of the wall-paintings, naturally, most have been destroyed; but it must be remembered that Romanesque architecture afforded wide spaces of wall, and it was the practice to cover these spaces with pictures. The earliest that have survived in France, at St Savin in Vienne, belonging to the end of the eleventh century, are worthy to be compared with the frescoes attributed to Cimabue, two hundred years later.[2] He and his predecessors of the thirteenth century worked on an older mediæval tradition, just as Leonardo worked on a later, and Raffael worked on Leonardo.

Furthermore, there is one form of painting, the painting with small cubes of glass upon walls and other surfaces,

[1] J. A. Symonds, while ascribing all Italian ' Renaissance ' sculpture to the influence of Niccola Pisano, is full of admissions : he " could not wholly free himself from the defects of the later Romanesque manner," he " resorted to his native Tuscan models," he introduced " a stir of life and movement, and felt his subjects with an intensity alien to the ideal of Græco-Roman sculpture." (*Renaissance in Italy*, 1882, pp. 106, 113.) Niccola also introduced the new Gothic cusps into his pulpit at Pisa, and his son Giovanni was intensely Gothic, as Symonds agrees.

[2] Discoveries in recent years show that these beautiful paintings were by no means exceptional. We know also that mural painting went on in France from as early as the fifth century. Romanesque examples have been found in Germany. In Italy there are the noble frescoes at San Clemente.

called mosaic, which belongs in the main to the Middle Ages, and is at its greatest in the earlier centuries, though it lasted at Venice and elsewhere into the modern period. Rising to perfection in the great Byzantine churches of the fifth and sixth centuries, it was not less fine in the Greece of the eleventh, in the Sicily, Venice, and Rome of the eleventh, twelfth, and thirteenth, and in Constantinople, where in the fourteenth century there was an independent renaissance of painting—a movement of great promise, cut short by the Turkish conquest. Mosaic is a noble form of the pictorial art which is beyond us to-day, with its glittering lights, its soft, dusky shadows, its depth of colour, its majesty of vision and vastness of design. The painting of the thirteenth century sprang out of it.

In other words, there had been a continued development of art from ancient Egypt, Crete, Greece, through classical and Byzantine Rome, and through the Middle Ages; interrupted sporadically by the barbarian invasions during the first half of the Middle Ages, but reinforced from the Eastern Empire, and from Syria and Armenia. There was a quickened development from the eleventh century to the sixteenth, which survived the so-called Renaissance—the reaction of the doctrinaire upon art—by about a century, and then declined. This great movement was, admittedly, not a reconstruction of the antique; but there had been a real continuation of the antique throughout the Middle Ages.

III

Based on a misapprehension of history, the theory of the Renaissance vitiated generations of criticism and still poisons the minds of artists to-day—the theory that there was a gap between the paganism of the antique and the

154

neo-paganism of the Renaissance. In Symonds' words, " No true form of figurative art intervened between Greek sculpture and Italian painting."

This theory of the gap was held more intensely in France and on the Continent: it was an indictment not only of the Middle Ages, but of Christianity. Because of it, the art of the Renaissance itself ran quickly into decadence; because of it, in part, arose the Puritan opposition to art; because of it, the modern world has been confused, wandering without any working philosophy of æsthetic (except the false one that the end of art is to give pleasure), without any working principle by which to live—for if the moral excellence of Christianity is opposed to the æsthetic excellence of the body and of art, then the spirit of man is torn asunder. Therefore still to-day the world outside the artists follows its own business—its commerce, science, and measure of well- and ill-doing; while those who care for beauty still in large measure (and more so abroad than here) have regarded themselves as rebels against our common civilisation, living in a peculiar pale of their own, often in a ' Bohemia ' aloof alike from the sphere of ethics and of knowledge. To be an artist, they had been told, was to be ' pagan,' since art was not possible till men went back behind the Christian era at the Renaissance; and paganism meant a crude notion of following one's own impulses and discarding the accumulated wisdom of the last two thousand years. It ignored the fact that the mind of man has been profoundly changed, and that we cannot go back to some imaginary age when men were supposed to be like beautiful untroubled children. The result was that artists were often trained in centres of great shallowness and narrow-mindedness, and in a real ignorance of the world. They had made a world of their own, they were out of touch with the great mass of human tradition; and as a consequence they have failed to convert the world back to an understanding of beauty, while often the most accomplished work has lacked the power which comes from adequate spiritual impulses.

Now the truth, of course, is that there was no gap. Men followed art in the Christian era as well as in any other, and there are extant Christian paintings as early as the first century. They did what they could. Sculpture, indeed, did almost disappear in the pagan empire of the second century, between Hadrian and Constantine. It revived under definitely Christian inspiration after Constantine, and produced beautiful reliefs in marble and ivory in the fifth and sixth centuries—sculptures about which connoisseurs would have raved—such has been our snobbishness—had they been found buried beneath the ruins of some ancient Greek city. The Byzantine ivories continued to be made throughout the Middle Ages. Side by side with this representation of the human form went decorative sculpture, the Byzantine capitals, for instance, of the sixth century—more beautiful than those of Greece, infinitely more varied and full of life—these capitals we find still being made and developed at Venice in the twelfth century. In that century also France entered the first stage of her great development. Need I remind you of the Gothic decorative art in thirteenth-century France and England; or of the great French statuary? "Twice," says Professor Lethaby, "in the history of art has sculpture reached a mark which placed it apart from that of all other periods "—Greek and Gothic[1]; to which I would add the Italian sculpture from the thirteenth century to Michelangelo.

[1] *Mediæval Art*, 1912, p. 216.

But the illusion about a gap has this amount of foundation. Between the fifth century and the tenth the whole of Europe (except the Eastern Empire, whose turn came later) was overrun by successive hordes of barbarians. They were, indeed, tamed, converted, civilised, in a marvellous way; but before their conversion they were giant destroyers, and, after it, they required some centuries of education. As a result, we do find, especially in the north-west, art almost as base sometimes as that in the London of to-day.

Up to the year 1000, art was either Byzantine or barbaric; but after that date Europe—or rather the patch of free Europe outside Moorish Spain, outside the still heathen north-east, and the Slav line where Tatars and Turks were later to get dominion—that patch of Europe, which looks small enough on the map, was to settle down and have peace enough to express itself. We forget the lurid centuries in which our forefathers struggled against an all-prevailing Bolshevism. Well, this little Western Europe expressed herself quickly enough—in communes, in free-cities, in guilds, in nationalities, and in art. Already in 985 the Othonian ' Renaissance' had begun. Meanwhile, from the earliest beginnings of Christian education, the art of Constantinople, its beautiful ivories, miniatures, enamels, metal-work, textiles, had never ceased to penetrate the West, like rain, causing such passing efflorescences as the Ruthwell and Bewcastle crosses in the eighth century, inspiring men like Benedict Biscop in the seventh, or the artists of the Carolingian revival in the ninth, and supplying the models which led the men of the Romanesque period toward the perfection of Gothic sculpture.

All the time, the Christian Church had been no enemy of the representation of the human form. On the contrary the Church needed this representation and demanded it;

157

for without this representation it was impossible to express the central principles of Christianity; and therein she differed from Islam, as Christian art always has differed from the purely decorative art of the Muslim peoples.

I have mentioned the Church in order to restore the balance and arrive at the truth—not to encourage, but rather to prevent that reaction against our pseudo-classical grandfathers which would exaggerate the virtues of the Middle Ages. Nothing is more exasperating, indeed, than the attempt to make ecclesiastical capital out of the art of the thirteenth century.

There were doubtless bishops without æsthetic understanding in the Middle Ages, as there are, I understand, to-day. There was also a strong ideal of asceticism among the monks; yet the monks covered our Europe with a ' white mantle of churches ' in the Romanesque period. Such a mighty outburst of beauty had never happened before ; and their monasteries were great workshops— workshops which were studios. Yet mediæval art did not reach its zenith till it had passed out of monastic control by the thirteenth century into the hands of the burghers and the guilds. But it was still Christian art, still the expression of the Christian inspiration: the sculpture of French Gothic, of Donatello and Michelangelo, was still the art of the Church. For the Church is not the clergy, nor is it bishops and popes: it is the people. And it was the people then—men to whom religion was indeed a great reality—but cheery, and indeed beery, fellows in leather aprons, who, amid all the wars and oppressions, laughed and thrived, and banded themselves together in their crafts —in Constantinople many centuries earlier than in the West. The towns swarmed with these workmen who happened to be artists—these artists who were content to be workmen. The idea that their interests were in sadness and suffering, or that their art was gaunt and emaciated, has long been exploded.[1]

IV

Let us come to architecture. It is the fundamental art. Without it, you may have a few brilliant men painting pictures for a few brilliant picture-dealers; you may have many profiteers recognising that a gilt picture-frame *must* have something in it; but you will not have art as a vital principle of life—you will not find the people seizing a great picture and carrying it in triumphal procession down the Strand. Clever artists will continue to arise, both in painting and sculpture, and a few discerning people will rejoice in them; geniuses will break through from time to time—generally under intense discouragement. New schools will try new experiments, and be intensely bored with the experiments of the schools before them. But you will not make art again secure and inevitable, as it always had been, everywhere in the world, before the Renaissance broke the tradition and expired together with its victim— you will not establish art again as the habit of mankind, until you set men's paths about with beauty again; and this involves two things. It involves architecture, the mightiest and most serious of the arts, and costume, the lightest and most capricious—yes, if Pericles had worn a top-hat and

[1] The cultivation of false pathos appears in the fourteenth century, and increases with the decline of intellectual leadership in the Church. In its wake follows the humanist reaction, but also the *macabre*. " Il semble," says M. Mâle in *L'Art Réligieux de la fin du Moyen Age*, 1908, p. 76, " que désormais le mot mystérieux, le mot qui contient le secret du christianisme, ne soit plus ' aimer,' mais ' souffrir.' " The absolute reserve of early Christian art is in the most striking contrast with the morbid emphasis on the Crucifixion and Passion during the past six centuries.

spats, where would Pheidias have been ? How much of the prestige of our ancient universities is due to their architectural beauty, and to the fact that in the academic habit some relics of mediæval costume are retained ? Yet I notice in some modern universities a tendency to regard even the humble minimum of a black gown as something to be discarded as much as possible, because it happens to be both convenient and graceful. It is characteristic of our age that men affect to despise costume, and then spend much money, care, and time in making themselves look nattily ridiculous. The beaux remain, though the beauty has gone. But until the streets we live in, and even the men who walk about in them, are tolerable to the vision, our eyes will not recover from their distortion and become normal again.

Fortunately, I need not take up your time with pleading the virtues of mediæval architecture. That battle has been long won. In the young days of this College, when it was regarded as the latest echo of the Parthenon, any gathering here would have believed that, as with painting and sculpture, so with architecture, there had been a great gap—say between the Coliseum and St Peter's at Rome—a gap precariously filled with the barbarous litter which our great-grandfathers called ' Gothic '—meaning what we should mean by the word ' Hun.' That illusion has disappeared, though the majority of our professional architects still act as if it were true.

There are, however, two facts about mediæval architecture which are, I think, not yet quite generally realised.

1. Gothic occupied only some three or four centuries out of our period of a thousand years, and that only in Western Europe. The East was untouched by it; in Rome it was a foreign fashion which never seriously interrupted Romanesque work; even North Italy remained on

the whole a land of basilican and Romanesque buildings. Europe between the fifth century and the fifteenth had five great kinds of architecture, Basilican, Byzantine, and Byzantinesque,[1] Romanesque, and Gothic, and within these main styles an unprecedented number of varieties which testify to their amazing vitality. These styles include nearly all the greatest buildings in the world; they include what most artists agree to call the greatest of all—St Sofia at Constantinople, where all the problems of architecture were solved into perfection at the beginning of the Middle Ages; they include the loveliest and most graceful of the basilicas from the fifth century to the eleventh—Ravenna, Torcello, Fiesole; they include the Byzantine of Venice and Aquitaine; the splendid Romanesque schools of Pisa, Florence, and Sicily; the cluster of great churches along the Rhine and in Lombardy; the several mighty schools of France, and masterpieces like our own Durham. And these classes of architecture culminated from the end of the twelfth century in our Western Gothic—reaching, shall we say, to the crown of Beauvais—an architecture so wonderful that it has about it something which we moderns, with all our admiration, have not been able even to *see*, as our attempts at restoration or revival so painfully testify.

2. All mediæval architecture has this common characteristic—it is free. Compared with it, the art of other periods is as crystals are to plants. Ancient Roman architecture had indeed partly extricated itself from the close limitations of ancient Greece: it had introduced the arch, but, excepting in its aqueducts and other works of utility (which form the real greatness of Roman architecture), it fails between two incompatible principles—that of the lintel which takes pressure direct and that of the arch

---

[1] Cattaneo's word, ' Italo-Byzantine,' is unnecessarily ugly.

MEDIÆVAL CONTRIBUTIONS

which spreads the pressure: its columns and entablatures are therefore usually only a veneer. Roman ornament, also, is seldom free from heaviness and vulgarity; Roman domes and vaults are giant lids of concrete: it was reserved to the architects of St Sofia to invent the true dome. In architecture, science is always struggling with art; and the ultimate perfection is only obtained when the two are reconciled, as they are in St Sofia, as they are in the final structural triumphs of Gothic.

The architects throughout the Middle Ages worked as free men, that is to say, as real artists. They were never enslaved, as we are to-day, by any superstition about correct Vitruvian orders. Look at the capitals of Ravenna, Salonica, Constantinople, and Venice, of French Romanesque and English Gothic; they invented for their new necessities new capitals, of infinite variety. They did this because, without ever breaking from the past, they used the past to make the present. They lived and grew, they dared, they experimented; their art was dynamic; in every age, in every province, they were themselves, and never the shadow of something that had once lived and was dead. As Sir Thomas Jackson says, " Byzantine and Romanesque art was in fact a revulsion from convention to the unaffected expression of natural law and methods of construction "; and he adds (too indulgently) that some of us, " the strict classic " purists, " value consistent obedience to authority and precedent, to strict canons of orthodoxy, correctness, and propriety, according to certain accepted formulas." [1] They do, indeed ! But this is not art. It is the negation of art, the corpse of art.

And how was architecture thus killed ? It was killed

[1] T. G. Jackson, R.A., *Byzantine and Romanesque Architecture*, ii, 268 (1913).

by what is called the Renaissance. Men discovered that a certain Roman named Vitruvius had laid down certain " canons of orthodoxy, correctness, and propriety "; and this became to them a gospel. Modern scholars have discovered that Vitruvius was not an architect at all, but just a literary gentleman, with an atrociously obscure style, who chatted about architecture. But he was set up as the evangelist, infallible for all time : nothing that could not be read therein or proved thereby was henceforward to be orthodox. Here, as in the other arts, great men did greatly within the formulas : the spirit of the Middle Ages did not die at once—it lived, for instance, still in Christopher Wren and his school, as the spire of St Mary-le-Strand, and dozens of other mediæval spires with classical detail, bear witness.

But a fatal blow had been struck at architecture. It had become mimetic—so mimetic that when the Gothic enthusiasm arose in the nineteenth century the revivalists could not free themselves from the central error of the Renaissance. They also were mimes, they tried to capture the Gothic spirit with rule and measure. They imitated Gothic in everything but this—that Gothic is not an imitation. They were mediæval in everything except in being mediæval. The Gothic revival was the last stage of the Renaissance, and the worst. For art is life : it is not revival.

At the present moment London, and the world, is thickly strewn with shams, Roman shams, Greek shams, Gothic shams—there was even an awful moment of Venetian shams—and now Roman shams again. Whenever we try to be grand, we become dull. Our only living architecture—and it is worthy to be considered with that of any age—is that of our country cottages and country houses; because here we build for our comfort and convenience, we build what we like and not what we are told we ought to like, and we give no shadow of thought to the pages of Vitruvius—or of Pugin. Yes, here in our beautiful country homes we are truly Gothic; here we are really mediæval, and here the spirit of the Middle Ages does contribute to our own time. May new schools of architecture arise now and be mediæval altogether, since to be truly mediæval is to be entirely modern !

I have spoken of the Renaissance as the reaction of the pundit upon art, and the consequent destruction of the free mediæval spirit. The word, indeed, has too many meanings; and I do not mean the new learning, nor the partial emancipation of the intellect from certain phases of tradition and authority. I mean simply that trammelling of intuition which accompanied it, which established a freezing scholasticism in the studio and put young and old alike under the rule of pedantic schoolmasters. It is this tyranny of the ' correct ' in art that is the reason for the universal absence of beauty in the modern world which we all recognise and deplore.

V

But, alas! if we climb out of our pedantry in architecture, as we have long done in painting, as we are doing in sculpture, there will still be one thing lacking. Before I mention it, I would ask you to add to architecture ornament, and the various minor arts and crafts which architecture encloses and protects.

The one thing lacking would be democracy—to use the only word we have got. Briefly, that interruption of tradition which we call the Renaissance was, as we say nowadays, undemocratic: it was the conscious, artificial work of a small class of grammarians, princes, and rich merchants. It had nothing to do with the people: it robbed the people of their art, till artists had to be the parasites of the rich, and the people relapsed into barbarism. The art of succeeding ages, beautiful as it has often been, has been the art of the drawing-room, not of the street; and the parish church has long ceased to be what it once was, the centre of beauty in every little village, the living home (not the mere museum) of an exquisite and popular art. Of course, parish halls might have taken the place of parish churches; but as a matter of fact they did not. The people of Europe have had their art stolen from them by the rich; and to-day there is hardly a scintilla of the divine understanding left among them.

Now, I would put it to you as an axiom that the paralysis of art among the people creeps upward to the whole body; that an art which is the art of a class must always be more or less artificial; and that you cannot have a great, living, and stable art, growing steadily from age to age, unless it is shared by all the nation, loved in all the nation, recruited from every class of the nation. And I would suggest to you that the present instability of our living art of painting, its somewhat reckless experiments, its abiding discontent, is due to the fact that it is not rooted in the common life of Europe.

This, then, is the second great contribution that I desire from the Middle Ages to the art of to-day: the first was liberty, the second is life. Indeed, they are one.

Now the art of the Middle Ages comes between an art resting on slavery, which we call classical, and an art resting on exploitation, which has been the art of recent centuries. With all its crimes, ignorances, oppressions, with all its still unsubdued savagery, the mediæval period

165

was, after all, an age of gradual emancipation, a period during which the shackles of slavery and serfdom were falling away, and workmen were learning to respect themselves and to combine. Wherever and whenever society was sufficiently settled, combine they did; and wherever their trade involved the making of permanent things, we find them to be craftsmen, artists in their degree—and not less artistic than the overlords, but more. Certainly the common folk of the Middle Ages loved the art which was created around them, and shared in its beauty. We know this best of that period which to most artists *is* the Middle Ages, the second half, when the worst disturbances were over, and society had a chance of expressing itself. Romanesque architecture (and therefore, of course, Gothic, its derivative), as Choisy and Enlart have shown, was due to the abolition of slavery—briefly, because, in the absence of slave labour, smaller stones had to be used.[1] In the eleventh and twelfth centuries the communes arose, city after city became free, the craft-guilds were formed. Gothic art sprang from Romanesque, and contemporaneously there arose the first assertions of nationality and the recognition of public liberty. Gothic is the result of the democratic movement in the twelfth century, and in Gothic, as Ruskin has shown in that great chapter, " The Nature of Gothic," [2] men had pleasure in their work, and therefore did not look to wealth as the only means of pleasure.

The never-ceasing action, the undying strain of thrust and counter-thrust which lies hidden under the quiet grey

---

[1] Auguste Choisy, *Histoire de l'Architecture*, ii, 142–5. *Cf.* Camille Enlart, in *Histoire de l'Art*, i, 443 (A. Michel, 1905).

[2] *Stones of Venice*, 1886, ii, 151–231, especially p. 163. I venture to think that the time has come for us to repudiate that depreciation of the art-writings of Ruskin, which was brought about by the next generation of writers, men who seldom reached his level of intelligence and discernment.

stones of those soaring cathedrals, was indeed itself the assertion of freedom, as it was of the strength of those masons who so unconcernedly handled the dangerous powers they were unloosing. There were no ' architects ' in those days, only guilds of masons, with a master-mason, who had worked his way up, to direct the building, at which he had started, perhaps, as a poor apprentice. No incitement to pedantry there ! And the enormous output of the thirteenth century rested on a great popular enthusiasm. Gothic was not the work of the monks, as Northern Romanesque had often been: it was the work of the people, of the peasants and the burghers, of the guilds; and the sculpture, the wrought metal, the glorious carved screens which astonish us to-day in our remote country places, were the work of the village mason, the village carpenter, the village blacksmith.

In the eleventh and twelfth centuries there was already a passion for building and for all the arts that go with architecture—leading incidentally in the twelfth to the invention of a new art of painting, the wonderful art of painting glass windows. Men did not build from necessity—there were on the whole plenty of churches already: they built because they had a passion for building and for the daughter arts; and that passion was certainly not the sentiment of any one rich or cultured class. In the thirteenth century nearly every important town was again at work upon a gigantic cathedral—and in the fourteenth or fifteenth—though hardly a city of Europe then had a population of more than twenty thousand souls. And, with the building, there went on rapturously every form of painting, sculpture, metal-work, and of all the crafts, now raised to the highest point of delicacy and loveliness. This was not monastic, it was not merely clerical; it was civic, it was the self-expression of simple burghers and peasants and artisans; and the pulse of the people beat so truly that the expression varied in each nation, nay, in each province of countries like France and Italy.

By contrast I have used the word 'exploitation' of the modern period. We remember our own 'Great Pillage' in the reign of Edward VI, which was an act of vandalism against art, as well as the robbery of the poor by the rich, and the destruction of workmen's unions; we remember the enslavement of Italy; we remember what happened to Germany in the Thirty Years War; we remember the social conditions of France before the Revolution; and Mr and Mrs Hammond have reminded us lately, with an abundance of new illustration, of the bitter serfdom of the English artisan a hundred years ago. Still, fifty years ago there remained the resulting ignorance, and what Mr Tawney calls "an almost animal incapacity for responsibility." [1] We know, indeed, that in many other ways the world has progressed enormously during the modern period. We do not wish to be back in the Middle Ages; but I submit that, in the matter of art, civilisation has drifted from its moorings, and that those moorings are, as William Morris rightly taught, in labour—the freedom of the workman to realise himself, to express himself in his work and to rejoice in it. Many are annoyed at the labour unrest of to-day; but at the bottom of it is an impulse of the utmost promise —the desire of labour for its share of human recognition and human responsibility. If, in the last generation, as Mr Arnold Bennett says of the art museum at Copenhagen, people " were never guilty of inadvertence. Their instinct against beauty in any form was unerring," [2] we have to

[1] R. J. Tawney, *The Sickness of an Acquisitive Society*, p. 71 (1920).
[2] Arnold Bennett, *The Log of the Velsa*, pp. 129–30.

remember that beauty is part of the Divine Absolute, and that in this as in other things we cannot serve God and Mammon.

Of the great cathedrals Professor Lethaby says: " They are more than buildings. . . . The work of a man, a man may understand; but these are the work of ages, of nations. . . . Nothing is marked, nothing is clever, nothing is individual nor thrust forward as artistic; they are serene, masterly, non-personal, like works of nature—indeed, they are such, natural manifestations of the minds of men working under the impulse of a noble idea." Their use "had been perfected by the daily practice of a thousand years, and was linked to a music that belonged to it as the blast of trumpets belongs to war. All were parts of a marvellous drama, the ceremonial life of a people." [1]

Of the towns themselves one need hardly speak. A few have in part survived the Vandals of our modern era, to show us in what magic streets the feet of our forefathers used to walk—Bruges, Domfront, Estavayer, Rothenburg, some towns in the Riviera, in Spain, Italy, the Balkans. Their beauty is confounding. Modern designers, in our good, new zeal for town-planning, are trying to catch some portion of their spirit—some have even tried to discover a hidden scientific formula in those turns and curves, those sudden breaks, and happy groupings of perfect gables, walls, turrets, spires, bridges, which are but the expression of an unerring instinct for that which is fit and beautiful.

Such towns as these had each its craft-guilds; and these guilds were the universities of art. When the workman sent in his 'masterpiece' for examination, he became, if it was passed, literally a master of his art. There were graduates in art, as well as in ' arts,' under that system;

[1] W. R. Lethaby, *Mediæval Art*, pp. 142–4 (1912).

and everyone recognised the master's worth, the honour of his rough hands. To-day, art is a frill upon the edges of life; it was then the stuff of life itself. It was then no factitious adjunct to work, but the very manner of work, and the impulse.

We have seen our civic beauty fallen to ruins. In the fourteenth century men sought for municipal office to promote the utmost development of communal life, to increase the municipal magnificence. To-day, the best of those who stand for election seek rather for the removal of municipal degradation: they no longer take office in the local council " because they are proud of their city, but because they are ashamed of it."

We cannot copy the Middle Ages—neither their guilds nor their cities, nor their Church, nor their art; but by ceasing to copy and by making art the friend of the poor and not the mere lacquey of the rich, we can recover the old spirit, which is the eternal spirit of humanity, and therefore will most surely arise again

> feeling out of sight
> For the ends of Being and ideal Grace.

VI

The spirit of ancient Greek art was flowing through Europe during the Middle Ages; but it had already changed and become Hellenistic, and it was changed again into a deeper wisdom and a new power by the spirit of Christendom. Across the history of art during the first half of the mediæval period lay the shadow of the barbarian invaders. Other savage incursions had destroyed what they overthrew; but the power which had now come into the world was deathless: Christian civilisation turned and subdued the conquerors, transmuting their strength into sweetness. Of all this, the mediæval art of Europe was the expression; to this it owed its infinite variety and its ultimate mastery of every human craft, including that of melody in music, and above all its spiritual depth. The subject of music would need another lecture, like that of poetry; but we will not forget that the unrivalled acoustic properties of the great mediæval churches were not thrown away: music of singular beauty existed all the time, and developed, though more slowly. Music is the most spiritual of the arts; and it is spirituality that gives to the whole realm of European mediæval art, overwhelmingly vaster in mere production than any other, its supreme mark of greatness. For mediæval art compares with all other as the art of more spiritual beings, of men who believe that they are but little lower than the angels, of men who are always striving after something which is beyond them in the eternal reality of the spirit. It is tremulous with aspiration, humble even in its majesty. The art of ancient Greece is, after all, only young with the physical perfection of youth, its satisfaction with what life can give. In another sense it is old with the finality of age. The statues of the great period of Greek sculpture express the beauty of the human form and of glorious drapery: their faces are often the faces of very noble animals. Let it be admitted—for we have been a little uncritical about classical art, our Bible, our Old Testament—they sometimes wholly lack expression. But the statues and paintings of the Middle Ages give us human beings with souls—men like ourselves, heavy with thought, bright with hope, tender with love, perturbed by some intensity of vision. A soul has crept into the marble. And when Michelangelo seems to be reviving the old classical tradition, he remains a child of the Middle Ages: the soul cannot be banished—in the words of his famous sonnet—

> Non ha l'ottimo artista alcun concetto
> Ch'un marmo solo in sè non circonscriva
> Col suo soverchio, e sola a quello arriva
> La man che obbedisce all'intelletto.

His paintings and his statues are eloquent beyond the capacities of speech; they seem to groan and travail with strivings that cannot be uttered—even by his supreme genius.

So the art of the Middle Ages is really the art of youth. It has no finality, because that which it expresses cannot ever be finished. It lives with unmeasured potentialities still before it. Until the Renaissance, and men's subsequent concentration upon commerce and science, it seldom rested in the West, but grew from one stage to another—as in our still living arts—of painting, and music, poetry, and the drama—we still move and change and grow.

The Middle Ages were the age of youth. I do not mean merely of young nations, but of men who were building up the future and had unlimited development before them. It was *our* youth, and we are growing from it. In so far as our art lives—the art of our *intelligentsia*—it is growing from that stem. In so far as it is dead, it is in those forms of art which have ignored their own parentage, such as architecture, ornament, the crafts, and much sculpture, and have tried to form themselves from ancient models in the pedantry of the schools. They are cut off from the stem, and they languish. But painting, like music and poetry, has gone on without a break and is alive to-day.

172

TO MODERN CIVILISATION

Over four centuries have passed since the real severance began; but the mediæval tradition still lived in England three centuries ago, still lived unfashionably among the people two centuries ago, has lingered last of all in folksong. It is not a very long period; and men have risen to vast achievements in other spheres, though they have been more concerned during it with truth, and some forms of goodness, than with beauty. But the severance has never been complete: the sap has never ceased to flow: there is no break between the mosaics of Ravenna and the warpictures of Mr Rothenstein. Let us take heart. We are the heirs of those old craftsmen. They have left us the next stage of their work to do, and they have shown us how to do it. The nineteenth century made the world ugly and debased. We can still make it beautiful again.

PERCY DEARMER

VI

THE MIDDLE AGES IN THE LINEAGE
OF ENGLISH POETRY

I

MY theme is English literature of the Middle Ages, and some few salient features in its relation to the more modern periods. There is a growing tendency at present to disparage the literature of the Middle Ages. Indeed, the farther off these Middle Ages happen to be, the more severe is the disparagement. To my mind, the perspective of English literature is often altogether distorted, because the relationship of Early English to later literature, and the component elements of the literature of the Middle Ages, are not clearly understood. One of the main causes of this attitude of some critics and historians is due to the fact that the literature of England goes back to a far-off age, long before the Norman Conquest, and that in consequence its language is so archaic that it cannot be readily understood without careful study.

Chaucer's spelling may be bad enough, yet he can be read without much difficulty; but in the case of Chaucer's predecessors by some five or six hundred years it is not merely a matter of spelling—the language itself seems utterly different, with its strange vocabulary, syntax, and

[1] *Cp*. Sir A. Quiller-Couch, "The Lineage of English Literature" and other chapters, in *Studies in Literature*. First and Second Series. Cambridge University Press.

grammar. I fear that one has often to fight against what is tantamount to a plea for ignorance. Because the ancient literature of England can be traced so far back, and because its language is so archaic as to necessitate serious study, it is dismissed as unworthy of consideration. The main object of my observations will be to dispel, if possible, some of these errors in respect of the place of older English literature, and of poetry in particular, in the lineage of our literature from the period of Chaucer to more modern times.

The term 'Middle Ages' is vague indeed. Writers in the eighteenth century would comprehensively describe previous ages, including even some part of the Elizabethan age, by the convenient epithet 'Gothic'—by which term was meant what was opposed to classical, what was rugged, what was well-nigh barbarous. The thirteenth and four-teenth centuries are generally called up to mind when one speaks of the Middle Ages with reference to English literature; but there were the earlier Middle Ages, the so-called Dark Ages, centuries before the Norman Con-quest, a period of no little interest for students of English literature. It is this Old English period which is more particularly singled out for the disparagement to which I have referred. Yet the extant remains of this literature from the seventh to the eleventh century are striking mani-festations of the genius of Old England in its strength and its simplicity, before the later alien elements had become infused. We are able to judge therefrom the spirit of that old English folk to whom are due not only the basic elements of English speech, but also the foundations of English institutional life, and much that is most characteristic in English ideals.

What do we discover from a rapid survey of this literature

of the early Middle Ages ?   We are not confronted with
the rude beginnings, the rough scaffolding, on which a
noble structure was to be built up.   We see rather a
finished effort of a special type, the culmination of a long
previous period of development, on special lines and with
marked characteristics.   In the productions of the Anglian
poets of the eighth century we have a poetry remarkable
for a certain stateliness, from which is absent what is uncouth
or rudimentary.   It is marked, too, by a high seriousness,
as though the poets felt that the purpose of their art
was to edify and to instruct.   Indeed, this hall-mark
of earnestness often testifies to something deeper in spirit
than can find expression in form.   In the heroic poetry
of this age the minstrel held up a mirror of heroic life,
showing how a young warrior should behave, how he should
comport himself, how he should regard life as of no value
when honour was at stake.   The burden of *Beowulf* is
that " death is better than a life of reproach."   It is not
only in the Christian poetry of the Anglo-Saxons that we
find the fine note of seriousness.   True, *Beowulf*, when
compared with the *Odyssey*, may easily invite disparagement, but it is surely a strange attitude for those who deal
with the history of English literature to argue that because
the Teutonic heroic poem is altogether inferior to the
Greek epic, it is therefore of no value whatsoever in the
pedigree of English poetry.   Æsthetic consideration is
one thing; the right appraising of a document in genealogy
is apart from æsthetic consideration.   At all events, the
business of the critic is to attempt to understand why and
in what respects the Teutonic genius differs from the
more glorious genius of Greece.   If the search is for
enchantment, one must look elsewhere than among the
remains of English poetry of pre-Conquest times.   In tone

176

and spirit this poetry is severely epic. It calls for no apology, but it demands study. From the seventh to the early part of the ninth century, until under King Alfred the centre of literary activity passed from Anglia to Wessex, Anglian poets produced work well worthy of the recognition that should be given to some notable achievement preserved miraculously from ancient days to our own time.

II

Anglo-Saxon civilisation was not suddenly put an end to by the Norman Conquest, though by that time it had come to its full development, and was passing into its decline. It is true that toward the end of that period the English muse had become anæmic and weak; she needed new strength, new forces of vitality.

Let us turn to the fourteenth century. During the second half of the century the arresting figure of Chaucer claims our first attention. Born in London, associated from his youth with the brilliant court of Edward III and the higher social life of his time, Chaucer was the disciple of the gracious poets of France. Finding nothing to quicken his poetic sense in contemporary or earlier English poetry, he turned to France and set himself the congenial task of bringing into native English the measures, the inspiration, the charm and delicacy of the French poets, with their joyance, picturesqueness, and delight in dreams of beauty. The magic of the *Romaunt of the Rose*, and of the school of poets under the spell of that Poets' Bible of the Middle Ages, must have won his heart in his boyhood. When he had tarried long enough in this Temple of Glass, he turned elsewhere, and dwelt with the greater intellectual forces of Italy. Dante, Petrarch, and Boccaccio, through

Chaucer, became part of English literary tradition. Having learnt what he could from these mighty patriarchs of Humanism, Chaucer discovered the full strength of his own genius as the inimitable story-teller in verse. His pre-eminence as poet was acclaimed in his own time, and through the centuries to our own day he has stood forth with undiminished fame.

From the historical point of view, as Tennyson well put it, Chaucer " preluded . . . the spacious days of great Elizabeth." He is the forward link in the lineage of English literature. In the first place, he was the poet of London, the centre of the social life of his time—the poet of the East Midland district of England. His greatness obscured the position of those of his contemporaries who belonged to more provincial parts of England, and who could not escape the oblivion that overtakes mere local fame. The place of these poets in the perspective of English literature it is my purpose to emphasise.

Along the Welsh Marches, up to Lancashire and Westmorland, as in many other districts of England, there lived those who held strongly to the older traditions of the English race. There were families in these regions who treasured their memories from ancient times, and who prided themselves on having lived in these parts long before the coming of William the Conqueror. Among these the English element predominated, even as the Norman among those of higher social life in London and the great social centres near. While Chaucer was singing his delightful ballades, charming the ears of courtiers and ladies by his French love-songs in English verse, there was a voice to be heard other than that of " the new gladness of a great people, which utters itself in the verse of Geoffrey Chaucer." It was a sterner voice, that disdained the gauds of rhyme and the harmonies of the French school of poetry. For let us think of the real conditions of the time. At the court there was the pomp, extravagance, and display of chivalry, the luxury and splendour of a revived Camelot. The glamour was truly great. But between Crécy and Poitiers there was dire national tribulation. There were grave economic and social problems, due partly to the Black Death, which in 1349 carried off large parts of the population, and also to the continuous wars with France. The splendours of the Order of the Garter proved no antidote to these ills. The condition of the country was bad; there was corruption in Church and State. Then it was that a stern voice arose in the West Midlands, the voice of Langland, like that of some Hebrew prophet-poet of old, telling the people, in language that went readily home, in the rhymeless alliterative metre of the old days before the Conquest, the stern truth that their sufferings were due to national shortcomings, and that a guide should be found to lead them to the shrine of Truth. Perchance from among the lowly, the humble tillers of the soil, such a true leader might be found. This was the purpose of *The Vision of Piers Plowman*. By the intensity of its lesson, the Vision seems to have spread far and wide throughout the land; Langland appears to be the only poet of the West Midland school who gained recognition as a national, and not merely local, poet. The school of West Midland alliterative poets, of whom there were many, though hardly a name other than Langland's has come down to us, holds a distinctive place in the lineage of English literature. These poets, in respect of metre, manner, and spirit, for the most part harked back to the time before the Conquest. I do not mean to say for a moment that they were acquainted with the writings of Cædmon or Cynewulf, or any pre-Conquest literature ; yet they were something more than the spiritual heirs of the older English poets. In some way or other—the problem is a difficult one—the Old English alliterative metre lived on during the centuries that followed the Norman Conquest, and suddenly, about the middle of the fourteenth century, to judge from extant poetry, there was a great revival of this archaic form of poetry. Even where these poets chose their matter from France or from Latin sources, the spirit of the handling is characteristic and altogether differentiated from the Chaucerian method. All the West Midland poets may not have the technical skill and finish attained by the poet of *Cleanness* and *Patience,* but where the treatment shows a weaker hand, the purpose is none the less marked, namely, that the lesson is the first consideration, transcending all effort in search of the artistic and æsthetic. In common with Langland, the whole school of West Midland poets represents the backward link in the genealogy of English poetry, that is, they link the age of Chaucer, in spirit as well as in form, to the far-off days before the Conquest.

Nor was the alliterative revival, as we shall see, a mere barren antiquarian freak. The voice of William Langland was not a passing voice; it re-echoed down the ages. *The Vision of Piers Plowman* cannot with any appreciation of the facts be regarded as " the last dying spasm " of Anglo-Saxon literature, as Sir A. Quiller-Couch, University Professor of English Literature at Cambridge, futilely, in my opinion, attempts to demonstrate, in his zeal to maintain the worthlessness of Middle English poetry, save that of Chaucer, in the lineage of English literature. " I shall attempt to convince you," he states, " that Chaucer did not inherit any secret from Cædmon or Cynewulf." As though, forsooth, it were necessary, at this time of day, to prove what no sane person would for a moment contest! The fundamental error in all these discussions seems to be a failure to understand that there were these two schools of poetry, the Chaucerian and the West Midland, representing two great voices in the harmonies of English poetry, the one with its quest for beauty and melody, and the other, by utterance more homely and direct, seeking primarily to enforce the lesson. In their attitude toward Nature the two schools may well be contrasted, the Chaucerian with its conventional bright May mornings and landscapes of joyance, the West Midland poets with their interpretation of Nature in her more rugged moods, with their fondness for storms and tempests and lowering clouds. Even in Chaucer's own time one poet at least sought to harmonise the two voices. The poet of *Pearl* was a West Midland poet who sought to blend the spirit of exalted religious aspiration with the beauty, harmony, and picturesqueness of the Romance poets. With one hand, as it were, toward Langland, and one toward Chaucer, he, in a sense, more truly than Chaucer, is the herald of the Elizabethan poets; certainly so, if Spenser is to be regarded as the Elizabethan poet *par excellence.* As the author of *Gawain and the Green Knight,* this West Midland poet is the prophet of *The Faerie Queene,* and stands on the very threshold of modern English poetry, in the fullest sense of the term. If Chaucer was "the father of English poetry," and the old title may well remain, let us at all events understand the place of his contemporaries in the pedigree of his descendants.

III

Let us come to the Elizabethan Age. The Elizabethan Age may roughly be described as the meeting-point of the Ages of the world. We pass from the Middle Ages to what we call the modern time. True, the Middle Ages were not far off, and their glamour was still a potent source of inspiration. Antiquity had been rediscovered—the great literatures of Judæa, Greece, and Rome. The Revival of Learning was not only the revived interest in classical antiquity; the Bible became an open book, and the Reformation in England, as elsewhere, was one manifestation of this aspect of the Renaissance. It is of Edmund Spenser that one thinks as the poet of the Elizabethan Age in spirit, in form, and in apparel ; and the secret of Spenser's poetry, I am inclined to hold, may perhaps best be understood with reference to the theory I am propounding. In text-books on Spenser critics glibly enumerate the poet's limitations, as well as the marks of his greatness, instead of endeavouring to understand some of their difficulties in dealing with a poet who is perhaps the truest representative of the greatest age of English poetry. There can be little doubt that his latent poetic genius was stirred into life by turning over the pages of a black-letter folio of Chaucer, and that instinctively the London schoolboy, for Spenser was a poet while still at school, fell under the spell of the older poet, and learned from him something of the true beauty of form and harmony. And yet, great as was the disciple's debt to his master, would it be possible to find two geniuses more utterly different in spirit and character than the poet of *Troilus and Criseyde* and the poet of *The Faerie Queene*, of whom Milton said he was " a greater teacher than Aquinas "? One thinks of the smile that would have played across the features of Chaucer, had some one hinted to him that he was primarily a great teacher, or had any qualifications or aspirations for that office. But with Spenser it was otherwise; and the secret of Spenser is this, that whereas as regards beauty of form and the technical art of poetry he was truly the disciple of Chaucer, in spirit he belonged rather to the West Midland poets, the school of Langland. This explains why it is that, although he gives us creations steeped in beauty, sparkling with light, dream pictures, armour of richest damascene, his object is to protect and save and exalt the human soul. You may well say that Spenser, as Chaucer, was a Londoner. What had he in common with the old poets of the West Midlands, with the spirit of Langland, even though he may have read a black-letter edition of *The Vision of Piers Plowman*? My answer might be that the spirit of a work is a thing apart from its immediate environment. But one need not dismiss the question so lightly. It is a fact that the family to which Spenser and all his forbears belonged lived in Lancashire; and this is significant as regards those marked elements in the spirit of his poetry which link him with the West Midland school. In this Elizabethan poet *par excellence* there lived on, spiritually, much that differentiates him from Chaucer and the Chaucerians, even as an analysis of his archaic English reveals a most significant attempt to blend words due to his reading of Chaucer with native mother-words belonging to the family Lancashire home. To illustrate some of these dialect words, one must turn to the alliterative poems written by Chaucer's contemporaries of the West. *Gawain and the Green Knight*, as I have already suggested, might well have stood as a canto of *The Faerie Queene,* and indeed the Gawain legend has its analogues there. In beauty, in technical skill, and in picturesqueness that fourteenth-century poet is the counterpart of Spenser, though the poet of the Renaissance had richer stores of knowledge to draw on. Yet, steeped as Spenser was in all the New Learning, in the glory of the philosophy of Plato and Aristotle, and in the inspiration of Neoplatonism, it is remarkable that his close kinship with the fourteenth-century poet of the alliterative revival is so unmistakable. Spenser, indeed, blended successfully, even as the poet of *Pearl* attempted to blend, the two main voices in the great harmony of English song. It is not without significance that he himself, when first he came before the world as the new poet, with due humility indicated his literary progenitors :

> Dare not to match thy pype with Tityrus hys style,
>   Nor with the Pilgrim that the Ploughman playde awhyle ;
> But followe them farre off, and their high steppes adore :
> The better please, the worse despise ; I aske nomore.

And what of Shakespeare and the Elizabethan drama and their debt to the Middle Ages ? The Elizabethan drama perhaps owed its greatest debt to the Middle Ages in being rescued, through the freedom and ease that characterised the earlier drama, from slavish adherence to the conventional classical forms of tragedy and comedy, from the tyranny of Seneca and Plautus and Terence, from the unities of time and place and action. In respect of matter, it might be an easy thing to point to the mediæval sources of Shakespeare and the Elizabethan drama. The matter of Britain and France, mediæval romances and tales, chronicles, ballads, and folklore all contributed materials on which the dramatists worked. As regards the chief instrument of expression, blank verse, which was originally a purely academic importation from Italy, it became the plastic instrument able to bear the impress of varied human emotions, only when it had become, as it were, thoroughly Teutonised. Shakespeare, and to some extent Marlowe before him, unconsciously rediscovered that freedom which characterised the Old English metre, and imposed it on this alien blank verse. Of course, in reality it was the English spirit resisting slavery to an academic convention, and naturalising an alien metre. Yet whatever one may adduce tending to link Shakespeare's work to the Middle Ages, and although he may wear the apparelling of his own age, his powers transcend altogether the stuff on which his genius worked. And so it is that I have chosen Spenser, rather than Shakespeare, to illustrate the underlying purpose of my discourse. Much as I would wish to dwell on the varied forms of poetry, the sonnet, the lyrical measures, complaints, and other forms of Elizabethan poetry derived from earlier ages, as these do not help forward my main contention, I pass them by with this brief reference.

Taken comprehensively, as Taine well put it, the Renaissance in England was the renaissance of the Saxon genius. From this point of view it is significant that Shakespeare's greatest achievement, *Hamlet*, is the presentment of a typically northern hero, the embodiment of the northern character:

> Dark and true and tender is the North

IV

In the period known as the Romantic Revival, antiquarianism holds almost as great a place as the 'return to nature.' The instinctive protest against 'good sense' led to the groping for far-off things and for the truer understanding of nature apart from convention. The various elements of mediævalism that were contributory sources of inspiration to the poets of the period of the Romantic Revival have been ably dealt with by more than one historian of English literature. Percy's *Reliques*, and Macpherson's *Ossian*, the Runic poetry that inspired Gray, Chatterton's infatuation, all represent phases in the effort to recapture the matter, spirit, and form of far-off days. Very often that return to the past meant a return to the Elizabethans, and to Spenser in particular, and through Spenser men unwittingly got much of the spirit of the Middle Ages. Then came Coleridge and Wordsworth, and their efforts to regain something that had been lost to English poetry. *The Ancient Mariner* and *Christabel* are the manifestations of the effort of the new poetry in its adventures in the eerie realms of mediæval lore. But for my purpose, as enforcing my theme, I would for the moment rather dwell on Wordsworth's poetry, in which there is so little of direct inspiration from mediævalism. There is no wild Gothic terror and wonderment that one can point to as linking him with mediæval machinery. Yet in his very canons of poetic diction, his early contemning of artifice, his exaltation of spirit, aiming seriously at the truth of things, his placing of the lesson over and above the form, his treatment of Nature especially in her sterner moods, his attitude as prophet-poet dealing with the realities of his time, the very limitations noted in him as poet, help to remind one that we are not here dealing with a poet of London, but one bred among the solitary cliffs, among the

> Presences of Nature in the sky
> And on the earth,

among the " visions of the hills, and souls of lonely places."
It is of no small interest that the chief of the Lake Poets
is a West Midland poet, and belongs to about the same
district as that assigned to the poet of *Pearl* and of *Gawain
and the Green Knight*.

Mediæval beauty revealed itself truly through Keats,
who through Spenser passed on to Chaucer, and touched
with his own genius mediævalism, even as he transformed
the myths of Hellas. Keats entered into the land of faery,
his poetic soul untouched by mere antiquarianism, and for
sheer inimitable mediæval glamour nothing can exceed
his transmuting touch:

> I met a lady in the meads
>   Full beautiful, a faery's child ;
> Her hair was long, her foot was light,
>   And her eyes were wild.
>
> I set her on my pacing steed,
>   And nothing else saw all day long ;
> For sideways would she lean, and sing
>   A faery's song.

"The Wizard of the North," on whom the spell of mediævalism worked so mightily, restored with marvellous
precision the panorama of mediæval life. It is not here a
matter of the poet's own spiritual outlook. Yet one may
recapture much of the matter of mediævalism without
being affected by its spirit.

The theme of King Arthur is perhaps of all others the
most abiding and inspiring in English literature; but the
artistic beauty, delicacy, and charm of Tennyson's *Idylls*
are a long way off from any antiquarian revival. He
feels himself inheritor of the great mediæval theme,
and applies thereto his own ideals and workmanship.
Through Keats, back through the ages to Chaucer,

187

Tennyson links himself to those poets who gave the first place in the art of poetry to the quest for the beautiful in harmony, diction, and picturesqueness—a contrast to his contemporary Browning, whose alleged obscurity and neglect of *finesse* remind one of the other type of the poetic mind, caring more for the message than the form.

V

The Pre-Raphaelite movement manifested itself in literature as well as in art. Rossetti, if not Holman Hunt, belongs to, and was not merely associated with, English literature. But one of the brotherhood, William Morris, represents better than anyone of the age that has passed some of the main aspects of the subject here dealt with. In memorable lines addressed to Chaucer he hailed that poet as " the idle singer of an empty day," a refrain which later on he applied to himself. He, the poet of " art for art's sake," found his own heart near to Chaucer, " great of heart and tongue "; and in his first published book, *The Defence of Guenevere*, we find him stretching out his arms to capture the fancies of mediæval romance and repicturing them with new artistic charms. The spirit of Chaucer is on him in this volume, which was the earnest of even greater achievement. That spell still held him as the poet of *The Life and Death of Jason* and *The Earthly Paradise*. Then came upon him the deeper spirit that set him pondering on social problems, and " the idle singer of an empty day " became the protagonist of the cause of social reform and the dignity of work. Another spell possessed him, linking him to the spirit of Langland, or, at all events, of Langland's contemporary, John Ball, with his famous text:

TO MODERN CIVILISATION

> When Adam dalf, and Eve span,
> Who was thanne a gentilman ?

He brought into English literature the riches, not only of mediæval Romantic literature, but also of the Sagas and Eddas of old Scandinavia. As artist he had kinship with Chaucer; but there co-existed in his being that other spirit of the literature of Chaucer's time represented by his great contemporary, the author of *The Vision of Piers Plowman*. Translator of the *Odyssey* and the *Æneid*, he yet did not disdain to touch with his genius even the Old English heroic poem of *Beowulf*. The significance of William Morris in the lineage of English poetry will perhaps in the days to come be adequately understood.

As for the future, whatever may be the fortunes of English poetry, whatever experiments may be made by new schools of poets, whatever new ideas may be brought into English literature, inspiration will still come from the bygone ages, however the matter be treated. That inspiration will be heard in varied voices and in many strains. The quest for the beautiful will find expression in richest harmonies, and the teaching of the lesson will still be enforced by prophet-poets. As in the past, so in the future there will be many mansions in the great house of English Poetry, and one at least there will always be, richly storied from the realms of Mediæval Romance, with

> Magic casements, opening on the foam
> Of perilous seas, in faery lands forlorn.

ISRAEL GOLLANCZ

189

VII

EDUCATION

THE previous lectures of this course have told of the mediæval contribution to religion, philosophy, science, art, literature; lectures yet to be given will discuss mediæval society, politics, and economics. There is not one of these things which does not educate; and if those lectures satisfy you that the Middle Ages made substantial additions to human culture, then the case for mediæval education is already argued and proved. But there is a use of the word 'education' which confines its range to schools and to similar institutions; presumably the word was so interpreted by those who arranged the present series. Although I deprecate as strongly as possible this limitation of the term, I will try to keep within it.

Our subject is the mediæval contribution to education so understood; and I propose to use the word 'contribution' so as to include negative as well as positive factors. Any historical period may be regarded as a field upon which men experimented in the art of living; when men of a later age come to survey such a period from their own vantage-ground they will detect failure as well as success, weak points and strong points in their predecessors' experimenting. So regarded, our subject is of much more than antiquarian interest. The ultra-modern man who thinks of the Middle Ages as 'reactionary,' obsolete, or sunk without leaving a trace will discover in mediæval shortcomings matter suggestive of reform in the practice of to-day. He will have the added satisfaction of saying that he had "told you so." The record of defect is a negative contribution, but a contribution nevertheless. We ourselves are past doubt making similar contributions to the future.

But the historically informed man, knowing that his own age is the residuary legatee of the ages which have preceded, will attend rather to the mediæval successes, the positive contributions of the past, and these he will discover to be neither few nor unimportant, but fraught with instruction for the present time.

How has it come about that for centuries past all formal schooling in Western Europe has had a literary foundation, and a superstructure which, in the main, has also been literary—a business of papers, pens, and ink ? The answer goes back beyond the early limit of our period, to the pre-Christian time when the rhetorical education prevailed throughout the Roman Empire. Grammar— that is, the study of the languages and literatures of Rome and of Greece—was the staple of the instruction then given, its higher stages constituting a training in rhetoric whose chief merit was thought to be in style, whether of the written or the spoken word. The two literatures make a mirror of human life, of its highest ideals and of its lowest, poorest performances no less, as Greeks and Latins conceived or observed them. When Christianity reached the classes whose education had been of this kind, and the question arose, How should the converts' children be educated ? these adherents of the new faith were in a quandary. The only general public form of schooling available was that which they themselves had received in the State and municipal schools of the Empire. But the instruction there given was based upon, and largely consisted of, the study of literatures which were uncompromisingly pagan, and sometimes flagrantly opposed to Christian morals. " Hearts devoted to Christ find no room for the Muses, nor lie open to Apollo."

Tertullian (A.D. 150–230) reflects this quandary in an age when a Christian literature was only in process of consolidation, and therefore not yet available for school use. He held that it was impossible for a Christian to be a schoolmaster or to teach letters, since the exercise of that profession implied belief in a pagan theology and the daily practice of pagan rites and customs. But the pupil was in a different case. As a learner already fortified by knowledge of the Christian faith, " he neither receives nor becomes a party to " the paganism which necessarily forms so large a part of Greek and Latin letters. This is, of course, an entirely inconsistent attitude for Tertullian to take up. But note his reason for adopting it. " We know it may be said that, if it is not permissible to the servants of God to teach letters, neither will it be permissible to learn them. How, then, may anyone be trained to human intelligence or to any understanding or business, since literature is the record of all life ? *How can we repudiate secular studies, without which divine studies are not possible ?* Let us, therefore, appreciate the necessity of literary learning in its incompatibility on the one hand and its inevitableness on the other."

There was much life in Tertullian's paradox, since the necessity of studying Latin, if not Latin and Greek, became more evident as time advanced. On the break-up of the Roman Empire in the fifth century, Latin, and such knowledge of Greek as survived in the West in the original or in Latin translation, constituted the sole depositories of knowledge of all kinds, whether desired for the sake of a profession or for purposes of culture. St Augustine of Hippo toward the close of the fourth century declared that a knowledge of the Liberal Arts was necessary if the Scriptures were to be understood. Some two centuries or more later Virgilius the Grammarian gave the same reason for studying ' grammar.' Both were repeating Tertullian's dictum respecting " secular studies, without which divine studies are not possible." Since ' divine studies,' or divinity, meant the study of the Scriptures and the writings of the Christian Fathers, grammar, the systematic study of the languages in which these were written, was the indispensable gate of approach.

Thus, however unwillingly, the Christian Church for Christian purposes kept alive so much of the ancient pre-Christian civilisation as is revealed in Latin and, to a much less degree in the West, in Greek literature. The Church's recognised form of secular instruction was simply the rhetorical education of Imperial Rome as described by Quintilian. The politic ' conversions ' which took place after the reign of Constantine must have included many whose conversion was merely acquiescence, and amongst these would be found adherents to the old religion and culture. Of course, men, whether Christian or not, were not all insensible to the intrinsic attraction, beauty, and moral value of Latin and Greek letters ; there were Christians not a few of whom St Jerome was typical. The Saint was himself a distinguished product of the older culture as it existed in the fourth century. While lying ill in Syria, he turned for solace to Plautus and Cicero in preference to the Psalter. He dreamed that he was dead, and on the threshold of the other world was met by the challenge, " Who art thou ? " To his answer, " A

Christian," he received the reply, " No, no Christian, but a Ciceronian; where the treasure is, there is the heart also."

The dates of some early extant manuscripts of Virgil are significant from this point of view. Those at St Gall and in the Vatican Library belong to the fourth century, while the Florentine manuscript, which once belonged to the monastery of Bobbio, was written in the fifth. Virgil remained a favourite author throughout the Middle Ages; the part which Dante makes him play in the *Commedia* will be recalled. Such names as those of Donatus, St Augustine, Boethius are symbolic of the close interplay between the Christian and pagan civilisations. It is possible, nay, comparatively easy, to draw up a list of names of men who possessed a knowledge of ancient literature, the names traversing the centuries through the so-called Dark Ages right down to the revival of classical learning and the beginning of the modern period. When account is taken of the discovery by fifteenth-century scholars of ancient manuscripts of the classics in monastic libraries, it is well to dilate upon the dust and neglect of their condition; but it is not well to ignore the significance of the fact that they were there to be discovered.

The Middle Ages, then, continued the rhetorical instruction which had constituted the formal schooling of Latins and Greeks. But the word ' rhetoric ' (which literally should mean no more than composition, particularly of speeches), when used comprehensively as meaning a mode of education, involved much more than this. Quintilian describes the orator as " the good man skilled in speaking," and he certainly attaches as much importance to the goodness as to the skill. Moreover, he has a prejudice in favour of the view, not universally entertained by rhetori-

194

cians, that the orator should be a well-informed man who really has something to communicate when he speaks. In consequence, the education of the orator, as Quintilian conceived him, included instruction in a great variety of matters as well as in the art of composition. At the beginning of our period, early in the fifth century, the curriculum had become organised into the Seven Liberal Arts, which are sometimes subdivided into the three ' arts ' of the Trivium, grammar, rhetoric, dialectic, and the four ' disciplines ' of the Quadrivium, geometry, arithmetic, astronomy, music. The all-round character of this course of study will be noted, although all the seven terms are not synonymous with the same words as used to-day. Dialectic, which at its best meant what we now call philosophy, at its worst meant formal logic, a dry and somewhat sterile form of which was in great favour in mediæval schools and universities. Grammar, as already said, was the study of both language and literature; the Middle Ages were over when the word acquired its present-day meaning. Arithmetic under Boethius, the master-mathematician of mediæval students, stood for the study of the properties of numbers, particularly of the doctrine of ratio and proportion. Astronomy tended to wander into astrology. Music was not so much the practical art as the mathematical and physical study of musical sound.

Grammar was the universal entrance to all these arts, and beyond them to the professional studies of the theologian, lawyer, and medical man, since the matter of their studies was to be found in the works of Latin authors and of Greek authors whose books were known to the West chiefly in Latin versions. Accordingly, grammar was *par excellence* the work of the school, though in the later Middle Ages ' trivial schools ' aspired to go beyond it.

195

MEDIÆVAL CONTRIBUTIONS

The conditions of mediæval teaching called for the preservation and diffusion of books when printing was unknown; that art, itself a great mediæval contribution to education, was not invented in Europe till near the close of our period, the mid-fifteenth century. What was done during the intervening centuries? The word 'manuscript' calls up visions of splendid colour and of delicate craftsmanship in many minds, to the exclusion of all thought of cheapness or of multiplicity of copies. Yet there were cheap and, no doubt, poor manuscripts in ancient Rome and in mediæval Italy. These, like the earliest books printed outside these islands, were school books, books of devotion and of learning, books of standing which were comparatively in general request.

But the production of manuscripts on a large scale involves a settled order of life not easily found in the centuries which witnessed the prostration of Rome. In the middle of the sixth century Cassiodorus, who had been an Italian civil servant of the highest rank, founded a monastery in Southern Italy, and made the transcription of manuscripts part of the business of his monks. While the prime purpose was the preservation and extension of 'divine letters,' secondary objects were the study of 'grammar' as preparatory to divinity, and the pursuit of the Seven Liberal Arts as auxiliary to both. In other words, this particular form of monastic labour tended to the preservation and propagation of ancient letters and learning. Other monasteries and other monastic societies followed the example thus set. With the rise of universities in the twelfth century and the multiplication of schools, the copying of manuscripts became a trade exercised independently of monasteries and of the devotion of the individual scholar. At the close of our period there were in England Greeks, whose names and places of work are on record, who were employed in transcribing Greek manuscripts.

The writing-room of the monastery implied its book-room or library. Alcuin, at that time *scolasticus*, or director, of the cathedral school of York, has left an account of its library as it was in the late eighth century. It contained copies of the Scriptures and the writings of divines of Latin, Greek, and Hebrew origin; the Greek and Hebrew were very probably in Latin translations. It also included the writings of Christian Latin poets, and works by Aristotle (again, in Latin), Pliny, Cicero, Virgil, Statius, Lucan, as well as treatises by the grammarians. There were famous libraries in the great monasteries of Bobbio, St Gall, and Luxeuil, foundations of Irish origin dating from the sixth and seventh centuries. Bobbio in particular owned great store of manuscripts. Shortage of writing material, a strong desire to write what chiefly interested contemporary monastic readers, and a weakened sense of the worth of classical works united to favour the reprehensible practice of erasing the original handwriting and using the vellum skins afresh. These palimpsests afford a striking illustration of a possible danger lurking behind a consuming desire to be 'up-to-date,' since the second writing very rarely compensated for the loss of the first. Dr M. R. James thinks that these erasures seldom, if ever, were perpetrated after the eleventh century; manuscripts now extant show that there was great activity in transcribing classical authors during the ninth century, and that manuscripts were produced in great numbers during the twelfth century.[1]

Toward the close of our period the library catalogue

[1] M. R. James, *The Wanderings and Homes of Manuscripts* (1919).

of Peterhouse shows entries under the names of Sallust, Quintilian, Seneca, Ovid, Statius, Lucan—a few authors of the first rank amongst a great welter of forgotten mediæval writers. In 1439, and again in 1443, Humphrey, Duke of Gloucester, presented to the University of Oxford books in manuscript which included works by Cicero, a Greek-Latin vocabulary, and Latin translations from Plato, Aristotle, and Æschines. But in Duke Humphrey we have an amateur of the revived classical learning, and are therefore moving beyond the Middle Ages, his date notwithstanding. Still, his library marks the time of transition, the greater portion consisting of mediæval treatises on the Seven Liberal Arts, on divinity, law, and medicine. The fourteenth and fifteenth centuries saw the beginning of such great collections of books as those of the Louvre, the Vatican, and the Laurentian Library at Florence.

In these various ways the Middle Ages transmitted a knowledge and a certain appreciation of the civilisation of Rome and Greece. Parenthetically it may be pointed out that these islands played no mean part in this transmission. An inherent weakness in rhetorical instruction, its excessive admiration for form as such, reduced continental writing in the sixth and seventh centuries to a trivial pedantry and the neglect of literature, faults which were intensified by the comparative ignorance of Greek. Ireland never formed part of the Roman Empire. By ways on which authorities are not agreed, Irish scholars, who were invariably Christian monks, kept touch with the East, retained some knowledge of the Greek language as well as of classical Latin literature, avoided the stupid pedantry of their continental contemporaries, and in due course taught these virtues to the English of Northumbria. Both Irish and English, but the former especially, com-

198

municated these benefits to Gaul, to Alemannia, and to the Frankish kingdoms.

So it came about that the literary, bookish type of education, established originally within the Latin civilisation, was maintained and made the system of the mediæval schools, the system which flourished down to our own day—if indeed it is appropriate to speak of it in the past tense. The Middle Ages, however, supplemented this literary culture in a way to be described presently.

The present-day curriculum is greatly indebted to that which was in operation under the Roman Empire; and we owe the transmission chiefly to mediæval solicitude for the study of divinity. The same interest also caused the Middle Ages to produce a system of institutions and of their administration from which the main lines of modern public instruction have been evolved.

When the Christian Church became an integral part of the Roman imperial polity, its bishops were usually drawn from socially prominent families, whose sons had received the customary rhetorical education. In such cases the bishop's seat formed a local centre of culture, clerical and lay. When Church and Empire fell upon evil days, this concentration of culture was intensified. Missionary work amongst barbarian populations and theological controversy with pagan fellow-citizens made great demands upon the teaching function of the Church. Education was particularly conceived as a training in divine letters, to which grammar and the Liberal Arts were necessary. The supreme educational authority and administrator within each diocese was the bishop, or his representative. From time to time councils of the Church laid the duty of education upon cathedral and collegiate churches and upon the greater monasteries. It was held that the instruction given in these capitular and monastic schools should be gratuitous. Teaching in grammar and divinity was necessary for those who were to become priests; the choristers must be able to read the Latin Psalter and service-book and to sing. Divinity developed into theology, and the latter involved obvious relations with philosophy which, under the influence of Aristotelian teaching, became scholasticism. At the base of this theological and philosophical learning lay 'grammar' and the Liberal Arts. Thus, a cathedral or a collegiate church or a monastery which was active in discharging the function of teaching contained in embryo both a grammar-school and a university. In favourable circumstances, such as those of Paris, Orleans, Chartres, those institutions were actually evolved from the ecclesiastical centre. The song schools, which taught music and the mere *reading* of Latin as the language of worship, had powers of development which sometimes carried them beyond their own modest function and into the sphere of the grammar-school.

At an early period the supervision of these ecclesiastical schools was delegated by the bishop, or abbot, to a member of the chapter (in most cases, the chancellor), who in respect of this duty was known as the *scolasticus, archiscolus,* or *archiscola.* He might, or might not, actively exercise the office of teacher; but in all cases he licensed all schoolmasters within the diocese, determined whether a school was needed in a particular district, and took measures intended to prevent overlapping and excessive competition. He claimed to supervise schools of lay origin, such as those founded by town councils and guilds, and schools attached to hospitals. His jurisdiction naturally extended to the numerous schools which were associated with chantries either by express foundation or by custom. In short, the Middle Ages gave to later times not only a substantial part of the curriculum, but also schools, universities, and the conception of public education locally administered by a director. Gratuitous instruction and the licensing of schoolmasters without exacting a fee were principles of that administration which were not observed at all times and in all places; nevertheless, when fees were charged they were always low. Board and lodging were, of course, paid for by pupils who were not ' on the foundation,' and therefore had no claim upon it beyond instruction.

The university is a peculiarly mediæval institution in point of origin. Athens, Alexandria, Rhodes, and other centres of the ancient civilisation possessed places of higher education which attracted young men from distant lands. But they had little in common with universities as we know them, on their administrative side especially. The division of teachers and of students into faculties, the ordered systems of curricula and of corresponding degrees, the government of the university society, are all forms of development which took shape in mediæval times. The very name ' university,' *i.e.*, *universitas* or guild, is a re-minder of the fact, since guilds were a characteristic feature of mediæval society. The technical name for a university was *studium generale*, within which the *universitas*, or guild, whether of teachers or of scholars, built up the university life.

The earliest universities, Bologna, Paris, Oxford, were never ' founded ' in any formal sense, and the date of their origin is uncertain; by the last quarter of the twelfth century all three were recognised *studia generalia*. Cambridge held that status in the opening years of the thirteenth century. But advanced teaching existed certainly at Bologna, Paris, and Oxford, possibly also at Cambridge, before those times. For example, Paris is associated with the scholastic philosophy and theology of Peter Abelard, teaching which, by attracting crowds of students, made inevitable the establishment of a *studium generale* and a teachers' guild. Yet Abelard died in 1142.

Colleges in universities are another mediæval invention. In their early period, the *studia generalia* confined themselves almost entirely to the business of teaching; board and lodging were matters personal to the teacher and student. But circumstances did not allow this easy attitude to be maintained for long. The great majority of the teachers and students were sojourners amidst a town population rarely friendly and frequently hostile. As a rule both teachers and students were poor; the former derived their living from their teaching and its appurtenances. Usually destitute of ecclesiastical benefice, they were, though ' clerks,' virtually professional lay teachers, not, as a class, especially loved by the ecclesiastical authorities. Some boarded and lodged students; the earliest university statutes (Paris, 1215) noted the relationship between ' clerks ' and those, not being members of the university, who let lodgings to students. In course of time hostels for poor students were established by charitable persons. The advent of the friars, Franciscan and Dominican, introduced the conventual house, with its common life in chapel, hall, and dormitory, its library and tutors. The object-lesson had an immediate effect. In the second half of the thirteenth century the first colleges were founded at Paris (the Sorbonne), Oxford (Merton), and Cambridge (Peterhouse).

As is well known, the twelfth century saw a great revival of learning which affected medical and mathematical science, philosophy, law, and letters. The French schools

202

seemed to be divided in their interest between letters, as at Chartres, and philosophy, as at Paris. But the great and popular instructors at Paris taught dialectic, logic, theology—in a word, scholasticism; and the practice of Paris determined that of most universities for the succeeding four or five centuries. Yet scholasticism at Paris and law at Bologna implied at least a minimum of grammar; the literary foundation remained everywhere. It is true that what we should to-day call 'scientific subjects' were included amongst the Liberal Arts, and natural philosophy was *read* as part of the course for the degree in arts. But the method of study preserved its bookish character. Science was learned from encyclopædias, works based on Greek originals known through Latin translations; these elementary manuals had in some cases been compiled for the purpose of preserving the *débris* of ancient learning, sometimes expressly to make it unnecessary to consult the original sources. In either case it was science founded not upon observation and experiment but upon authority, in harmony with the legal and theological methods of the day. This remained true in spite of the friars, Roger Bacon and Albertus Magnus, and other early students of science as now understood.

The art of printing is a contribution of the first rank made by the Middle Ages to those which followed. It furnishes some striking illustrations of the cardinal defect of education as then practised, namely, the unquestioning deference to authority, with a correspondingly slow, almost imperceptible advance in the content of studies. The three standard books on the Liberal Arts which were in use throughout the mediæval period were the work of Martianus Capella (fifth century), Cassiodorus (sixth century), and Isidore of Seville (seventh century)

respectively. They were in the nature of brief and rudimentary encyclopædias. Of the first, eight editions were
printed between 1499 and 1599; the second was printed
as late as 1580. Isidore's *Origins*, which was compiled
in order to make it unnecessary to consult pagan originals,
appeared in six or seven editions between 1472 and 1577.
The *De Arithmetica* of Boethius held its place as an authoritative text-book for a thousand years after its first appearance in 502; the printed editions issued after 1488 were
innumerable. The standard text-book of universal history
was a compilation from the Bible, Livy, Tacitus, and from
earlier compilers, made about the year 417 by Orosius.
As its title implied (*Seven Books of Histories against the
Pagans*), its purpose was to maintain that the Divine
Providence was manifested in the disasters which befel
the Empire in consequence of its paganism, a type of
controversy which was rife in the fifth century. Not
unnaturally the adherents of the old religion retorted by
blaming the Empire's conversion to Christianity. The
well-nigh universal elementary text-book of grammar in
the mediæval period was the work of a fourth-century
teacher, Ælius Donatus, *On the Eight Parts of Speech*;
it was one of the earliest books to be printed more than a
millennium later. Another favourite elementary grammar
book was the *Doctrinale* of Alexander de Villa Dei, produced
about the year 1200; there were two hundred and sixty
editions in whole or in part printed between 1470 and
1520.

It should be noted that all the works above named
survived beyond the close of the period 500–1500, and
that they were *text-books*, not great literary classics—that
is, they survived not in virtue of their purely literary merits
(which in truth were few), but as exponents of knowledge

as it existed at the times of their publication. Here we have the characteristic failing of mediæval education as it was practised in schools and universities, namely, an overweening respect for authority as set forth in the written word. The consequence was either comparative stagnation or sterilisation; these books made no progress beyond the stage at which something had been saved from the ruin of Roman civilisation. And this was in spite of the presence of much educational machinery both of institutions and of administration. It needed the revival of classical learning during the last century or so of our period to effect a drastic change which the genius of individual men had failed to bring about.

In the early days of universities, owing to the comparative scarcity of books and the great cost of classical and other standard works, much of the teaching took the form of lecturing to large audiences. The lectures were very frequently dictation lessons for the same reasons; the practice became traditional, and was continued when conditions made it less excusable. For example, the University of Louvain, founded in 1425, employed disputation and the dictation of texts, glosses, and commentaries as late as 1475; students memorised their notes and, like schoolboys, repeated them to their instructors. Disputation grew out of the wholesome method of teaching by dialogue, by conversation, by question and answer. The mediæval text-books respected the convention by putting the questions in the mouths of the learners; thus, in the Donat it is the pupil who asks, " How many parts of speech are there ? " Scholasticism in theology and philosophy was elaborated by the method of dialectic or disputation; and scholasticism directed the practice of the universities. Since the formal exercises leading to a degree were steps in the training of a university teacher, it was natural that *disputatio* should play a prominent part in those exercises. The method afforded a welcome relief from the tedium of the lecture; so long as it was genuine it was a better form of teaching, since it required the pupil's active participation. Later times kept up the tradition, but turned the disputation into a farce. We learn from Stow, the antiquary, that as late as 1535-40, when he was at school, London boys on St Bartholomew's Day disputed publicly in Smithfield. The only available material lay in the grammar book; and it is safe to infer that ' exceptions ' and ' exceptions to exceptions ' were freely drawn upon by the disputants to discomfit opponents. In that case these schoolboy wranglings had their share in creating the belief that ' exceptions ' were of far more importance than ' rules.'

The institutions thus far considered concerned themselves with learning Latin, reading books written in Latin, teaching in Latin, and this irrespective of the mother-tongue of teacher or taught. In other words, the instruction which they gave belonged to the spheres of what we now call secondary and higher, or university, education. Did the Middle Ages make no contribution to popular education, to teaching rudiments in the vernacular without reference to any alien tongue ?

The answer is, in the first place, that public instruction in reading, writing, and summing originated within that period under economic pressure. It is a mere prejudice, the child of ignorance, which ascribes the origin of this kind of instruction to the influence of Luther, Knox, Calvin, and others, whose principles logically required every child to be able at least to read. Principles are not infrequently in advance of practice. Elementary instruction of this kind existed long before the Reformation outside the systems fostered by the Church and the universities.

In strictness, it was not the business of the schools to instruct in the 'three R's.' That part of mathematics now found in arithmetic books, so far as it then existed, was regarded as a practical art, useful chiefly to tradesmen. Reading meant the ability to read Latin words. The school had no use for the former, and it very frequently expected the pupil to bring the latter ability with him, just as he brought the ability to talk. But the strict view could not always be maintained with respect to reading and writing, arts which found their way into grammar schools and song schools. In the later Middle Ages these often were part of the studies of the lower forms occupied by the 'petties.' There were also other and less formal ways, chiefly under private teachers, by which children, girls as well as boys, learned to read and, less often, to write.

The origin of the elementary school as such is to be found in the demand made by commerce and industry for junior clerks and for workmen who could read and write the *vernacular* and, in fewer instances, make out or at least understand a bill. Such schools, quite distinct from grammar or song schools, grew up in the great commercial and industrial centres during the fourteenth century in Italy and in Germany; they appeared in England in the following century, when the country passed from an agricultural to an industrial and commercial status.

While the Church had no special interest in this purely utilitarian instruction, it was not unmindful of the education of the great majority of the people. Councils and individual bishops admonished parish priests to keep schools in which all comers might be taught gratis. The object in view is expressed as follows in a papal document of the second quarter of the thirteenth century. "Let every parish priest have his clerk to sing and to read the epistle and lesson, a man able to keep school [a gloss adds "to teach children the Psalter and singing "] and [let the priest] admonish his parishioners to send their sons to church to learn the faith and that he may chastely educate them." The purpose, then, is religious and liturgical; and it is religious because it was held that education must be a religious education, or, conversely, that religion is education. We can very easily be unfair to our ancestors on this point. After all, it is no small part of true education to teach and to train a man to act up to his duty to God and his fellows. The great expansion of knowledge, especially of scientific knowledge, during modern times tempts us to attach more than its due importance to ' knowledge ' in a scheme of education. But these parish schools had possibilities of development. They were open to girls as well as to boys, and their object was not so rigidly stated that there was no room for a particular interpretation of it by a given priest or his parishioners. In France certainly that development took place; the priests' or parish schools, especially those in the great towns, became in due course charity schools, which taught reading and writing, sometimes also summing and, more rarely, drawing.

But again we are unfair to the mediæval world if we regard its universities and schools as its only educational institutions. Apart from the parish schools, the mediæval schools were addressed to the needs of the scholar or professional man, the theologian, lawyer, or doctor. Their business was not with girls or women, but with boys and men whose minds were of the scholarly type, an *élite*, not of birth or of wealth, but of a certain type of capacity, the type which is apt to arrogate the term 'intellectual' to itself. It did not include a very powerful body of persons, women as well as men. The man of action, the soldier, the great landowner, the sovereign prince, and their respective women-folk received little or no help from grammar-school or university, though it must not be assumed that the men and boys of these social classes never resorted to either.

The needs of these men and women 'of affairs' were not coincident with those of the clerkly person. Further, while one sort of human excellence fitted the scholar for his career, these men and women could apply many sorts of excellence in their daily lives. Moreover, they were in a position to give some effect to their varied ideals.

The 'chivalric education,' as it is called, was given within the domestic circles of the royal court, the castle, and the feudal or semi-feudal household of the territorial magnate. The pupils in the first instance were the wards of the head of the house, but their number was increased by the sons and daughters of his greater vassals and of others of similar rank. The system of chivalry was certainly developed in the eleventh century, but its beginning can be noted as early as the eighth. The chivalric education existed down to the close of our period, when it came under the influence of the classical revival and passed into the 'doctrine of courtesy,' the body of principles which governed the nurture of the socially distinguished for three centuries at least. Under purely feudal conditions the chivalric education of the boy was largely devoted to physical exercise, to the management of arms, to horsemanship, sport, and the outdoor life generally. The tournament was often the occasion of great international gatherings of men and women, who, irrespective of nationality, were practised in the etiquette of the tourney and who could not fail to educate and be educated by the daily intercourse with their fellows. But the education of chivalry also included in its sphere the social amenities, behaviour in hall and bower, table manners, and indoor games. Girls and women shared this with boys and men, while the girls and women also received a practical training in the government of the household and in simple medicine and surgery. Unlike the schools and universities, the chivalric form of education held vernaculars in honour; the early literatures of France and of England especially are full of the romances and poetry which helped to shape the culture of dame and knight. In its later phase, the doctrine of courtesy, the chivalric education laid stress upon modern languages, literatures, and history, and upon modern studies as the extension of knowledge gave them birth. In this form courtly education had a sounder claim to be called 'humanist' than could be put forward for some types of upbringing to which that term is applied without hesitation.

In sum, the Middle Ages made a substantial contribution to the modern course of instruction, and in so doing it transmitted a knowledge of the ancient civilisation, so much of which had disappeared by the fifth century. The mediæval curriculum distinguished between professional studies and general culture, the latter being represented by the faculty of arts in the universities; the conception of a general education as the necessary preliminary to such professional studies as theology, law, and medicine became established at Oxford during the thirteenth century. The Middle Ages gave us public instruction on the great scale, chiefly 'secondary' in character, but 'elementary' also, meaning by that word instruction confined to the 'three R's' and the mother-tongue. The local administration of this public instruction dates from the early times of the period A.D. 500–1500. Last, but by no means least, the ideas latent in the practice of knightly education may be applied directly to national systems of universal, compulsory instruction. Indeed, these latter will both fail and involve prodigious waste of time, brains, and money so long as they ignore the root principle of chivalric education, the principle that every type of human capacity calls for cultivation. It is not enough that a nation educate its scholars only.

Negatively, this same period of history demonstrates the abuse of authority in education, an abuse especially harmful in the field of physical knowledge. Mediæval science was credulous and superstitious, and, without examination, repeated the mistakes as well as the truths of an earlier age. This, however, is mediæval education at its worst; at its best it trained men to a critical temper which in the end proved the undoing of much which was characteristic of itself.

J. W. ADAMSON

VIII

SOCIETY

A CERTAIN French historian, M. Paul Viollet, wrote a well-known book[1] on the history of the political and administrative institutions of France, mainly during the Middle Ages. That work is in three volumes, and its text, exclusive of index, table of contents, and so on, fills more than fourteen hundred closely printed pages; its gradual publication extended over a period of thirteen years; its scope is wide, including Church and State, royal, seigniorial, and municipal institutions, machinery for peace and machinery for war, finance, justice, legislation. The author of such a book not only has abundant material for forming an historical creed of his own, but, indeed, if he be worthy the name of historian at all, must inevitably do so. What, then, is the belief to which M. Viollet's labours have led him?

"We issue," he said, "from the Middle Ages. . . . The roots of our modern society lie deep in them. . . . What we are, we are, in great measure, because of the Middle Ages. The Middle Ages are alive in us. They are alive all round us." When, nine years after the completion of this first work, its author published another, relating to a more modern period, his preface shows that further researches had only confirmed him in his views.

[1] *Histoire des Institutions politiques et administratives de la France* (1890–1903).

212

CONTRIBUTIONS TO MODERN CIVILISATION

" The Middle Ages were fertile," he says. " They were creative. . . . Whatever is most living and most resisting in the national character is inherited. Modern society strikes its roots deep into the past: the dead are alive in it."

That is a point of view which has been held very generally by historians. There is a classical, if hackneyed, example to be found on this side of the Channel, in the much-quoted sentences from Bishop Stubbs' preface to his *Constitutional History*. " The roots of the present lie deep in the past, and nothing in the past is dead to the man who would learn how the present came to be what it is."

The task imposed on me is to examine such a point of view especially in relation to society—to the life of man as a social being, a member of a community. What does modern society owe to the Middle Ages ? What link binds a man's life in the twentieth century to that of his forefathers in the thirteenth ?

That is no new question. It has been asked again and again. Historians in particular, perhaps, have thought about it, since to them, whose minds dwell much in the past, who, as Sir Thomas Browne says, " daily command the view of so many imperial faces," analogies and contrasts and speculations must constantly be suggesting themselves. But there are few of us who have not, at some time or other, with more or less seriousness, with more or less knowledge, with more or less genuine desire to seek truth, asked ourselves similar questions : and to them, no doubt, we have found answers varying as widely as our own temperaments.

The answers most frequently returned stand at one or other of two opposite poles.

One set of inquirers comes to the conclusion that modern society owes nothing to the Middle Ages, except an instructive object-lesson in what to avoid. They pillory mediæval ignorance, superstition, brutality, and violence, the discomforts of mediæval life, and the imperfection of mediæval manners. Or they patronise the Middle Ages, and, while denying them the right to a man's full stature, are willing to admit the charm of their childlike innocence, and their skill in constructing beautifully such toys as pleased them.

The other set of inquirers takes a directly opposite line. Society as we find it now, they say, is unwholesome, over-complicated, distressed, and impotent. Society in the Middle Ages was regulated, finished, secure in its own outlook, satisfied with its works and ways. Salvation lies in a return to the past. The world of to-day is covered with the hot lava of an eruption: we must make it anew, with its cool streams and green hillsides, as it was before it underwent that ordeal by fire.

Among the enemies, or patrons, of mediæval civilisation there are undoubtedly some great names. If you read, for example, the Lowell Lectures[1] which the late Provost of Trinity College, Dublin, delivered at Boston some years ago, you will find that, not content with describing to his American audience very finely, very justly, very impressively, the services rendered to modern civilisation by the Greek genius, he constantly, by implication or by direct assertion, derides and belittles the contributions made by the Middle Ages. He speaks of the way in which " the gloomy splendour of Dante, the mightiest outcome of the Middle Ages, had put out the cheerfulness and light of Greek life, even as Virgil understood them, with a cruel and relentless creed." He contrasts the Gothic cathedral,

[1] J. P. Mahaffy, *What have the Greeks done for Modern Civilisation?* (1909).

" the ideal gloom," as he says, " in which to worship a relentless God and a tortured Christ," with the Renaissance palace, " a place of light and gladness." Dr Mahaffy was a great scholar, though in other than mediæval fields. So strong a prejudice in a trained mind is rare. But there are hundreds of people who paint contrasts just as vivid, without having any basis of scholarship on which to rest them. Their main interest is in the world in which they are alive. Possibly, until the classical tradition in education fades entirely away, they may continue to admit that to the making of that world there went something glorious that was Greece and something grand that was Rome. But the Middle Ages, the thousand years between the fifth and the fifteenth century, represent to them a period in which men's works were unproductive and men's thoughts incomprehensible, a period of whose whole character they are vaguely, and faintly, suspicious.

One of the disciples of guild socialism devotes a whole chapter in his most recent book [1] to what he calls "the conspiracy against mediævalism." " Among a certain class of writers," he says, " it is the custom to designate as mediæval anything which they do not understand or of which they do not approve, quite regardless of the issue as to whether it actually existed in the Middle Ages or not." The accusation may stand if it is modified. There is no conspiracy, surely. There is nothing so definite, no such armed enemy to detect and arrest. What there is is indifference, vague terminology, and uninformed repetition of meaningless phrases. Even a slight acquaintance at first hand with the Middle Ages as they really were ought to destroy generalisations so sweeping.

Let us turn, then, to the other set of inquirers, those

[1] A. J. Penty, *A Guildsman's Interpretation of History* (1920).

to whom the mediæval construction of society represents a lost ideal. That school of thought began with Ruskin; William Morris carried on the tradition; and to-day the guild socialists have taken up the torch. It is only quite recently that most of us have added 'guild socialism' to our vocabulary of political terms; and we are apt to forget that the views of the guild socialists, propagated vigorously since the War, were conceived long before the War, and are linked very closely with the whole process of thought which started in Ruskin's lifetime. One of the earliest expositions of guild socialism was set forth in 1906, in a little square book which, with its decent coat of dark blue buckram, its wide margins, firm paper, and admirable type, recalls even in its physical appearance the works of William Morris.[1] There is a much more intimate mental connexion. The modern flame, indeed, burns with a harsher and more glaring light than Ruskin's, but it is fed by the same fuel. Time has developed an attitude of mind into a political creed, and the social crisis hastened by the War has led its exponents to offer their theory as a practical solution of present ills. But the spirit that informs the dogma has been the same throughout.

Broadly speaking, the idea of the guild socialists is to reorganise modern industry on lines similar to those which they believe existed in the Middle Ages. They select as most characteristic of mediæval society the organisation of guilds; and guilds they would restore in the world of to-day. But, as they admit, such guilds would differ from their mediæval predecessors in at least two important respects. In the first place, their organisation would be national, not local; in the second, their basis would be the trade unions, which have no historical continuity with

[1] A. J. Penty, *The Restoration of the Gild System.*

the mediæval guilds, and are in some ways markedly contrasted with them, since they are societies of workers, not of masters, have no monopoly in their respective trades, and take no responsibility for the quality of the wares they produce.

The guild socialist movement, then, is in the main economic, and its most important aspect lies altogether outside the scope of the present lecture. But the advocates of the movement would be the first to claim that it involves wide social issues. " It has been well described," says one of them, " as a religion, an art, a philosophy, with economic feet." " The majority of people to-day," he says elsewhere, " feeling that the tendency of modern civilisation is to add more to the sorrow than to the joy of life, are beginning to ask themselves what Carlyle and Ruskin were asking themselves fifty years ago—whither modern civilisation goeth. . . . The failure of modern society to realise itself will result in an effort toward finding lost roads. The people will come to connect the Golden Age with the past again, rather than with the future. . . . A reverence for the past, then, is the hope of the future."

No mediæval historian is likely to belittle the work of Ruskin and of Morris. He must recognise in them preeminently two qualities—complete sincerity and a passion for beauty. They led a crusade where it was sorely needed, and they won some bitter fights. They left the world lovelier than they found it—" surely that may be their epitaph of which they need not be ashamed." And in their modern disciples, too, there is the same earnestness, the same revolt against squalor and ugliness, the same idealism.

Yet even the mediæval historian—indeed, perhaps particularly the mediæval historian—is driven reluctantly to criticise a certain unhistorical and artificial outlook in this school, to which it might seem at first sight that his sympathies would be so warmly attracted. Many of its disciples are mediævalists by instinct rather than by training, and their attitude is the result of a combination of natural affinities with carefully cultivated tastes. The former often lead them nearer to truth than the latter. William Morris was closer in type to his mediæval forebears when Burne-Jones found him " embedded in iron, dancing with rage, and roaring," because the vizor of a helmet he was trying on had come down and refused to go up, than when Rossetti visited his house in Red Lion Square and discovered him surrounded by " intensely mediæval furniture " and " chairs such as Barbarossa might have sat in."

The historian who reads the works of this school is constantly brought up short by the unreality of the picture presented to him. When he finds William Morris talking of London, " small, and white, and clean," he remembers mediæval London as he has met it in record and chronicle, with its muddy lanes and filthy gutters, its dirt and disease, its gates bristling with the heads of criminals, its jostling and rioting crowds. When Mr A. J. Penty tells him that " bureaucracy was a peculiarly Roman institution, and hardly existed in the Middle Ages," he thinks of English constitutional history as it has been rewritten during the last twenty years in the light of fuller knowledge of the records of these bureaucratic offices which managed—or mismanaged—the affairs of mediæval kings and kingdoms. The enthusiasts tell him that " according to the old conception, art, religion, ideas, integrity of work, the pursuit of perfection, were looked upon as the serious things of life, while business and money-making were subservient things, considered relatively unimportant, for men had a reverence for the truth and abhorrence for the false." The historian would be glad to believe it, but if he is to preserve his own respect for truth, he must say sadly that such a theory of an altruistic and ideal society is utterly at variance with the Middle Ages as he sees them in their writings and their doings. There is no such simple formula to explain their infinite variety. He must say rather with Sabatier that the Middle Ages had every vice and every virtue, " every vice, except vulgarity, every virtue, except moderation."

But it is time that we forsook destructive for constructive criticism. If the contribution of the Middle Ages to modern society was neither to act as a dreadful warning, nor to serve as an ideal for imitation, what was it ?

It was, I think, something gradual and rather elusive. It consisted in a long and slow process of historical development, which prepared the way for the structure of modern society. It can be best represented by that favourite metaphor, of whose use by historians I have already quoted two examples. " Modern society strikes its roots deep into the past," said M. Viollet. " The roots of the present lie deep in the past," said Stubbs.

That is a very exact metaphorical description, and can be pressed and elaborated in a way few metaphors could bear. The Middle Ages produced, in lavish quantity, a flora all their own. What it was like we know partly by description, partly by rare survival, partly by certain specimens artificially preserved. Many of its characteristic examples died out altogether. A gorgeous blossom of theory like the Empire, for example, weighed down and snapped a stem of practice too slender to uphold it. Fruits that had seemed at first tempting and sustaining became in the end insipid or even poisonous. Feudalism, for instance, first became the mere shadow of itself in chivalry, and then ceased altogether to meet man's needs. Some trees grew so tall that other life near them was stunted and stifled—so it was with the world-power of the Papacy. By the end of the mediæval period what had once been a fair garden was rank and in confusion. Natural decay, the neglect of the cultivator, the tramplings of enemies, the thefts of the greedy, the strong pushing of weeds among the flowers, had played havoc with what was at first sweet-smelling, orderly, and vigorous. Clearing and burning followed, before new seeds could be set.

But—and here is my point—it was into the old soil that those seeds were dropped, and the soil was richer, warmer, and more fertile than raw uncultivated ground. Moreover, in its very substance were the remnants of the plants which had sprung from it. The new roots spread themselves in the mould of centuries. And further, even while the displaced plants were still in full vigour, they had had beside them seedlings different in type from the parent tree. Now that the clearance had been made, these had their chance, and soon were spreading their flowers so gaily to the sunshine that men failed to recognise in them the offspring of the plants they had destroyed.

The fact was that all through the Middle Ages two processes were going on. One was immediately constructive, and by it was made the prevailing type of civilisation which we call mediæval, and which reached its most complete form during the twelfth and thirteenth centuries. To meet the practical needs of life it evolved feudalism, and, with feudalism, a society in which men were ranged in order of privilege according to their greater or smaller share in that chief wealth, the land. That method of construction produced a world in which large groups of human beings were inarticulate and unnoticed, blotted out from historical view by the commanding figures of earls, barons, and knights who stood in front of them. The only lay type we know well in feudal society seems extraordinarily remote from anything familiar to us to-day. The duties, prejudices, recreations, code of honour, and works of piety of the average feudal baron seem as different from those which present themselves to the average man of this age as the feudal castle is different from the modern house.

The immediate process, then, constructed something unfamiliar to us, which has passed away. Yet what we are is based on what we were, and even with that vanished civilisation we have more links than we always realise. That is the first part of my metaphor, the soil in which the roots are spread.

The second process, which it is easy to overlook, was going on side by side with the other even in the heart of the Middle Ages. There never was a time when the order of society which we call mediæval was as consistent, as unchallenged, as complete as it looks to us when given a false unity and security by our own remoteness from it. Experiment and criticism were unceasing; theory and practice never closely fitted each other; absolute uniformity was unknown. Again and again in the Middle Ages, more and more as we look closely into them, we shall find suggestions, and sayings, and actions too, which strike us as amazingly modern. That they do strike us in tha way is because we have that innocent and universal conceit with which man in every age has regarded his own as the touchstone of all the rest. We reject what is unlike our own world in the world of the Middle Ages as antiquated and alien. What is like our own, we regard as the happy prophecy of better things, vouchsafed to a few chosen spirits. A more historical view would be to see in such examples the manifestations of a second process, less immediately successful, working beside the first, a minority beside a majority. The minority is produced by the age it lives in as much as the majority; and its theories or its practice, if eventually results come of them, are just as much part of the creative faculty of that age.

Let me illustrate my general view of the mediæval contribution to modern society by taking a particular instance. Selecting from the most modern of ages, that in which we live, the newest social phenomenon we can find, let us examine it in the light of mediæval theory and practice.

There is nothing much newer in England's life to-day than the removal by law of women's disqualifications from sharing to the full in the obligations and privileges long confined to men. There has been an immense and general upheaval of opinion as to women and their place in the world, and it has taken this practical shape. So much for 1920. What would 1220, or 1320, have thought about it ?

The general theory of the Middle Ages undoubtedly conceived of woman's position in society as completely subordinate. Hear St Thomas Aquinas, greatest of mediæval teachers, supreme embodiment of the mediæval spirit.

" The woman is subject to the man, on account of the weakness of her nature, both of mind and of body. . . . Man is the beginning of woman and her end, just as God is the beginning and end of every creature.

. . . Woman is in subjection according to the law of nature, but a slave is not." Finally, and perhaps most astonishing of all, " Children ought to love their father more than their mother."[1]

Much mediæval history shows us women accepting and endorsing that official estimate of their importance. Take, for example, the case of a lady who in 1301 was prioress of the Cistercian nunnery at Whistones, on the north side of the city of Worcester. Archbishop Winchelsey, in that year, was about to undertake a visitation of the diocese of Worcester, and had instructed the bishop to summon clergy and people to meet him in the cathedral church on a certain day in March. The bishop accordingly sent notices to the cathedral chapter, to the collegiate churches, and to the monasteries, and among the latter to Whistones. What did the prioress do ? She wrote to the archbishop to explain that on that day the convent chaplain would act as its representative, " since it is not fitting that women should mix themselves up with men's meetings."[2] The occasion, be it remembered, was one of great importance, possibly of danger, for religious communities in the diocese; the convent was close at hand, so that there was no question of travel or expense; but it was " not fitting that women should mix themselves up with men's meetings," so she stood aside.

That is, perhaps, hardly a fair example, for in the case of a man there were special conditions to be taken into account. Yet the chronicles, the records, the romances, and the poems of the Middle Ages give a general impression that

[1] *Summa Theologiæ*, I, xciii, 4, II, pt. 2, xxvi, 10, Supp. xxxix, 3, lxxxi, 3. I owe these references to Mrs M. Beer.
[2] Rose Graham, " The Metropolitical Visitation of the Diocese of Worcester, 1301 " (*Trans. Royal Hist. Soc.*, Fourth Series, ii, 66).

most mediæval women would have taken the same point of view as the prioress of Whistones. They performed their own duties adequately, they received a great deal of outward respect, they may have found life on the whole rather dull, and they did not meddle with what did not concern them. The first process of construction, that is to say, had produced a theory in marked contrast with that held by the world of to-day and a practice in many cases consonant with that theory.

Yet, if we care to look below the surface, we shall find a second process also at work. We shall find that not even all theorists thought alike, and that practice did not always fit the more usual theory. Position counted, and brains counted; even in a woman; even in the Middle Ages. The heiress to a great fief, for example, was a person of importance and independence, and, if she added personality to her other endowments, might act with considerable freedom. A few real individualities of this sort stand out against that rather impersonal background to which our imperfect knowledge of the Middle Ages at present condemns us. Such, for example, was Joan of Acre, second surviving daughter of Edward I. Joan lived for thirty-five years only, for she was born the year her father came to the English throne, and she died the year he left it. Yet that short space was long enough to show her mettle, and to differentiate her from more conventional women. At twenty-five she was left a widow by the death of the elderly Earl of Gloucester, to whom she had been married for political reasons. For similar reasons, Edward I was on the point of arranging a second marriage for her, when she confronted him boldly with a statement that she intended this time to marry the man of her own choice, who happened to be a mere knight, Ralph of Monthermer. He stood right outside the narrow circle of great earls and barons, and Edward I could find no words strong enough in which to express his opinion of Ralph's ineligibility for such a match. But Joan, says the *Opus Chronicorum*, argued the point vigorously. " It is not humiliating or disgraceful," she said, " for some great and powerful earl to marry some poor and unimportant little woman; and so, contrariwise, for a countess it is neither blameworthy nor difficult to promote a strenuous youth." She followed up words by deeds, and, after a first tremendous explosion of anger, Edward I accepted the situation and gave to the second husband that same title, Earl of Gloucester, which the first had held.

A less well-known example of Joan's courage and independence occurred in 1305, when her young brother Edward, Prince of Wales, fell under the displeasure of his father, who cut off all supplies. The Prince's only idea of meeting this situation was to write lamentable letters to his friends and relatives, and to trail miserably about the country, as near as he dared to the court, in the hope of some sudden relenting on the King's part. A good many people wrote sympathetic letters, or invited the Prince to visit them, but the only person who took practical measures was his sister Joan. She placed at his disposal all her goods, and all her husband's, and she sent him her seal, by means of which he might be able to secure much that would not have been forthcoming at his own discredited order.[1] She risked, that is to say, in eager partisanship, all that she had gradually recovered of her father's favour. Fortunately the trouble blew over within a month or two.

Turning from the world of the court and castle to the world of learning, there too we can find instances of women's activities. As early as the eleventh century more than one

[1] *Exchequer Miscellanea*, 5/2, m. 7.

woman doctor was practising, lecturing, and writing in the medical school at Salerno in Italy. Two hundred years afterwards, Pierre Dubois, a French lawyer, was foreshadowing the modern medical missionary by suggesting that women should be taught languages, surgery, medicine, and the rubrics and canons of the Church, as a preliminary to work in the East. It is only fair to add that Pierre Dubois was full of ideas which astounded his contemporaries. Moreover, his ends were more mediæval than his means. He wanted to recover the Holy Land. His women doctors were to marry intelligent infidels or schismatics, cure their bodily diseases first, and then take advantage of their gratitude to wheedle them out of their theological errors.

Coming to a very recent and controversial question, the ministry of women, there is matter for thought in a tale told by the St Alban's monk, Roger of Wendover,[1] at the beginning of the thirteenth century. It is as follows: There lived somewhere in Burgundy a certain maiden who had all the advantages the world could give her—noble parents, riches, and the promise of a desirable marriage. "But from early youth," says the chronicle, "she had been instructed in liberal studies," and when the time of her wedding came unpleasantly near she slipped away to take refuge, not in a nunnery, but in a convent of Franciscan friars. She cut off her hair, put on the serge habit and rope girdle, went barefoot, and tried (but, says legend, quite unsuccessfully) to do away with all her natural attractions. No austerity was too great for her, no prayer too lengthy, no task too hard. She "preached the Gospel of Peace through cities and villages, more particularly to those of her own sex." The biography has no final chapter,

[1] *Flores Hist.*, iv, 108–112 (Eng. Hist. Soc.).

for no one told Roger of Wendover the end of it; but, as he truly said, what he had related already was quite sufficient.

The way in which the St Alban's monk tells that story is itself instructive. He lifts his hands in admiration of his heroine's saintliness, but he does not raise his eyebrows in astonishment at the peculiarity of her career. Not a word in his account suggests that he regarded that feature of the story as curious, abnormal, or interesting. We should think his attitude an evidence of the indifference of the mediæval mind to breaches of accepted etiquette, if it were not that we have an immense number of examples in other connexions which prove the exact opposite.

At any rate, whatever Roger of Wendover's views may have been, that lady—if, indeed, she ever existed—was certainly an exception to rules. She falls into line with other instances, some of which I have given, many more of which could be found, of women whose opportunities and ambitions were far wider than was usual in the age in which they lived. Add to such practical examples the theorising of Dubois and others, and you have an illustration of the second part of my metaphor. The seedlings are growing beside the parent plant, but they are so unlike it as to be hardly recognisable. For the time being, they remain almost unnoticed; but by and by, when the shadow of the stronger growth is removed, they will shoot up and call attention to themselves. Women doctors, women preachers, women at liberty to develop their own talents and tastes, were rare phenomena in the Middle Ages; but they were there. Moreover, their presence might be of real historical importance. Let me quote you in illustration of that a passage from Dr Rashdall's *Universities of Europe in the Middle Ages*.[1] He has been describing the

[1] Vol. ii, pt. 2, p. 712.

227

way in which precedents were sought in the mediæval university system, and illustrates his point as follows :

> The University of London, after being empowered by royal charter to do all things that could be done by any university, was legally advised that it could not grant degrees to women without a fresh charter, because no university had ever granted such degrees. We have seen that there were women doctors at Salerno.

In a footnote he adds :

> I have been informed by an eminent judge who was one of the counsel on whose advice the university acted, that a knowledge of this fact would have modified his opinion.

The position of women, then, may serve on the whole as an illustration of my general contention—that the Middle Ages on the one hand evolved a social order of their own, different from, but linked to, the social order familiar to us to-day; while on the other hand they made suggestions and experiments to which the modern world would respond more readily than the mediæval.

That is a single illustration. There are others. There are many others. There are more than we know of, or shall know of, until we have carried our investigations of mediæval conditions much farther than any point as yet reached. Before that can be done, there will have to be a general and sincere recognition of two facts, at present very imperfectly realised. The first is, that the study of the Middle Ages is not an antiquarian pursuit, quite unconnected with present-day interests and problems; it is the examination of a stage as essential as any other to the making of the world we live in. The second is, that our knowledge of that stage at present lags behind our knowledge of others, because there are not as yet nearly enough workers in the field of mediæval history.

Let me conclude by examining a little more in detail
these two statements. To the first, witness is being borne
by the whole series of lectures of which this is a part.
Moreover, the fact perhaps needs less demonstration by
argument than it would have done six years ago. We
have been fighting a war on fields well known to English-
men of the fourteenth and fifteenth centuries; in the course
of it we have tried some experiments which differed in degree
rather than in kind from some they knew well; and we are
now faced with a social reconstruction of a sort which
suggests at every turn comparisons with the mediæval
world. Shall we ever again be as national, or as insular,
as we were before 1914? Do we not hear talk on every
hand of internationalism, and is not our class warfare
organising itself on lines that recall those horizontal strata
of mediæval society? The social chain of the mediæval
world did indeed bind in mutual dependence different
classes in a single country: but in mutual affection and
co-operation it bound each class to the same class all over
Western Europe. Again, take the question of travel and
transport, so vital in its importance to a community. Are
not our roads and our rivers being utilised to an extent
unparalleled since the introduction of steam traction? The
motor-lorry, indeed, is an animal both swifter and uglier than
the mediæval packhorse, but he serves the same purposes.
Of late years we have tasted by personal experience some
minor mediæval discomforts. We have stumbled through
unlighted, and unmended, streets; we have gone to bed
betimes of necessity, and not of choice; we have done
without numbers of things which under peaceful modern
conditions seemed the normal accompaniments of every-
day life. Finally, across the Irish Sea at this moment
scenes are being enacted which recall the Middle Ages at

their worst. Men are standing by inactive while their fellows are murdered before their eyes, just as men stood and watched while the Treasurer of England was done to death in London in 1327, or while many another victim, more obscure, perished *multis astantibus et admirantibus*.

Mediæval society, then, had many features for which we may be half prepared by what we ourselves have seen and heard. For thorough investigation, of course, we should have to add to that general interest the examination of huge masses of manuscript material, the technical training which is preliminary to such an examination, and the patience, concentration, and enthusiasm required for any serious occupation.

It is the enthusiasm which is chiefly lacking. The material, and the training, are readily accessible. I speak to you in a college to which the University of London has assigned its only chair of mediæval history. Close at hand is the Public Record Office, with such a store of material for the history of mediæval England as can hardly be described in language which will not seem exaggerated. Before next year is far advanced, we shall have in Bloomsbury the modest beginnings of what in time will be, I trust, one of the most important centres of historical studies in England. Among those studies mediæval subjects should play their proper part; they can only do so if there are forthcoming both workers prepared to labour in those fields, and endowments to facilitate their labours.

And when we have our workers, and the tools are ready to their hands, and their task is on the way to accomplishment, what shall we have secured? First, clearer knowledge of the past; next, clearer vision for the future. The Middle Ages, we have said, had every vice and every virtue; and among the virtues none was greater than the

TO MODERN CIVILISATION

energy with which they concentrated upon realising their ideals. Let them, then, leave us that legacy. Let us bring to the solution of our own problems the patience and the passion they brought to theirs. We can find our determination voiced for us, once for all, not indeed by a man of the Middle Ages, but by a man who was heir of all the ages:

> Bring me my bow of burning gold!
> Bring me my arrows of desire!
> Bring me my spear; O clouds, unfold !
> Bring me my chariot of fire !
>
> I will not cease from mental fight,
> Nor shall my sword sleep in my hand,
> Till we have built Jerusalem
> In England's green and pleasant land.

HILDA JOHNSTONE

IX

ECONOMICS [1]

IN the Middle Ages it was the fashion for every good chronicler to begin a history of his own time with an account of the creation of the world; even in this chilly age of scientific research there is still something to be said in favour of this principle, for by so doing it is possible to explain the present by the past, to emphasise in the past those tendencies which we, looking back with the superior wisdom of a later century, know are going to mould the mind of the present, determine its political likes and dislikes, and fashion the main lines of its economic life. This may offend the sense of those historians who hold that history should be written with a mind swept clear of all knowledge of after events, but all the same it produces valuable results: it brings into relief what is really permanent in the life of a people, it marks out the lines along which it has progressed in the past, and, if approached in an optimistic spirit, it may hold out some hope of a tentative

---

[1] Further information can be gathered from any standard text-book. Cunningham's *Growth of English Industry and Commerce* covers both mediæval and modern periods. Lipson, *Economic History of England*, and Ashley, *Economic History*, both deal only with the mediæval period. Lipson is an accurate and rather dull work; Ashley is possibly not so reliable, but far more brilliant and suggestive. Ashley's *Economic Organisation of England* is a slight but vivid sketch of the whole period. G. O'Brien's *Mediæval Economic Teaching* is useful for economic theory. For guild socialism the works of G. D. H. Cole are valuable, especially his *Chaos and Order in Industry* and *Self-Government in Industry*.

232

solution of the problems of the present, and even of the future—at any rate, it is often willing to teach us what to avoid, though we, far too frequently, turn a deaf ear to its warnings. For the life of a people is continuous, and therefore its history must show a gradual progress from one stage of existence to the next, with few, if any, cataclysmic changes: every institution we possess, every form of industrial or commercial activity, can show a steady and unbroken development, so that it is strictly true to say that the Middle Ages must influence most profoundly the life of to-day, because the life of to-day is in the broadest sense the product of mediæval conditions; but if the two extremes in the series were placed side by side, if the institution of to-day were compared with that very different germ in the Middle Ages from which it has sprung, no one could profess to discover the faintest resemblance between the two.

What similarity is there between the mediæval gild, with its profound and intense local feeling, its stringent regulation of its members' industrial activity, its fixing of prices, the religious feeling which permeated its every aspect, its charities, its liveries, its festivals, and the great capitalistic organisations of to-day, of world-wide scope; a Port Sunlight, for example, with its factories, its fleet of ships, its tropic islands to feed it with the essential raw materials, its distributing agents in every part of the habitable globe? And yet there is a broad road of historical development that leads straight from the one to the other, for out of the corruption of the gild system capitalism in industry developed; commercial capital, which was probably one of the earliest forms to arise, was able to secure the subordination of allied crafts, and, long before the Industrial Revolution came with its power machinery, capitalism was a vital factor in industry, and in certain trades the factory had already become the industrial unit. The Industrial Revolution merely selected and emphasised those forms of economic organisation which were most suited to its rapid development, and so laid the foundation of the industrial system as we know it to-day; on this foundation, steam and electric transport and the development of international finance have built that ostentatious and somewhat insecure edifice of large-scale production which has divided the world into the antagonistic classes of employers and employed, and which at present is threatening immediate collapse and the engulfing with it of the whole system of our industrial organisation; if a tree is to be judged by its fruits, this is not a disaster greatly to be deplored.

Or if we regard that most conservative of all industries —agriculture—what possible resemblance can be seen between the great farms of Canada or the United States, with their enormous fields tilled almost entirely by power machinery, from the ploughing of the land to the harvesting of the ripe grain, and the two- or the three-field system of the Middle Ages, with fairly large fields indeed, but each field split up into acre or half-acre strips, with each man's land scattered throughout the common fields, a strip here and a strip there, with its primitive and rigid system of agriculture, its crude ox-drawn plough, its co-operative cultivation, its sowing and reaping and threshing by hand, its dependence on the waste and the woodland, its manorial services, its normal condition of self-sufficiency? And yet, once more, the Middle Ages live still in the most modern methods: to prove this, it is not necessary to stress mere verbal survivals—the fact that we still use the term furlong, the length of the mediæval furrow, and chain, the breadth of the mediæval acre-strip, for long before the Middle Ages were drawing to a close there were growing up side by side with those scattered strips the more convenient compact farms, consisting sometimes of land enclosed from the waste, sometimes of a bundle of neighbouring strips gradually and painfully gathered into the same hand; to a few minds that rose above the common agricultural ruck, these compact farms, which had grown up almost as it were by accident, were not long in demonstrating their superiority, and they began to be consciously imitated; books were written advocating their creation, a general feeling arose that land in severalty was necessary for progressive agriculture, especially as, at this time, the balance that had held in the Middle Ages between arable and pasture land was being completely reversed by the realisation of the profits that came from intelligent sheep-farming; enclosing became the fashion, and when science began to lend its aid to the agriculturist, when root crops, fodder crops, and the more careful preparation of the soil began to be regarded, the Agricultural Revolution exercised the same selective power as did the Industrial Revolution some years later. To the compact farm its methods could be most easily applied; therefore it was primarily to the compact farm that it brought prosperity; the strip system and the open fields had to give way, and contemporary industrial conditions soon turned their defeat into absolute rout. Therefore the compact fields were the prevalent type to which the application of the simpler forms of agricultural machinery brought still greater prosperity, and, with the bringing under cultivation of the vast and level areas of the New World, the use of steam or electric power became common, and further mechanical improvements followed as of course.

MEDIÆVAL CONTRIBUTIONS

Thus both in industrial and agricultural practice modern conditions grew naturally out of mediæval organisation, and the latter must have contributed much to the form that modern life has taken. As much can be said of mediæval economic theory: it seems, indeed, a far cry from the prohibition of usury, which is stressed so much, and often so inaccurately, in economic text-books, to those philanthropic gentlemen of to-day, who, under ostentatiously English names, are prepared to lend us any sum from five pounds to five thousand on our note of hand alone. And yet there is really no break in the chain of development that connects the two, for the prohibition of usury was but the one side of the mediæval picture, and if usury was forbidden, interest was allowed: if on the one hand it was held wrongful to exact payment or usury from your fellow-man for a loan which he repaid punctually and in full, for any gain that had accrued to him by that loan was the result of his own intelligence or his own labour and not of yours, yet compensation or interest could always be claimed if you had suffered actual loss in consequence of making the loan, either because it was not repaid punctually, or because you had been yourself placed in difficulties for lack of the money, or because you had thereby been hindered from making a just and legitimate profit. As the opportunities for the employment of money in trade and industry increased, the chances that the making of a loan would react unfavourably on the lender grew greater—interest assumed an ever more prominent position at the expense of usury, which was gradually pushed into the background; the secular government, which had succeeded the Church in the regulation of economic activities, considered that enough had been done when it had laid down maximum rates of interest, and finally even that precautionary measure was abandoned, in England at any rate, with the repeal of the usury laws in 1839, thus allowing free scope to the activities of those who lend out at interest. But it is extraordinarily significant of the way in which a regulation which is based upon sound principles will persist or, if for a time abolished, will later be revived, that, by the Money-lenders Act of 1900, once more was there imposed a limitation on the rate of interest that could be charged, and once more was there a legal difference between that and usury, not certainly the same as existed in the Middle Ages, but based upon essentially the same idea, that of a reasonable justice between lender and borrower.

Here you have had the same fundamental idea leading to much the same conclusion in both mediæval and in modern times, but that was by no means always the case.

If one desired to show that there was any real connection between that central doctrine of mediæval theory—the idea of the Just Price—and the doctrine which was equally vital to the England of the late nineteenth century—that of the free competitive price—one would, on the face of things, have considerable difficulties to meet. Yet if one were to read " Buying and selling seem to be established for the common advantage of both parties, one of whom requires that which belongs to the other and *vice versa*," one would be tempted to exclaim: " Ah, yes, from Adam Smith no doubt, and from this he will prove that as both parties benefit from the transaction there is no sense in trying to impose restrictions upon it; every man will then be at liberty to seek his own profit, and the sum of the profits of each will be the profit of all, that is, of the country at large; hence the value of free trade and competitive prices." But it is nothing of the kind; the quotation really comes from St Thomas Aquinas, the greatest exponent of economic theory in the Middle Ages, and he goes on from it to prove the value of the Just Price, not of the competitive price. Therefore, different though these two things be, they obviously have something in common; Adam Smith and those predecessors of his who were preaching these doctrines through the whole of the eighteenth century were merely harking back to one of the fundamental truths that underlay the idea of the Just Price and of the legislation that strove to enforce it, not only in the Middle Ages, but also under the Tudors and earlier Stuarts; Adam Smith approached the problem from the soulless standpoint of the economist, St Thomas from the more human one of the moralist and the theologian, but their problem was much the same in the two cases, the medley of conflicting interests under which trade groaned, and the lack of some sound principle upon which economic theory could base any doctrine as to the trade relations of man with man.

And so one might go through the whole gamut of the economic theory and practice of modern times, but within the limits of a brief article it would be impossible to trace this steady, and at times almost imperceptible, development which has changed the mediæval organisation into the fundamentally different one of the twentieth century.

Rather is it desirable to turn our attention to the limited and more precise sense in which it could be said that the Middle Ages have contributed to our present civilisation; of these contributions there seem to be two: a direct influence by the survival down to modern times of some typical mediæval practice or idea, and a more indirect influence arising from the conscious imitation by men of the present day of some mediæval institution which they have learned to respect.

The survivals are actually few in number, and are often

more interesting than important, but some at least still form an essential portion of our civilisation. In the realms of industry we sometimes confide ourselves to the provincial make-to-measure tailor or bootmaker, who is often a handicraftsman employing his own capital to supply his small stock-in-trade of cloth or of leather, possibly with men working under him, but none the less supervising and often working with them himself. Then there is the small dressmaker in the back street who makes up her customer's goods, and so requires no capital but her needle or her sewing-machine. She represents another phase of mediæval industry which we still have with us and which plays a not unimportant part in our appearance as a nation. Tailor, bootmaker, and dressmaker alike have survived the competition of capitalism and large-scale production, although there are signs even now that their doom is not far distant, and they still remain as mediæval in their business organisation as they are but too often in their methods and their ideas of current fashions.

Or consider the west of Ireland and the west of Scotland tweeds; they are still made to some considerable extent in the people's own houses, the industry is still domestic, very comparable to that which was growing up in the wool-trade throughout the period of the later Middle Ages, and which reached its full importance with the decadence of the gild system in the fifteenth century. The centuries have passed them by, and to-day they have an importance as having done something by the force of example to assist in the revival of village industries to which I shall presently refer.

All the examples of survivals that have hitherto been given have been taken from the realm of industry, but commerce can provide an even more important one: the great fairs that are still held on the Continent serve precisely the same purpose as they did in the Middle Ages; thither merchants still bring their wares and set them out before the buyers who flock from all corners of the country, sure of finding the class of goods for which the fair has become famous: such are the great book and leather fairs of Leipzig, the fairs of Nijni-Novgorod, where the furs of the North, the tea and silk of China, are purchased by the merchants of Western Russia, and in a lesser degree the more famous of the markets in some of the great capitals, the Billingsgate and Covent Garden of London, or Les Halles of Paris, which bear to the town somewhat the same relation as a street in the great mediæval fair bore to the whole country.

And even high finance has its mediæval survivals, some still in a very flourishing condition; possibly lending to kings is not practised so much to-day when crowns are falling too fast to be pleasant, but the Bardi and the Peruzzi of the fourteenth century have worthy successors in the Rothschilds of the nineteenth. But it is in less exalted spheres that the survival is most striking: the pawnbroker is a useful member of society who is still with us. In the early days he was usually, though not always, a Jew, and occasionally he received rather quaint pledges: one can conceive that he would have little objection to taking charge of the plate of Lincoln Minster which Bishop Chesney pledged with Aaron of Lincoln in the middle of the twelfth century, but when William of Walterville, Abbot of Peterborough, in 1175 broke open the reliquaries in his own church and pledged the relics of the saints together with the arm of St Oswald, king and martyr, with the Jews, the least that might have been expected was a miracle in which the arm of the wrathful Oswald should have played the principal part; alas! the chronicler is silent as to any such sequel. But that the path of the pawnbroker in those early days was often a thorny one we learn from the following tale, culled from the middle of the twelfth century:

"A mighty noble and robber pledged his carriage for twenty deniers with Reuben. Now Simeon desired to go on a journey, and asked Reuben for the loan of the carriage. Reuben said: 'You must first ask permission of the lord.' But the lord being out, Simeon asked his lady, who gave him leave. It happened that on their journey Simeon and his wife passed the lord's castle in the carriage, whereupon the lady, seeing this, declared she would never sit in the carriage where a Jewess had sat. She sent for Reuben and demanded the carriage back, to atone for the profanation, and declared that she would make one of her servants swear that it had suffered more than twenty deniers' damage. When Reuben pointed out that she had given Simeon permission, she denied it." Now the problem arises, who ought to stand the loss of the twenty deniers—Reuben or Simeon? But unfortunately our curiosity must go unsatisfied, for the question is left unanswered.

But Christians did not long leave the Jews unrivalled in so lucrative a field as pawnbroking, and just before the end of the Middle Ages we actually hear of a religious order—the Franciscans—entering the ancient and honourable money-lending profession, though, be it said, from the worthiest of motives. In 1462 they founded the first of their *montes pietatis* at Orvieto in order to loan money to the poor at reasonable rates; so popular did they become that eleven more were founded in Italy during the next thirty years, and to-day the Mont de Piété—or State pawnbroking establishment—of Paris preserves the name and, to some extent, the laudable objects of the houses set up by the excellent Franciscans.

But, after all, interesting as these survivals are, important as may be the part they play in the daily life of some of us, their influence upon modern economic conditions seems almost negligible in comparison with that which has resulted from the study of the Middle Ages and the conviction that followed in the minds of many eminent men of the later nineteenth century—a conviction that is still a very living thing—that the Middle Ages had much to teach us, much that would lift us out of the sordid materialism into which we had sunk, much that might aid in solving those social and industrial problems that were crowding thick and fast upon England at the end of the last century.

The first fifty years of the nineteenth century found England profoundly steeped in an indolent and insular spirit of self-satisfaction, an England given up to the grosser forms of money-making, lacking in æsthetic appreciation or in any honest sympathy with the world that surrounded her, an England like nothing so much as that fine flower of her artistic effort, her horsehair-covered furniture—smooth and sleek and shiny and exceeding loathsome to the touch. We were, indeed, a nation of shopkeepers, and shopkeepers of the sanctimonious type that praised God daily that they were not as other men. The corrupting finger of trade had touched everything; it was the Englishman's boast that he turned out good solid stuff; with its beauty, its originality, even the measure with which it met the convenience of his customers in other lands, he was not concerned—what was good enough for him must indeed be good enough for the rest of the world; even if the name originated in the early eighteenth century, the conventional picture of John Bull might well have been first drawn during these years, so much does it reek of their typical beef-fed self-complacency.

With those whom he was pleased to call the lower classes he did not have much concern; they had certainly given trouble earlier in the century, but by 1850 they seemed to have been successfully hypnotised by their mechanics' institutes and their politico-socialist discussions, and it was once more safe to treat them as so many cogs in the industrial wheel, for why should they not be fully satisfied so long as regular wages rewarded the years of their toil and a strictly just workhouse system tended their grey hairs to the grave?

Against all this a small group of idealists revolted. Ruskin and William Morris were led by their desire to introduce more beauty into a drab and material world to strike at the root of the evil and find some means to breathe fresh life into industry, to make each worker feel that he was producing something worth while. It was impossible to do this, they soon came to the conclusion, so long as the workman was regarded as so much labour material, so long as machine production was allowed to crush out all individuality. This quarrel with the current methods of industry drove them and those who thought like them to seek inspiration from the past. Just as the Pre-Raphaelites sought to recover the art of the later Middle Ages, Ruskin and Morris, enthralled by an idealised picture of mediæval industry in the heyday of the gild system, strove to re-establish such conditions as they thought might secure that economic independence and that freedom to follow the lure of his own spirit which they imagined the mediæval craftsman to possess. And therefore arose that movement for the establishment of arts and crafts, for the revival of village industries. As Walter Crane well says in his article, " The Revival of Handicrafts and Design ":

> The movement indeed represents, in some sense, a revolt against the hard mechanical life and its insensibility to beauty (quite another thing to ornament). It is a protest against that so-called industrial progress which produces shoddy wares, the cheapness of which is paid for by the lives of their producers and degradation of their users. It is a protest against the turning of men into machines, against artificial distinctions in art, and against making the immediate or market value, or possibility of profit, the chief test of artistic merit. It asserts, moreover, . . . apart from the very wholesome and real pleasure in the fashioning of a thing with claims to art and beauty, the struggle with and triumph over technical necessities which refuse to be gainsaid.

Along with the arts and crafts movement went the revival of village industries. It was just as mediæval in its inspiration, for it sought on the one hand to recreate the master-craftsman working for himself with his own materials, and largely guided by traditional or conventional models, but in no way precluded from making his own variations from them; and on the other, to snatch industry from the grime and drudgery of large towns, from the slavery of machinery and the routine of the factory, and by transplanting it into the country to breed another type of worker, who fashioned things with his brain as well as with his hands, who was his own master and sound in body as in mind; a man who could say with Touchstone even more truly than Shakespeare had foreseen, "An ill-favoured thing, sir, but mine own," for he would be speaking not merely of possession, which after all is little enough,

244

but of that god-like power of creation, of loving the work of your hands, that you have moulded from shapeless clay to a thing of beauty or of use.

This is mediævalism right enough, but mediævalism seen through a golden haze, with all its petty failings wiped out, its local jealousies and small discomforts ignored; mediævalism with the emphasis laid on every feature that contrasted most strongly with modern industrial methods, and because of that very contrast, rather than by reason of inherent value, its every feature pronounced worthy to redeem the world from the parlous condition into which it had drifted for lack of a due observance of the fundamentals of mediæval life.

But by teaching these fundamentals much that was best in the Middle Ages was brought to bear on modern civilisation and influenced it profoundly, for, though William Morris did not really know the true Middle Ages at all, and did not see them with the eyes of the people who lived in them, yet in a way he knew them better than we do, with all our knowledge of their infinite variety, drawn from painful research into the records they have left behind them, for, an idealist and a visionary himself, he could speak across the centuries with men of like substance; we are too prone to stress the exceptions, we know too many details always to estimate fairly the broad light and shade of the picture; we are a little too ready to describe the Middle Ages from its lists of crimes and misdemeanours, to delineate society, as it were, from a Newgate Calendar. Religion was then a living force, and its precepts guided a man in every walk of life, whether sleeping or working, eating or fasting; if one wants to know the economic theories of the day it is to the moralists, the theologians, the scholastic writers, that one goes, and merely to say that their theories were often violated proves little; that there are thieves in London does not prove that no man's goods are safe; indeed, every breach of a law that is recognised as such but serves to emphasise the reality of such a law, and many of the broad fundamental truths upon which the Middle Ages based much of its life have, of recent years, gained acceptance once more by moralists and economists alike. Sometimes there has been conscious imitation, sometimes merely a revival of past ideas unconsciously evoked by similar circumstances and emotions. When Morris and his followers preached the dignity of labour they were intentionally treading the path already traced by many mediæval footsteps: what the Benedictines taught by their example, Trithemius at the very end of the fifteenth century expressed in words: " Man is born to labour as the bird to fly, and hence it is contrary to the nature of man when he thinks to live without work."

Mere similarity between mediæval precept and modern practice does not, however, always imply any continuity or even any attempt by men of the present day to imitate what seemed good to the fourteenth or fifteenth century, and it is necessary, even though it be difficult, to remember that there is no direct connection between the Profiteering Act or the Food Control of to-day and the doctrine preached by that same Trithemius when he writes: " Whoever buys corn, meat, and wine in order to drive up their price and to amass money at the cost of others is, according to the law of the Church, no better than a common criminal. In a well-governed community all arbitrary raising of prices in the case of articles of food and clothing is peremptorily stopped; in times of scarcity merchants who have supplies of such commodities can be compelled to sell them at fair prices, for in every community care should be taken that all the members be provided for, and not only a small number be allowed to grow rich and revel in luxury to the hurt and prejudice of the many." These ideas are not precisely those that would have commended themselves to the economist of a hundred years ago. How then is it that they find favour to-day ? It is merely that the Just Price is coming to its own again, based, indeed, on very similar factors to those that determined it in the Middle Ages— wages, cost of material, and a reasonable profit to the producer. This is no doubt partly due to the artificial conditions created by the War, but yet, at bottom, even this is the indirect result of the mediæval influence which was brought to bear on English economic theory by the school of William Morris. One of the changes which he did a great deal to stimulate, although he cannot be said to be its sole author, was the reassociation of ethics with economics; in the Middle Ages there had been the closest union between the two—in fact, it would not be too strong a statement to say that all the fundamental principles of economic theory were part of the ethics of the day. And this lasted for some considerable time after the Middle Ages had passed away, much of the government regulation of the Tudors and even of the early Stuarts being set up on a definitely ethical basis. But as religion became more individualistic with the advent of the Reformers, as the master and apprentice became more definitely employer and employed, and the employer no longer shared in the actual craftsmanship, and so was less capable of understanding the needs of his workmen, commercial and industrial practice began to overcome the authority of general theory, and new theories that were evolved owed their existence to an attempt to explain and justify existing facts rather than to establish any general basis for economic activity. This became much more pronounced during the eighteenth century and culminated in the great school of English theorists who looked to Adam Smith as their progenitor. Then came that chilly abstraction, the economic man, divorced not only from all ethical considerations but even from human and psychological ones as well. Against all this the teaching of William Morris inaugurated a revolt which joined hands with the better aspects of the humanitarian movement, and began that stressing of other than purely economic considerations in the world of industry and commerce which has culminated in the attitude of the present day, in the pressure for an improved standard of life and a minimum wage, in the treatment of employees as human beings with tastes to be studied and bodies and minds to be cared for, as men and women and not as mere cogs in the industrial machine. It looks a far cry from the Middle Ages to these essentially modern doctrines, and the road that connects the two is often obscure, but it does exist, and had mediæval economic theory made no other contribution than this to the solution of the problems that face our civilisation of to-day it would amply have justified itself.

But, in fact, much more can be said in its praise. To us who live in the midst of industrial turmoil, of strikes for higher wages, of strikes for shorter hours, strikes for nationalisation, and strikes for local self-government in the factory, the world seems caught in an infernal labyrinth from which there is no escape. But all the same we do struggle to escape, and to some of us, groping wildly after light, the thought comes that the experience of the past might provide suggestion and precept. It was but natural that those who had already been deeply influenced by the ideas of William Morris, ideas which had achieved a certain amount of success in spite of the rather patronising attitude that was taken by many of their exponents toward the unenlightened masses, should turn to that same epoch which had already been the source of his finest inspiration. And this was all the more natural because the most evil of the conditions they sought to destroy was capitalism, and it was one of their fondest beliefs that the characteristic institutions of the Middle Ages were the sworn enemies of the capitalist; moreover, the leaders of this new movement were not, as a rule, men who had been at all influenced by the scientific study of mediæval times that had been made since the days of William Morris, a study which has shown that many of his historical conceptions would not stand detailed examination.

I need hardly tell you that it was in the gild that this small group of writers saw salvation. Morris had justly realised that the gild was the central feature of industrial life in the Middle Ages, that the craftsman as a unit was as nothing, that he attained to the full measure of his existence only as a member of his gild; that in his gild he enjoyed some of the advantages of corporate life, that he learnt some of the lessons of self-regulation, if not of self-government, that there he enjoyed the support of his fellows without sacrificing his industrial independence; it was the gild that strove for good quality and fair prices, honest work and a decent living for all. What Morris failed to realise was that, while in theory the gild was all this and more, in practice it fell far below such a standard; its members were but human after all, and as full of human failings as their less favoured brethren of the twentieth

249

century. They scamped their work on occasion, they evaded the gild regulations when they could, they put their best cloths on the outside of a bale and the poorest in the middle, they moistened groceries to make them heavier, they soldered together broken swords and sold them to confiding customers for as good as new—indeed, they would have found themselves thoroughly at home in the present age. And even the gild itself loses some of its glamour when viewed at close quarters; its regulations often proved oppressive and unfairly restrictive, and, as the Middle Ages wore to a close, it often steadily tended to become an exclusive body of masters, careless of the interests of the craft as a whole, thoughtful only for the gain of that particular section from which its members were drawn.

But the protagonists in the movement for the revival of the gilds—the industrious Mr Penty and, in a lesser degree, Mr Orage—were not hampered by too close an acquaintance with the economic history of the Middle Ages. Even in his latest work, *A Guildsman's Interpretation of History*, Mr Penty remains the same guileless enthusiast that he was in the beginning; he can still believe in the pure and undiluted communalism of early society, in its degradation by a foul conspiracy of lawyers, capitalists, and religious reformers, and he can still write of it in a way reminiscent of nothing so much as Fenimore Cooper in praise of the noble Redskin. " Looking at Feudalism from this point of view," he says, " it may be said that while its existence was due to the depredations of robber knights, and though these knights would have certain groups of workers at their mercy, there would be other knights or lords, who came into being as protectors of the communal rights of the people. Such were the

250

chivalrous knights of romance and legend. . . . The serfs of the robber knights would be tyrannised over, because the robber knights would never feel their position to be secure; but the serfs of the chivalrous knights would enjoy all the advantages of a communal life, for the chivalrous knights, owing their position to popular election, would have no desire to tyrannise."

Now, a man who can write such unmitigated nonsense as this would seem little likely to found a movement that would prove of any real importance. And yet, while these early advocates of the adaptation of gilds to the needs of modern industry—Penty, Orage, and Hobson—possessed none of the genius and little of the literary ability of a Ruskin or a Morris, they were dowered with that enthusiastic belief in themselves and their cause which is eminently necessary if a new doctrine is to gather converts to its side. And converts they made, most notable among them being G. D. H. Cole, the present leader of the guild socialist school. With the appearance of Mr Cole a very material change comes over the whole affair; he was a man of considerable historical reading who was not likely to commit himself too openly to the rather wild statements of his predecessors; therefore much of the mediæval idealism was dropped; it was felt that the truth about the mediæval gild was after all a minor problem, if attention was to be concentrated on improvement in modern conditions, and, though the Middle Ages were still recognised as the original source of inspiration, it was laid down quite clearly that the emphasis was to be on adaptation and not on mere imitation, that, though the mediæval gild would not meet the needs of modern industry, it might provide suggestions for what is really to be a new organism specially devised to administer the industrial world after the

251

elimination of private capitalist ownership. All the workers concerned in a particular type of industry, in coal-mining, in railway transport, or in cotton manufacture, for example, are to be gathered into a national guild which is to include those who work with their brains as well as those who work with their hands; and these guilds are gradually to be evolved out of the existing trade unions, so soon as they can be persuaded to reorganise themselves on industrial instead of on craft lines. The factories, or the mines, or the railways are to be owned by the State, that is, by the community at large, but to be administered and controlled each by its respective guild; while the whole organisation of the guild from shop-foreman up to central committee is to be based on democratic election, though it is recognised that experts in various departments must be appointed on sound business principles, and not as the result of the votes of their fellow-workers. Side by side with this industrial organisation of producers, there are to be national and local organisations of consumers and producers alike, as there are to-day—a central parliament, municipal authorities, county councils, and so on, and prices are to be regulated by the guilds in conjunction with these local or national governmental bodies. At the basis of the whole edifice, as the prime motive for any industrial action, Cole sees the principle of free social service, of work not for private profit but for the community at large.

This guild socialism tacitly recognises that trade unions, as they exist at present, are dying institutions, that they are essentially bound up with the wages system, and that, having achieved what they set out to do, they are liable to embark on all sorts of new ventures and extravagant claims in order to retain the active adherence of their members; to this guild socialism says, by implication and only very deferentially, for of the support of the trade unions it has great hopes: " If you will reconstruct the world, you must first reconstruct yourselves; provide yourselves with a new organisation and, what is far more difficult, provide your members with a new and more efficient stimulus to labour."

Merits this new idea of guild socialism has in plenty, but this is not the place to discuss them; it will be sufficient to point out the vast difference that exists between these guilds and the mediæval ones: the mere accident that these guilds are national, 'and the earlier ones local, is after all not the most vital distinction; that lies in the equality of every member of the guild and the democratic government of the industry as a whole, for it is very doubtful if there ever was for any length of time in mediæval craft-gilds either equality or democracy, as we understand those terms. But, though this sketch of the proposed guilds shows many other obvious differences in matters of organisation from the mediæval gilds, yet one must not be blinded to the share of the Middle Ages in this guild socialism movement, for it arose out of a study of mediæval economic and social history, and it still retains a considerable number of essential qualities which were fondly believed by its originators to be derived from the craft-gilds of the fourteenth century.

By the arguments that I have developed and the examples that I have quoted during the course of this paper I have tried to show the really vital bearing that mediæval economic history has upon the most intimate and important aspects of our modern life; how mediæval industrial and commercial methods are surviving even down to the present day; how a study of these dead institutions and discredited theories has led men to find good in them, to see remedies

253

for some of our most pressing economic problems; how almost every institution that we have, industrial or commercial, financial or agricultural, owes something to the Middle Ages, how its present shape has been determined not only by the hands of time, but also by the nature of the original clay from which it was moulded.

But such an argument as this, while possibly curious in itself, would be arid indeed, were not the just moral drawn from it. It was that moral with which we started, and to it we return, and we return the more readily because just at present it is of vital importance to bear it in mind. Our universities are turning out scores of people—mostly earnest young women—who have gained a smattering of historical knowledge, and are possessed with the determination to do their duty by the world, whether the world likes it or not; and the spirit of the age leads their minds to the study of economic and social problems. But all they will consent to listen to are the most modern thinkers on the most modern topics, and the more diffuse the thinker the better they like him. If we suggest to them that some foundation may be necessary, some real knowledge of the past desirable, they scornfully remind us that basements have gone out of fashion, that we live in a rapid age when the arduous spade-work necessary to foundations is no longer esteemed. Let the dead bury their dead. They want to produce something modern, and to produce it now.

And so it is to them that I would give my moral, though I doubt if they ever listen nowadays to such mid-Victorian things: let them ever remember that the past must be studied if the present will be understood, for it is out of the past that the present has been made.

E. R. ADAIR

X

POLITICS

I HAVE been asked to speak of the political conceptions of the Middle Ages under a heading which implies that those conceptions are, or have been, contributions to our modern civilisation. I do not know in what sense that is so. Everything that we are and have has developed from the Europe of the mediæval period, with some additional assistance direct from the world of Greece and of Rome. But that fact hardly helps me. The Middle Ages do indeed contribute directly to our civilisation a wonderful legacy of artistic achievement, of which we, in the last few centuries, have largely proved ourselves unworthy. But when I come to political thought I am at a loss what to say in this connexion. All I can do is to ask the question, What value have, or may have, the political ideas of the Middle Ages for us here and now? I can ask this question, but I cannot answer it.

There is an initial difficulty. I might ignore it, but I do not feel disposed to do so. I do not know what is meant by mediæval political thought. If what is meant is all that was thought about politics as such in the Middle Ages, I don't know where to begin. The more I study the writings of those times the more I become convinced that most of the questions that have been asked since the fifteenth century were asked then, and that most of the political ideas developed in modern times are to be found

255

there. In fact, speaking generally, such study of the history of political thought as I have been able to make is gradually producing in me a conviction that ever since men began to think in general terms they have been asking much the same questions and giving much the same answers. The differences between the questions and answers of one age and those of another are very frequently differences of form rather than of content. And specifically with regard to the Middle Ages I get an impression that the more one looks the more one finds. I have, for a long time, been telling my pupils that the theory of climate expounded by Jean Bodin in the sixteenth century was practically a new thing; that there is nothing similar to be found earlier except in some mere suggestions in Aristotle and Plato. My excuse is that the books say so; but it is not true. A theory of climate in Bodin's sense is explicit—I do not say fully developed—but quite explicit in the writings of Pierre Dubois very early in the fourteenth century. How much further it may go back I do not know.

Many people I am sure are under a quite wrong impression about it. People talk sometimes as though all through the Middle Ages men kept saying the same things or nearly the same things. The fact is, I think, far otherwise. Even if we take the term Middle Ages in its narrowest sense as covering the period from the eleventh to the fifteenth century, we shall find change everywhere going on, and everywhere irreconcilable differences. There is a great change from the views of Hildebrand and his followers of the twelfth century to the views of Aquinas in the thirteenth, and between Aquinas and William of Occam perhaps a still greater change. This is a change that takes place in the thought of a series of men who all have

256

the same kind of ecclesiastical bias and training, and who
are asking the same questions as to the nature of secular
authority and its relation to the Church.   If we go outside
this circle we come at once to the sharpest antagonisms.
Between the views of Aquinas and of Pierre Dubois a
great gulf is fixed.   In truth, I think, the Middle Ages,
in this as in other things, are a period of harsh and violent
contrasts, of contradictions more hopeless, perhaps, than
exist among modern thinkers.

There are, of course, modern ideas you cannot possibly
find in the Middle Ages.   But theories of the sovereignty
of the people are there; and Marsilio—and not Marsilio
only—uses language, at times, that oddly suggests
Rousseau.   The conception of society and of government
as a co-operative effort to realise merely temporal and
material ends is in Dubois; and Dubois represents, I am
sure, the views of many other people besides the ministers
of Philip IV.   And if you want to find in the Middle Ages
the very latest thing in Bolshevist communism, you have
only to look at the record of John Ball, the mad priest of
Kent, who preached on Blackheath in 1381, or at what
is called the confession of Jack Straw.

We are too much inclined to take the writings of
ecclesiastics, of schoolmen, of the professed philosophers,
as expressing the whole thought of the Middle Ages.
Professed philosophers never do represent rightly the
current thought of their time.   The point of view of these
writers is at once too detached and too ecclesiastical.
The difficulty is that the mass of lay opinion on these
subjects in the Middle Ages rarely found expression.
There was, it is true, a school of juristic philosophy.
But we get only fragmentary glimpses of the views of
the governing statesmen of the twelfth and thirteenth

centuries, of the men in England who worked under Henry II, of the men who surrounded Henry III, and of whom Grosseteste wrote that they it was who were hostile to the Church and determined the impious and secularising policy of the Government. Yet these men had views, however unformulated or confused; but only their deeds speak for them. When, as in the writings of Pierre Dubois, you get as it were a sudden revelation of the ways of thinking of such men—and this, I believe, is the case—you get a shock and exclaim: " How un-mediæval ! " and even " How modern ! " Modern if you like, but not unmediæval. Just so when Machiavelli formulates, though very imperfectly, the assumptions and the perceptions that had governed political action in Italy more and more for the last two hundred years, we declare that he is the first of the moderns. I will add this : that the further you go into the thought of the sixteenth century the more mediæval you will find it. In England, in the last years of the century, Hooker is reproducing the views of Aquinas almost as fully as Suarez the Jesuit in the early seventeenth century. So far as there comes a real break-away from all mediæval conceptions, it occurs, I think, in the seventeenth century, with Hobbes and Vico.

If we wish to understand the thought of any political or any other sort of thinker, it is first of all necessary to make clear to ourselves what question or questions he is trying to answer. I have painful memories of candidates for honours who appear to think that the difference between Aristotle and Plato is that Aristotle was thinking about things and Plato about nothing. Such candidates are confounding the actual with the real, and have not reached the starting-point of philosophy. And people make the same mistake about the mediæval thinkers. Plainly they are not, most of them, writing about any existing state or about any state that ever had existed. After all, how could they? In the political welter of the earlier Middle Ages they could not discern any distinct outline of any state at all, unless it were Christendom itself; and that, visibly, was not actually a state. Gradually, indeed, outlines emerged and became more or less distinct, and when a writer in the fourteenth century uses the word 'emperor' he frequently uses it, as does Marsilio, to mean simply the secular authority anywhere as contrasted with the Church. But the earlier mediæval schoolman is forced to disregard the actual by the nature of the actual in his time. What he is concerned with are the fundamental questions that do not change with circumstance.

It is a mistake, I think, to regard mediæval scholasticism in politics as Aristotelian. The schoolman of the thirteenth century felt great reverence for Aristotle. He studied Aristotle as minutely as he could, and quoted and referred to him constantly. But I do not think he ever understood Aristotle. He treated the Greek philosopher's writings as a collection of texts which could be detached from their context and separately made use of: just as many people have treated the Bible. In this way he at once avoided all danger of assimilating or even understanding Aristotle's thought, and was enabled to adopt his maxims and fit them in to his own system. Nor did he hesitate, when he came upon a particularly tough and indigestible extract, to assert that here the philosopher was wrong. The schoolmen seem to me to have got little from Aristotle, for all their talk of him. They Platonised him and they Christianised him, but they never understood him. Aquinas in some aspects is a Stoic, in some a Neoplatonist, never an Aristotelian.

MEDIÆVAL CONTRIBUTIONS

In the main, so far as there exists real difference between the political thought of one age and another, this difference is a consequence of the fact that in one age a particular question is asked more frequently and insistently than in another. The difference is a difference of subject. Most questions are asked, perhaps, in most ages; but in one age the stress is on one, in another on another. The difference between the thought of two periods becomes profound only when questions are asked in one that could not have been put in the other.

Now, at last, I am coming to the essential subject of what so far may have seemed a rambling discourse. I may put it thus. What questions were asked in the Middle Ages that we should do well to ask now more often than we do? And what answers given to such questions by mediæval thinkers have or may have a real value for us?

It is not the thought of men like Dubois or Marsilio that has positive value for us now: it is, if anything, the thought, above all, of the schoolmen of the thirteenth century, detached, abstracted, forced into asking fundamental questions as to the basis of the State in a chaotic world. It is just these fundamental questions that need to be asked now and always. They are as unanswered now as they were then.

The main questions of that scholastic thought of the thirteenth century seem to have been these. What is the nature of obligation as between man and man, and, in connexion with and dependence on that, what is the nature of political obligation? What is the purpose which justifies to reason all that we mean by government? Or, in other words, what is the true function of government? And, finally, what is the character of that state the realisation of which will satisfy man's needs and aspirations?

260

This last is the question Plato had asked in *The Republic*. These questions, though not exactly in the form I have given them, are raised at every point in the writings of the twelfth and thirteenth centuries. The question of the extent of civil authority and law-making power was wholly bound up with the question as to moral obligation in general. The controversy as to the relations between Pope and Emperor, stripped of its non-essentials, was a controversy as to the end and purpose of life on earth.

The answer given by the schoolmen to these questions was a complete and coherent whole. It began with the assertion of the real existence of what was called natural law. The term was a very old one. It had come down from the Latin Stoics, and to the Fathers of the Church in the fourth and fifth centuries it connoted much what it did in the Middle Ages. The Fathers repeat continually that natural law is in the heart of all men, " written in the hearts of the Gentiles," in the phrase of St Paul. To the Fathers, though not to the true Stoics, natural law is wholly a moral law, a law of conduct. It is a God-given intuition of the absolute good.

The idea, in the Fathers, is a little vague and unrelated. In the thirteenth century it is much fuller. There are, says Aquinas, three modes in which God reveals Himself: one direct and verbal, in the Scriptures, given once for all; the other two continuous and unceasing, one in visible non-human nature, the other in the heart and conscience of man. The *Lex Æterna*, the plan of the world in the mind of God, he likens to the design of an unbuilt building in the mind of the architect. It is that to which all things move incessantly, and it is that by which they move. It can be known in its entirety to no man. But there is in every man a conscious participation in the eternal law

261

a partial consciousness of it, a sense of what he ought and ought not to do. This intuition as to right and wrong, this intuition of the Absolute, is formulated by reason as the law of nature. So far as man adheres to that law, so far his will becomes one with the will of God in the everlasting act of creation.

The term 'natural law,' then, implies and involves a philosophy of the absolute good : an assertion that right and wrong exist in the nature of things unalterably. If there be any conception eminently characteristic of mediæval political thought it is this. It is true that already in the fourteenth century the idea is losing its grip on men's minds; it is fading. Natural law means little to Marsilio: it means nothing at all to Dubois. To Occam—well, I am not sure what it meant to that very difficult and uncompromising intellectualist. But on his own metaphysical premises, if I understand them aright, it should have meant nothing at all. But in the twelfth and thirteenth centuries this conception of natural law dominates political thought. In relation to the State men find in it at once a basis for law, a limitation on authority, and a purpose for government. Logically it must have been so, for if the State does not create right, right must create the State.

" All human law," says Aquinas—I am translating from the *Summa*—" precisely to the extent to which it partakes of right reason, is derived from the eternal law," that is, of course, by way of the law of nature. And again: " Every law framed by man has the character of true law " —that is, creates obligation—" exactly to that extent to which it is derived from the law of nature." He will not admit that obligation to obedience can be derived otherwise. Law must be derived from the general moral consciousness, and enactment inconsistent with that has no binding force. The most he will admit is that, " for avoidance of scandal or disorder," it may be right to obey unjust law.

It follows that there can be no law binding on the conscience save that which is directed to the common welfare. " Law must be enacted," says Aquinas, " for the common welfare of men, and failing this it has no binding power." If a ruler, he goes on to say, makes, or rather tries to make, law " for the gratification of his own cupidity or vainglory," his enactments must be regarded as acts of violence rather than as laws. But he insists that if law be ordained for the common welfare and be consistent with the moral consciousness, it creates obligation and is binding absolutely. And this because every man is bound by the natural law to will and to work for the common welfare. I translate his words once more—words, this time, that recall the *Contrat Social* of Rousseau : " For as any one man is part of a multitude, all that every man has or is belongs to the multitude."

But Aquinas goes further. So clearly does he see law as the expression of a common moral consciousness that he asserts that law may be made and obligation created " by repeatedly multiplied acts, which make a custom," since " the reason and will of man is manifested in deed no less than in word." And similarly law made by enactment may be abnegated by " repeatedly multiplied acts " in a contrary sense. There can, in fact, exist no binding law which is not an expression of man's sense of right.

But it was not enough to conceive of law and of government as expressions of the moral consciousness and based on the law of nature. Law and government must, to justify themselves in the court of reason, be referred to a common end. And so the thirteenth-century thinkers elaborate the conception of an ultimate and absolute end and purpose of life for all humanity. To this end all politics, all law and government, must necessarily be referred. For if there be such an end and purpose of life for all men, it follows that all government must have this end in view constantly and universally. This proposition is, by itself, undeniable. But the specific mediæval assertion in regard to the question is twofold. Firstly, it is asserted, or assumed as too obvious for assertion, that failure to recognise such a meaning and purpose in life leaves all government purposeless, and means for society friction, waste, and chaos. And, secondly, it is asserted that the end and purpose of life cannot rationally be conceived as lying within the sharp edges of this material world. It must be conceived as transcending this world. Nothing, in fact, short of real and vital union with God will suffice to satisfy man and realise his potentialities. In any case the purpose of man's life cannot rationally be conceived in relation to any merely circumstantial and accidental needs or desires or in relation to anything merely external and temporary, but only *sub specie æternitatis*.

It is, of course, the Church, at least in the view of the ecclesiastics and scholastics of the twelfth and thirteenth centuries, that is the final authority as to the proper good of man. It is argued, therefore, that it is for the Church to judge of and to direct all State action. The distinction between temporal and spiritual disappears before the definition of a common purpose and an ultimate end for all forms of activity. Law and government can, it is asserted, be of real value only in so far as they conduce to the realisation of the purpose of each and every individual soul. Therefore, to the Hildebrandine school of the twelfth century, the Emperor becomes a mere sword in the Church's hand, a chief of police, a *justitiarius* under the Pope. Any secular Government that claims independence of the Church can base its claim only on an assertion that the end of man can be realised in this life and in relation to mere earthly and temporal needs. At the least it must claim real value for the things of this world. But no real value attaches to the things of this world in themselves. Real values are spiritual and transcendental. The claim of secular powers to independence is blasphemy and of the devil.

This is twelfth-century doctrine. In the thirteenth century men begin to see things differently. Aquinas finds a real basis for secular government in the fact that peace and order and a certain minimum of material well-being are necessities of the spiritual life on earth. Yet he too insists that government has no meaning or value except in so far as it conduces to that apprehension of God which is the end of man's existence.

The mediæval empire was conceived by these thinkers as a thing very different from that which we are accustomed to associate with the word. It was, to them, all but an ecclesiastical institution. Their idea of it involved the conception of a common purpose in human life, and this purpose involved, ultimately at least, an escape from the bonds of the material. The material world was antagonistic in many ways—not in every way—to man's spiritual self-realisation. The essential function of government is one of release. The duty of the secular power was to create and maintain conditions favourable to spiritual development. So far from being concerned solely with temporal affairs it was concerned essentially with spiritual affairs. For this very reason it was subordinate to the Church. Its business was so to order the temporal as to

265

strengthen man's hold on the eternal. Coming after Aquinas, John of Paris sees no need of an emperor at all. But he sees that secular government has a reason for existence. And emperor or no emperor, all secular government must be directed by the same final purpose.

And so we come to the last word in this system of politics: the idea of a world-state, based on the moral consciousness of mankind and on the recognition of a common end of existence. That ideal world-state could be called indifferently, in the language of the twelfth century, *respublica generis humani* or *ecclesia universalis*. But, granted the premises, nothing less will suffice, logically or morally. For the purpose is the same everywhere; the end of living is the same for all human beings; the real interests of all men are the same, or rather man has only one real interest. The desire of man is for completeness and for happiness. Neither can be realised here; but so far as realisation is possible on earth it is only in a world-state that it is possible.

Already in the fourteenth century this system of ideas is breaking up. On one side its metaphysical foundations are being attacked if not destroyed by the analytic intellects of Duns Scotus and of Occam. On another the new national states, territorial and racialised groupings, are emerging to self-consciousness, striving for independence, and drawing men's thoughts more and more to actuality. Gradually it is becoming apparent that Christendom is not a unity: that, in fact, there is no Christendom at all. It had always been so. Christendom was a figment born of the incurable optimism of humanity. Already in Italy is going on that separation of politics from morals which finds verbal expression in Machiavelli. The process goes on and on; till in the seventeenth century Hobbes is able to declare that the natural relation of any two states is war, and that natural law is simply that law of reason which forbids a man to do anything that impairs or will impair his security in the pursuit of pleasurable sensation. Gradually the whole system was sapped, and crumbled at its foundation; the belief, that is, in a natural law of obligation. Though at the end of the seventeenth century Locke still believes in natural law, the belief was being replaced. There was an increasing tendency to get rid of the transcendental element in morals, and to fall back on some form of utilitarianism. So also there was an increasing tendency to reject the idea of a transcendental purpose or end of human existence, and to seek a sufficient purpose for life within the walls of matter. Mechanical explanations of life and the universe had their vogue, and along with all that went an increase of pure scepticism.

But there was always reaction; and it has, I think, strengthened in the last century. We have still with us a philosophy of the absolute good. To say that the mediæval conception of natural law and of a transcendental purpose in life was demonstrably false would, I think, be demonstrably silly. There has been for a long time past a tendency to return to the mediæval conception of society as an expression of the moral consciousness. Equally is there now a tendency to turn toward the idea of a world-state. We are perhaps drawing nearer to the thought of the Middle Ages.

I suggest not merely that any separation of politics from ethics is fatal, but that a society which has lost belief in the validity of its own moral intuitions rests on rotting foundations. I suggest, further, that the idea that government must be directed to a recognised, common, and ultimate end, and refer to a standard of absolute values

267

or be radically purposeless, is perfectly sound. The end, perhaps, need not transcend this world. It may be possible to find a purpose referring only to this world that will satisfy the soul of man. But I suggest that no such end has yet been found.

We can strip from the mediæval system of ideas that I have tried to define in outline all that is not essential to it. We can eliminate the Church altogether, and it will still stand logically coherent. It is a question—it is perhaps *the* question—whether we can also eliminate God.

It may be that our civilisation is slipping down toward chaos and dissolution. Personally, I am under the impression that things are not so bad as that yet; but I am well aware that no man's impression on such a matter is worth much. But I do believe that we may yet learn from the mediæval thinkers. We need to consider what we, the State, are at, and why we are at it. Man never has known what he wants; but he won't be happy till he gets it.

J. W. ALLEN

ERRATA

On page 188 lines 14, 15 read "as not" instead of " as,"
and "humbly" instead of " later on."